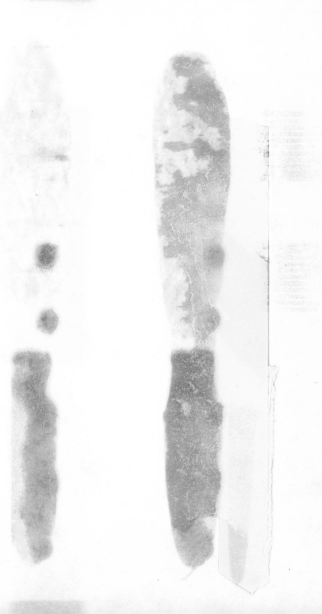

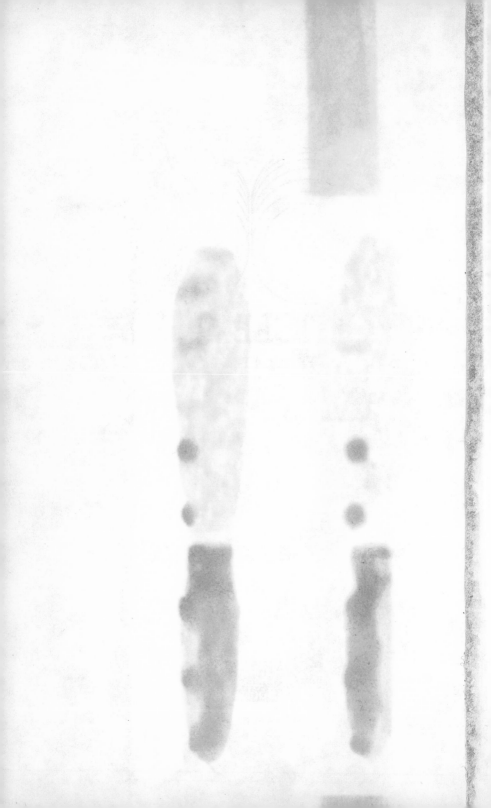

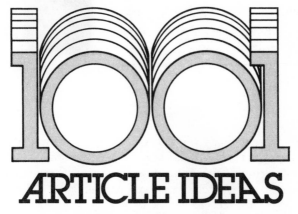

ARTICLE IDEAS

Frank A. Dickson

Writer's Digest Books Cincinnati, Ohio

Library of Congress Cataloging in Publication Data

Dickson, Frank A   1911-
   1,001 article ideas.

   Includes index.
   1. Authorship—Handbooks, manuals, etc.
I. Title.
PN198.D5   808'.066'07043   79-11602
ISBN 0-911654-64-X

To Mere and Jon Dickson

Foreword

Frank A. Dickson is an idea man. A great one.

I first became aware of Frank's ability to see an idea in even the *teeniest* topic when I was starting out as a freelance writer. Each month *Writer's Digest* arrived, and the first thing I would do—after clearing out an afternoon to soak my head in the magazine—was read Frank's "An Idea a Day" column.

I always came away with a handful of excellent article ideas to develop and sell to editors. Often there were multiple and reprint sales of the articles, too.

I can recall reading in one of Frank's columns the suggestion for an article on a doctor with an unusual hobby. As it happened, I knew of a doctor whose hobby was raising unusual animals: llamas, peacocks, exotic sheep from Africa, cattle from New Zealand—a cast of furry and feathered characters that made for appealing photos as well.

I sold that story, using different editorial slants and photos, to a medical publication, a state outdoors magazine, a Sunday magazine, and to *Grit,* the national smalltown weekly paper. And, as I think on it, this is my first opportunity to thank Frank Dickson for that income—for giving me the idea in the first place.

A writer is often uncertain or undecided about what he wants to write—just as a child doesn't know what he wants from Santa until he sees it in a store window or catalog. The book in your hands is just like that big, fat Sears catalog in a seven-year-old's hands one month before Christmas. The ideas keep coming at you, bouncing off your imagination, your know-how, your curiosity, your itchiness

FOREWORD

to write something but you're not sure what, until . . . Ah, hah! There's an idea I can develop . . . and you are off to do research, to interview, to write, to rewrite—and to sell.

Today, Frank A. Dickson—who syndicated his first newspaper feature in 1929—is still on the job at *Writer's Digest.* His "Looking Ahead" column appears regularly, jam-packed with ideas for the writer who must look months ahead on the calendar for salable ideas that appeal to editors planning issues six months in advance.

For a typical column, I ask Frank for thirty ideas. He usually sends fifty, minimum. "You pick the thirty you want," he says.

Thus, I was delighted when Frank started work on this book—the proper home for hundreds of ideas that could not be squeezed into the confines of a magazine's columns, and the best place to browse for an idea (or three) whenever that writing itch starts to act up.

Any *one* of the ideas in this book could lead to a sale many times the purchase price invested. The additional thousand are pure writer's gold—yours for the taking.

John Brady

Editor, *Writer's Digest*

Introduction

The article writer sits on top of the world these days because nonfiction is enjoying its greatest boom.

Whether you fashion your features for national or local and regional consumption, you face an unprecedented opportunity. General magazines of national circulation devote almost 85 percent of their contents to articles, while in the newspaper profession the editors of the locally edited Saturday or Sunday magazines use local or area features as about 90 percent of the reading fare. One magazine alone—*McCall's*—purchases between two hundred and three hundred articles each year, and one weekly paper—the *National Enquirer*—buys a thousand manuscripts in the same period. And the editors at *Good Housekeeping* will cross your palm with $500 for short articles and $5,000 for features.

Feature writing supplies the ever-varying dessert for newspaper readers, especially on Sunday when the subscribers expect something extra to fill their additional reading time. Although feature stories also pepper the weekday editions, the big attraction on Sunday is the bundle of local features, which many newspapers present in magazine form.

Feature subjects, like charity, begin at home—or right around the corner. Your own "backyard" can be a prolific vein of article material you can mine day in and day out, for exciting features to sell to newspapers ranging from weeklies to metropolitan giants and from state and regional monthlies to the behemoths among the general magazines of national circulation.

There are no substitutes for the local, sectional, and state angles in the Sunday feature sections or locally edited magazines of your state's dailies. Stories about regional personalities and celebrities who are visiting or making appearances in the area, as well as events either current or historical, stand as the rule instead of the exception.

So alert writers who live in a particular section have an edge over authors elsewhere, even the most successful in the business. The local author, familiar with the people and happenings of the community, holds the inside track, with no extensive travel necessary for the interviewing and/or research needed to gather an abundant supply of anecdotes and other data to turn into a fast-paced and polished performance.

The size of the storyteller's audience depends upon the scope of the story, whether it is local, regional, or national. But out of newspaper feature stories spring articles for large magazines, all the way to *Reader's Digest*. And a piece of national interest can concern the activities of a small community, such as the article by Stewart Dill McBride, "The Town That Took On the Corps of Engineers," which dealt with the town of North

Bonneville, Washington, that refused to be pushed around. First published in *The Christian Science Monitor*, the article was condensed in *Reader's Digest*.

Always bear in mind the national possibilities of a regional article, runs the advice of William L. Rivers, who worked his way from a Sunday supplement to the big-time magazines. "If your subject is unique and there is a story connected with it, you probably have a national article. If your subject is common and there is a story connected with it, you may have a national article."

One feature suggestion can be developed a dozen different ways, because the same story idea can be told in different ways for different audiences. First ladies of your state's supreme court would make excellent copy for newspapers of the state, but go a step further and develop a magazine article about the first ladies of the United States Supreme Court.

Solutions to the most pressing problems in cities, such as downtown decay, crime explosion, or teenage runaways, make good copy for local newspapers and magazines. But a writer can point the way to how an accomplishment can be duplicated elsewhere in the nation.

A newspaper feature can reveal how the local zookeeper shops for food for his charges. Likewise, a magazine editor might be in the mood for an article about unusual delicacies that must be obtained for the daily diets of the more exotic creatures in a zoological garden—where supplies are purchased, and how frequently.

How about favorite exercises of athletes, dancers, and coaches in your section? A fine newspaper feature, yes, but you could hit the magazine market with an article featuring famous figures; their hints on how to keep fit; and a sampling of exercises for such specific purposes as achieving slimness, to improve posture, and as an aid to better breathing.

Let's turn historical with the subject of Indian names. This can be covered on a local or a national basis—the history behind Indian place names and the tribes that still live in our designations for rivers, mountains, valleys, towns, and cities today.

What is the road from a local feature to a national one? Suppose you decide upon an anniversary angle—the opening of the Brooklyn Bridge to traffic on May 24, 1883. This sets in motion a long string of story ideas about bridges.

The names of your area's bridges, especially in honor of prominent persons, could be worked into a revealing local or sectional feature. The covered bridges in the state—now a rare species—and also the state's longest or highest bridges can be evolved into articles of statewide significance. Who is involved *today,* in your city, state or region, in planning the construction of a major bridge? What authorities must approve those plans? County? State? Federal officials? How about bridges that connect states—yours with neighboring states or interstate bridges elsewhere in the nation. Bridges that connect the U.S. with other countries.

What changes have there been in bridge construction since 1883? How does one test the safety and strength of a bridge after it has been standing for decades? Who designs bridges today, and where do the designers learn the art? Have gullible people really, as the jokes insist, "bought" the Brooklyn Bridge from New York con men? How many companies are involved in the building of a bridge? What are the housekeeping chores on a bridge—the road repair, rust removal, sanitation problems? Handling breakdowns on bridges.

A national angle in bridges struck Martin Abramson: Just how safe are bridges *throughout the nation?* He described an alarming situation in "Our Bridges Are Falling" in *Parade* with national statistics and examples, and listed ten states that led in the number of obsolete or unsafe bridges.

Take it from Will Oursler, one of the most successful magazine writers: "Everything on earth has a possible article for somebody. It's the slant, the handling, which makes the difference."

Your subjects in article writing—an actual total of 1464, not counting the spinoffs that open up new fields of subject matter—are in this book, plus extras suggested by special days, weeks, and months as well as birthdates and anniversaries of historical events listed in the introduction to each month.

The subjects are based on my column "An Idea a Day," and more recently "Thinking Ahead," in *Writer's Digest* magazine, which has been presenting my article ideas in column form since February, 1939. These subjects, which contain much new, revised, and expanded material, boast themes and anniversary angles that feature editors will welcome for their timeliness.

Each idea in this volume—be it historical, current, or futuristic—has been designed to enable you to give your readers—whoever they are—a *personal* interest and identification in the story. Not only newspapers and magazine article writers, but also photojournalists and television interviewers and news reporters can draw upon the subjects day after day for a wealth of ever-ready material.

I have no fear that this guide of article subjects will result in a steady stream of identical stories from the users. As Robert Stein, who has served as editor of both *Redbook* and *McCall's,* has observed, each writer has a way of seeing and reporting that is distinctively his own and because of this fact newspapers and magazines are able to cover similar events without repeating themselves.

"For example, if you gave a dozen writers identical instructions for an article—to report, let's say, on the largest maternity hospital in the city:

"One writer, whose beat is scientific, would come back with a detailed report on new medical techniques for delivery, and care of mothers and infants. Another, whose main concern is psychology, would write about natural childbirth and the emotional advantages of rooming-in. A third, with a sense of the dramatic, would bring back a narrative of the hospital's fight to preserve the life of a premature baby. A fourth, who sees the humor in every situation, would string together anecdotes of mothers and fathers who barely got to the hospital on time. A fifth writer might bring back an article on the high costs of maternity care. And a sixth could easily devote his entire report to the part that nurses play in caring for new mothers and their infants.

"Send a hundred writers—and no two of the resulting articles will be the same. Because no two writers have identical interests, curiosities, enthusiasms, or ways of expressing what they see."

Whatever the subject, or the slant, the article writer always borrows experiences from the lives of other people as well as his own, through the processes of interview and research. I hope you will make abundant and profitable use of what I lend you here.

Every day is a new adventure for the feature writer.

Frank A. Dickson
Anderson, South Carolina

Building an Article from an Idea

No matter what the marketplace the writer must knead his feature dough into one central idea with a slant that fits the style and the type of publication, whether a newspaper or magazine.

Give the idea all the strength possible, endowing it with an unusual twist. Take a subject and write down two dozen questions in order to explore thoroughly its possibilities. Probe the idea until you pull out a *real* story, because you must not confuse a good idea with a satisfying story.

The idea is a skeleton; fleshed out with a lead, a cohesive and well-developed body, and a conclusion, which should pack as much punch as the beginning.

Like the creator of short stories, the nonfiction writer plays on the reader's emotions and never strays from a central theme. Both kinds of writers share a common purpose and goal, for each spins yarns that carry a definite message and sparkle with drama and characterization. Both fictionist and fact writer lift the reader from the opening sentence and never put him or her down until the curtain falls.

"Be sure you have enough material," writer Will Oursler counsels. "Get plenty of anecdotes. A good article should have at least four or five first-class anecdotes, plus half a dozen minor stories worked in. You should get three times as much material as you can use. Then you can write a second piece.

"Arrange your facts and anecdotes dramatically to prove their thesis. You might begin with either a dramatic lead or a straight factual lead— an anecdote with sharp conflict is usually safest. But somewhere in the first few pages get in a bald, direct statement of your thesis."

Next listen to Carl Schuon: "Every article has its own best beginning. What kind of lead should you write?

"If you've got so much dope that you don't know exactly how to begin, stop right where you are and concentrate on all the facts.

"Now pull out the BIG one. There should be a big one. If there isn't, take one of the biggest and make it your big one! Now take all of your other facts and determine their relation to your big one. This isn't always easy, but it's necessary because you are going to use them in relation to your big fact, which has now become your theme. If these minor facts can be used to prove your big point, you have got it made!"

The newspaper feature is the little brother of the magazine article. "While the general make-up is the same, the format is much more compact," I.E. Clark, an authority on article writing, explains. "Both must have a timeliness and a fiction-like quality in telling, for example, why or how someone has done something important or unusual. Both benefit from a conversational approach, but the newspaper feature must be streamlined, unrambling. There is no room to elaborate as there is in magazine articles.''

The feature writer ensures his or her success by sticking to subjects inside the circulation area of the newspapers to which he or she submits the story. To understand why, the writer should learn some facts about the newspaper business.

The feature editor and the circulation manager of a newspaper team up in their efforts to increase the circulation figures and outclass the opposition—circulation salesmen expect help from the editorial department as they knock on doors to show residents that the newspaper gives them more and better attention than journalistic rivals.

Yes, Virginia, there are circulation wars.

In these battles the feature writer strikes for an exclusive just as the news reporter does. He or she turns every subject over and over in his or her mind to determine the greatest point of interest and emotion *in relation* to the readers.

My friend Dr. George W. Crane describes the secret of human interest in writing, in three short words: ME ... HERE ... NOW! Take it from the famous author, our primary interest is in our own epidermis and its contents—in our present location—at this very moment.

The more you move away from another person's immediate concerns, the more he loses interest; so for example the readers of your local newspaper are most interested in local or area inhabitants, particularly present ones. A person gives his greatest attention not to the distant past but to this very second. With this formula you can market practically everything you write.

Whether you're writing for newspapers or magazines, you can build a salable subject by taking an interesting person and dramatizing or exploring his or her occupation, experiences, or pasttimes. One big trick of the trade is to capitalize on superlatives—such as the youngest, the oldest, the smallest, the largest, the most expensive, and the fastest. You can't go wrong with leaders and champions!

Open up a new world for the reader. Offer strange slices of life. Take the reader behind the scenes in occupations. Serve up observations and opinions of the great and the near-great. Show celebrities at home. Other surefire subjects: New experiments; record-breakers; notables who come to town for visits with relatives and friends or to make appearances; rags to riches; battles against crime; wonders of science; domestic achievements; community projects; rural progress; financial eye-openers; fads and fashions; latest honors for leaders in agriculture, industry, and the arts; new ways of doing old things; a day with so-and-so; and confessions, or secrets, of an entertainer, bandleader, et al.

Success stories, particularly if obstacles or handicaps have been overcome, never go out of style. In this age when readers complain that good news is neglected at the expense of stories of crimes and violence, editors desire features about good deeds, heroes, and good neighborism.

Photographs, please. Visual communication flourishes as an indispensable ally of feature writing. Photographs can be a selling point of an ordinary article when the competition becomes stiff. Teacher of writing and photojournalism at East Texas State College, Otha C. Spencer once checked his records and found that 90 percent of all magazine articles sold by his students were illustrated with photographs—most of them taken by the students themselves.

Most writers have acquired the knack of good picture-taking, but some writers make arrangements with freelance photographers, on speculation, and others find it profitable to employ a professional photographer when the results really count.

"A photograph has the basic ingredient of believability and is a perfect parallel to factual statements in words of an article," Spencer stresses.

How is an article sold to an editor? Most editors of general magazines prefer to be queried by mail. An editor's go-ahead does not imply acceptance of the completed manuscript, but it does provide assurance that the editor will not assign another writer to the same subject.

Many editors consider an outline almost as important as the article itself, so prepare your query outline carefully. Avoid being too brief and too stiff. The outline should carry the suggested title, a sample lead, at least four points to be emphasized, a few representative anecdotes, and a summing up. Written in your own style, the query should explain why the subject is news and has regional or national significance.

You can offer an article to only one newspaper in a city, and if you submit the same feature story to a number of newspapers be sure that these newspapers do not have overlapping circulation areas. Some editors demand features on an exclusive basis. In syndicating your features, it is imperative that you give the release date near the top of page one of the manuscript, with the notification: "Offered at your standard rates."

Submit manuscripts to newspapers and magazines in ample time, three months or more in advance for editors of general magazines, a few weeks ahead for use in Sunday feature supplements or locally edited magazines, and at least a week beforehand for articles to appear on the feature page or pages of a newspaper's Sunday edition or run separately. Early copy always has preference. And keep *Writer's Market* in reach for latest requirements and rates of payment.

JANUARY

Month of Variety and Beginnings

January—named after Janus, god of doors and gates in Roman mythology—opens a bulging storehouse of subjects for the wide-awake feature writer who can sink his or her typewriter keys into the present as well as the past parade of life and find it full of excitement, color, and surprises. The name of the game with the feature editor is variety. January, off to a flying start with New Year's Day, offers more than its share of diverse article ideas.

January gives a mixture of customs, traditions, and sports on the first day of the new year, and the lively pace continues as the political scene comes loudly to life with the convening of state general assemblies. Special days, weeks, and months can inspire a stream of articles. Stephen Foster Memorial Day falls on January 13, the day of the composer's death; Thrift Week, an oldie, begins on Ben Franklin's birthday, January 17; National Printing Day proclaims the importance of printing to the world's welfare; and polka fans can thank the International Polka Association for National Polka Music Month.

In various states carnivals take over, and other events drop a variety of topnotch subjects into the laps of writers. For instance, in Indiana the Creole King Ball unfolds in Vincennes in January, and Tarpon Springs, Florida, highlights Greek Cross Day during the Epiphany season with the release of white doves and other festivities. Arizonans grab their share of the January spotlight with Gold Rush Days in Wickenburg.

New Year's Day introduces a patriotic note with the observance of the birthdates of Paul Revere and Betsy Ross. The month also offers the anniversaries of the birth of General Douglas MacArthur, Stephen Decatur, Robert E. Lee, Alexander Hamilton, Benjamin Franklin, Daniel Webster, John Hancock, Thomas Paine, Virginia Woolf, W. C. Fields, Franz Schubert, Edgar Allan Poe, Jack London, Thomas "Stonewall" Jackson, Albert Schweitzer, John C. Fremont, Edith Wharton, and Martin Luther King Jr. Four presidents have celebrated their birthdates in January: Millard Fillmore, William McKinley, Franklin D. Roosevelt, and Richard M. Nixon.

January days with special significance for Americans are: 1. Tournament of Roses began in Pasadena, California, 1890; 1. President Abraham Lincoln gave the Emancipation Proclamation, 1863; 5. Nellie Tayloe Ross, the first woman governor, took office in Wyoming, 1925; 6. President Franklin D. Roosevelt delivered Four Freedoms message to Congress, 1941; 7. The Bank of North America, the nation's first commercial bank, opened in Philadelphia, 1782; 8. General Andrew Jackson scored a victory in Battle of New Orleans, 1815; 10. League of Nations came into existence, 1920; 12. Hattie Caraway, first woman elected to United States Senate, 1932; 16. Government Civil Service system created, 1883; 21. The first atomic-powered vessel, the *Nautilus,* launched, 1954; 25. United States inaugurated transcontinental telephone service, 1915; 28. United States established the Coast Guard, 1915; 29. American League organized in professional baseball, 1900; 30. Charles B. King patented the pneumatic hammer, 1894; and 30. Germans elevated Adolf Hitler to office of chancellor, 1933.

1

What do the butcher, the baker, and the candlestick-maker have in common on New Year's Day? Besides watching the bowl games on TV, chances are they feast on collards, black-eyed peas, and perhaps even hog jowls, because such a menu is supposed to bring greenbacks and other forms of good luck.

New year, new sight. The latest person in your state to be rewarded with new vision through the eye bank, which receives eyes of donors immediately after death. Slant: The most beautiful sights, in the subject's opinion.

— First babies of past years in your city. Those who have married—and are grandparents. Compare pictures. Do the names reflect headliners of the various years? Doctors who have delivered quite a few of the "January 1 babies." Do any of the first babies celebrate their birthdays together? Have they formed a club?

New Year's Day finds new almanacs and calendars in homes. What the weathermen of the almanacs and calendars predict for the year, especially in your state. How the weather charts—and also the fishing calendars—are prepared, and their reliability. Spinoff: Local and national predictions on any subject.

2

Photography in local churches. The boon in membership directories with photographs. Slant: The minister's belief that a picture is worth 10,000 words. The photographers and their experience in such work; the number of states they have covered; taking pictures gratis in expectation of the subjects buying a number of copies.

The regional vehicle manager of the United States Postal Service. Slant: The essential role of delivery trucks and carts in getting the mail through, despite all weather obstacles. The most common repairs on vehicles; number of tires used; mechanics' toughest mending jobs; safety record of drivers.

A woman who is a well-known director of pageants. The most elaborate pageants she has produced; pageants for centennial celebrations; checking historical material. Is the director an actress herself?

Superstitions of farmers in your county. Old wives' tales and beliefs concerning the weather. Formulating predictions early in January. Crop planting by superstition. Slant: Old-time farmers as "weather prophets" with their signs. Weather proverbs, as a halo around the moon is a sign of rain and a gray sunset means a storm.

3

A racing car driver of your state who builds his own racers. Slant: In construction he puts emphasis on safety as well as speed. How he made a championship car. His fastest speed in competition; close calls in collisions. How he tests his cars. Does his wife give a hand in car building?

What drives millionaires crazy? A psychiatrist's report on the leading causes of mental illness among the rich. Do any wealthy men and women worry about losing their fortunes? Do millionaires worry more than average persons do?

— The federal judge of your state who has administered the oath of citizenship to the largest number of persons. Unforgettable experiences swearing in new citizens. How the jurist extended help to new Americans. Foreign-born persons in whose successes the judge has taken the greatest pride. The changing pattern of immigrant nationalities over the years.

The favorite capitals of the United States of the most extensive traveler of your city. The most outstanding architecture; the leading places of entertainment; the most spectacular sights. Libraries and museums; parks that made an everlasting impression. Making movies, slides, and photographs during the travels.

4

Do many prisoners have the heart of a poet? (The literary, not the graffiti division.) Poems that appear in the prison newspaper. Are women prisoners more prolific poets than male inmates? Spinoff: Inmates of the state penitentiary as journalists. The most prolific of the authors; sales to newspapers and magazines. Study of the craft of writing; books on the subject in the prison library. The editors and staff members of the prison newspaper; types of stories appearing in the publication.

A society for the preservation of old dwellings in your section. The battle to educate the public and prevent history from falling to progress. Houses that have been preserved; their historical importance. Tours to raise funds. The commercial value of the homes at today's prices; the historical worth.

The champion reader among the blind in your section. Average number of books a month; favorite authors and characters. How many Braille books are available? Today is the anniversary of the birth of Louis Braille, who invented the reading method for sightless people. Spinoff: Talking book programs for the blind.

Modern Portias in your state. Their rapidly rising number on the membership rolls of the state bar association. Women in partnership and their specialities. Women lawyers with the longest practices; their most colorful cases; longest trials. Their views on to-day's problems. Laws they consider urgently needed.

5

The forests of tomorrow. How a timber company plants trees to take care of future needs. Selecting the best stock of wood for planting; varieties that grow the fastest. Different trees for different uses; fringe benefits of forest plantings. Scientific forest management. The demand on the forest products industry during the past year.

Stephen Decatur; from a log cabin to a naval hero. Anniversary angle: He was born at Sinepuxent, Maryland, on this day in 1779. His most daring exploits and his declaration, "My country—may she ever be right, but right or wrong, my country!" How on March 22, 1820, he dueled with Commodore James Barron, who became enraged when Decatur refused to reinstate him after a court-martial.

What is in store for sports champions—both men and women—this year? Predictions by a sports authority, and how he or she reached the conclusions. Forecasts about record-breaking performances; outlooks for new sensations.

Reading material at the state mental hospital. The most popular magazines and books among the patients. Discussion of the most suitable literature by the superintendent. Spinoff: Remedial reading and high school degree programs.

6

Four Freedoms Day, which marks the anniversary of President Franklin D. Roosevelt's message to Congress in 1941 when he urged all settlements after World War Two be based on four freedoms—freedom of speech, freedom of worship, freedom from want, and freedom from fear. Former prisoners of war or immigrants can discuss what these freedoms mean.

A woman mayor or a councilwoman of your section. Her campaign platform, and her margin of victory. How she became involved in politics; her objectives during her present term, and her plans for future races. When does she predict a woman president or vice president?

Research in an ancient cemetery of a church in your area. Slant: How the graves form a mecca for historians and writers of family histories who are in constant search for data, particularly dates. The oldest graves. Maintenance of the cemetery.

Lifesaving in a jungle hospital, as related by a medical missionary from your state. The spread of modern medicine and techniques in the jungles. Combatting the most common diseases; the medicines. Villagers' reaction to surgery; the operating room. The activities of medicine men.

7

A glimpse into a playground equipment manufacturing plant. How the factory turns out products for nationwide sale; the machinery and the number of employees; the daily output. The types of materials used. How testing is performed. Changes in interest in the past decade or so. The best-selling models; the rush for the summer season. Spinoff: Community children's parks with homemade equipment; novel uses of natural material. P.O.

The city that reigns as the entertainment capital of the state. The largest theaters, and their longest runs. Touring companies that have made frequent appearances. The activities of the Little Theater, and the director's plans for the year. Other sources of entertainment, including night clubs.

The first presidential election in the United States, held on this day in 1789. The choice of General George Washington as a foregone conclusion. Other chief executives who were natives of Virginia, "the Mother of Presidents"—Thomas Jefferson, James Madison, James Monroe, William H. Harrison, John Tyler, Zachary Taylor, and Woodrow Wilson. The youngest and the oldest when they were inaugurated.

Taxi drivers' experiences with animals. Pets brought along by passengers; animals that cause the greatest ruckus; requests for transporting pets. Are most of the animals well behaved? Are the majority of cabbies animal lovers?

8

The pages in your state legislature. How they obtained the positions, and the number of hours they serve a week. Rubbing elbows with the lawmakers and government officials, the governor among them. Do any of the pages hope for a political career? Former pages and the value they place on the experience.

The dean of city attorneys in your section. The worst legal headaches during his term. Little-known facts about serving as legal adviser to a city. Old statutes that have been or should be repealed. Recollections of the most colorful lawyers of the past. The attorney's law library and hobbies.

An interview with a rare book dealer. How the books are obtained; the oldest volumes sold; old books in greatest demand. The process of finding books wanted by collectors; acquiring family libraries at auctions. Problems of maintenance.

Jackson Day, which the Democratic Party observes with banquets and speeches in tribute to President Andrew Jackson. Observances in your state. Old Hickory succeeded in paying off the national debt on this day in 1835, the only president to accomplish this.

9

A long-time secretary for the president of a local college. Slant: How because of her long service and close association she ranks as an authority on the college's activities and other matters of the institution. The presidents she has served; other duties she has carried out. Is she a graduate of the college?

Handle with care! Accidental breakage of fragile articles by customers in stores. Do children or adults do the most damage? Are warning signs effective? The most expensive objects broken; settling the mishaps.

Carrie Chapman Catt, leader for women's suffrage, in the role of lecturer. Anniversary angle: This native of Ripon, Wisconsin, was born on January 9, 1858. How, in 1890, she organized the suffrage movement in Iowa, where she was a school superintendent, and became state lecturer. Her lectures in the United States, Canada, and Europe.

Accidents will happen—and do to officials in sports. Spills and injuries during the excitenent of a game. Officiating can be as rough as playing. Why officials need the skill of an acrobat.

10

Mechanics who service the cars of the highway patrol. Keeping the automobiles in tiptop shape, including emphasis on safety. The most common troubles the mechanics encounter; patrolmen who are expert mechanics. Average monthly mileage of a patrol car. How often are new automobiles purchased? What happens to the old ones?

Sinclair Lewis, a Nobel Prize winner in literature, as a novelist who drew upon life for material. The Sauk Center, Minnesota, native died in Rome, Italy, on this day in 1951. In *Main Street* Sauk Center was portrayed as Gopher Prairie, and the character Will Kennicott is a country doctor, as was the author's father.

Mail of local ministers. The pile of daily correspondence. Unusual requests; the average number of speaking invitations received per week. How the secretaries stay busy. Slant: Clergymen must be luminous writers as well as speakers. Spinoff: What type of mailing lists do ministers find themselves on? Who tries to sell what by mail to the clergy?

Unusual experiences of a staff photographer for a United States senator from your state. The job of turning out pictures of the solon and his activities. The senator's belief in the importance of the photos and also of his newsletters to his constituents.

11

Reach for the phone—for help! Groups formed to aid persons in distress by telephone. Slant: How hot lines are rendering life-saving services in your community and elsewhere across the nation. How Alcoholics Anonymous goes to the rescue of alcoholics via telephone; fast telephone talk and action by members of suicide prevenion centers. How drug users and pregnant girls are urged to telephone proper groups.

The local police auxiliary. Slant: How the wives perform good deeds daily just as the husbands do in the performance of their duties. The chief projects of the organization during the past year. Spinoff: Wives' thoughts about their husband's chosen profession.

Use of mattresses and jars as banks. Is the origin of this unsafe practice distrust of bankers or a ploy to evade the tax man? See police and firemen about the extent of this banking system.

Colleges in your state that have badminton in their intramural programs. Competition in tournaments. The activities of the American Badminton Association. The game's popularity in the United States as compared to Canada and England. Comparison of badminton with tennis. Spinoff: Growth of other indoor court sports.

12

Inside a large newspaper library; the so-called morgue. The amazing amount of information and photographs available at the librarian's fingertip. The files on leading personalities, local, national, and international, with pictures and biographical sketches. Rows and rows of reference books. Clipping newspaper stories each day. Microfilm facilities.

Pawning of wedding and engagement rings in your city. Common and uncommon experiences of pawnshop operators in making loans on such rings. What percentage of the total number are redeemed? Are high school and college rings worth enough these days to be pawnable? Hard-luck stories unfolded by ring owners. Spinoff: Pawnshop activity as economic barometer.

Transporting perishable foods to grocery stores. The number of states from which the truckloads of fresh produce are driven; the drivers making the longest trips. The produce hardest to obtain during the winter and the demand for it. Kinds of products transported by railroads. Spinoff: Special treatments to extend the life of produce.

An interview with the state climatologist. Slant: How his wide knowledge makes him a "walking weather bureau." The climatologist's discussion of extremes of weather in your state and recent changes in weather patterns.

13

A local devotee of pigeon racing. How homing pigeons today are put to the principal use of racing. Winners and their time. The birds' amazing sense of direction and their service in wars. The devotee not only as a raiser but also as an authority on pigeons. Does he or she raise pigeons as show birds? Exhibits at county fairs; winning blue ribbons.

Tracing lost relatives. How people from other areas write the chamber of commerce, the court house, and the city hall about kinfolk. Extending help; reunions, as of relatives who have not met in a score or more years. Cases of amnesia and their happy endings.

A dancer of your section who has made a name for himself or herself at entertainments or on the stage. How dancing develops rhythm and coordination. The fun and exercise dancing brings to the entertainment. Is tap among the accomplishments of the dancer? Performances at benefits.

The top swine producer of your county. His years as a grower of hogs, and the prizes his animals have captured at county and state fairs. Developing leaner, or meat type, hogs; the sale of the swine and the prices. Pig byproducts. The producer's observation on the personality or intelligence of pigs. Any pet pigs?

14

The waiting list of policewomen in the local police department. Slant: The confidence of the chief of police in the Dick Tracy traits of the once weaker sex. Opportunities for policewomen in your city; assignments for the protection of women and children; duties with the vice squad.

The biggest chef in your city. Slant: How he looks like an advertisement for his cooking! A typical meal for him; his likes and dislikes. Average number of persons he cooks for daily; busiest days of the week. Spinoff: The chef and new recipes. Does he experiment?

An antique car club of your state. Slant: The growing appeal of such clubs to adults of every age. The officials of the organization; the leading collectors and their cars. The oldest vehicles of the members and their acquisition. Did any of the cars once belong to celebrities? Endurance contests; taking part in parades. Problems of maintenance; obtaining parts.

A woman probate judge. How long has she held this office? The number of couples she has joined in wedlock. Unusual marriages. Do people favor marriage ceremonies performed by a woman? Her advice to newlyweds. Other duties.

15

The ups and downs of a chimney cleaner. The demand for such services. Average time the chimney sweep spends in cleaning a chimney; the process and average charge. How large an area does the sweep serve? Wearing the traditional black suits with tails, black top hats, and red mufflers.

The birth of the steam locomotive in the United States. Anniversary angle: The first practical American-built locomotive, the Best Friend of Charleston, made its first run over the Charleston and Hamburg Railroad in South Carolina on January 15, 1831. The passenger capacity of the train and the speed; public reaction to this new form of transportation.

Athletes at the penitentiary in your state. How sports keep the prisoners physically fit and provide an outlet in confinement. Sportsmanship among prisoners? The kinds of sports played; the best players. Inmates who once starred as athletes.

The success of the organization known as Parents Without Partners. How members are single parents who are divorced, widowed, separated or unmarried. Proportion of men to women members. How often does the group meet, and what are the activities? Officers and their plans. The agenda for children at gatherings.

16

The publisher of a city magazine in your state. His or her credo in publishing a periodical devoted to the wide range of activities of the city. Stressing civic and cultural interests; your city's personality as developed in/by the magazine. The editor and the size of the staff. The public's reception of the publication; the trend in issuing city magazines. The publisher's magazine experience.

Built-up shoes. Facts from shoe store operators of your city. How persons of average height as well as the very short add height with heels. The psychological angle; professional reasons. Men versus women in the practice; problems encountered. Are most short persons self-conscious?

Dirt eaters of your section. Many adults are fond of a certain kind of clay and eat it regularly. A local doctor's opinion on the habit.

Spinoff: Odd foods craved during pregnancy; nutritional reasons.

Local church libraries. Persons who serve as librarians; the largest library and the average number of patrons per week or month; the most popular books in the various libraries. Donors of volumes. Any books not returned? Slant; The influence of the church libraries in forming the habit of reading such literature.

17

The ambulance service of the local rescue squad. Are more and more people of the county availing themselves of this service? Have operators of private ambulance services been "up in arms" over such competition? Average number of ambulance trips per month; life-saving missions; letters of gratitude.

The band director at a girls college in your state. His or her musical background; the instruments that the director plays. Favorite selections. Any sister musicians? The longest trips for performances.

Snowplows used on railroads. The frequency of use; worst snowfalls within the past dozen of years. How railroad workers are equal to any occasion, in winter and summer, with their diversified equipment. The use of track sweepers and weed burners.

The projection room of the newest motion picture theater in your city. The projectionist's description of the latest improvements in equipment. The size of the reels that the projector accommodates. Are movie projectionists scarce or plentiful?

18

The landscape gardener of the state house. How he takes care of the trees and shrubbery on the grounds of the capitol; the flora to which he gives the most attention. The amount of money spent for the grounds' upkeep. Trees with unusual histories; the oldest and the rarest trees there.

Children of professional wrestlers who appear in your city. The homes of the wrestlers, and the schools attended by the sons and the daughters. The wives' participation in community affairs. Do the kids take a leading part in a variety of sports? Cities with the greatest professional wrestling fever today. Spinoff: Same treatment can apply to other professional sports.

The custodian of the county courthouse. The task of maintaining the county offices; the most difficult sections to keep clean. The number of the custodian's assistants. Lost articles found by the subject.

A day at an auction for automobile dealers in your section. Sources of the cars; number of dealers generally in attendance; most automobiles sold in a day; frequency of the auctions. Do dealers ever get taken?

19

A psychology professor engaged in dream study. His or her most significant findings. How many times a person dreams in a single night. The average length of a dream. The explanation of nightmares. Precognitive dreams.

The child wife of Edgar Allan Poe, the poet and story writer, born on January 19, 1809. How, in 1836, he took as his bride the beautiful Virginia Clemm, fourteen-year-old daughter of his aunt, Maria Clemm. Slant: His love for Virginia as the sunshine of his strange existence. Her lengthy illness that ended in death in 1847.

The activities of the Society for the Prevention of Cruelty to Animals in your city. The organization of the national society in 1866; the founders and the outcome of their first efforts. The introduction of the society in your state; present leaders statewide and local. Cases of negligence and mistreatment of animals. What do local residents feel are the cruelest sports to animals?

The ten most popular bridal gifts. A survey of the sales staff at local stores. The average price of wedding presents. Does a bride often swap gifts because she has too many of the same thing? Spinoff: Treat other special-occasion gifts in the same manner.

20

A farmers' museum. The attractions for citizens and tourists. Did an agricultural or historical society establish it? The museum's chief promoters and the leading donors of farm tools and appliances. The progress of farming through the years shown by the various exhibits. The most recent additions.

The coach of a champion girls' basketball team. The first basketball game was played at Springfield, Massachusetts, on this day in 1892 under the supervision of the sport's inventor, Dr. James Naismith. Number of teams the coach has led to championships, and the stars. The mentor's rule of success, and his or her personal confidence in the players.

Breaking into journalism, thanks to the Scholastic Press Association of your state. Slant: Opening the doors of journalism to high school students through work in the advertising, circulation, or editorial departments of school newspapers. The number of schools that belong to the association; the body's activities, as the annual awards; newspapers that received top honors in the last competition. Stress on photography.

The history of the local city hall. The architect and the construction; the laying of the cornerstone and speakers for the occasion. Renovation or additions; officials with the largest quarters. The office of the mayor. Portraits and pictures of former officials on display. The municipal courthouse as part of the city hall.

21

The power of hypnotism put to professional use. A local physician who uses the hypnotic trance during childbirth. How a surgeon sometimes resorts to hypnotism as an operation aid, and you can report on a dentist who uses it in his practice. Uses by pschologists. Spinoff: Biofeedback.

The upkeep of lots in local cemeteries. The superintendents and their assistants. Maintenance for a fee; perpetual care. Slant: The heavy amount of work required to keep the Cities of the Dead beautiful throughout the year. Maintenance problems in the newer tombstone-less cemeteries versus problems in old-style cemeteries. Grave-decorating taboos or restrictions; complaints about flower and vase thievery; vandalism.

The origin of the nickname Stonewall for General Thomas Jonathan Jackson, a Confederate leader in the Civil War. Anniversary angle: The native of Clarksburg, Virginia, now West Virginia, was born on this day in 1824. How General Barnard E. Bee inspired disorganized troops in the first battle of Bull Run with the cry, "There is Jackson standing like a stone wall."

"My hardest words." Query a score or so of well-known residents of your city about spelling. Include city officials, ministers, and professional and business leaders. Memories of spelling bees. How the National Spelling Bee has been conducted by Scripps-Howard Newspapers and other newspapers since 1939. Children under sixteen years of age as contestants.

22

Senior citizens on the go. No longer do old-timers sit in a corner and rock. Instead, they belong to groups and take trips to faraway places. The longest and the most enjoyable trips; the highlights; capturing the scenes with the camera; buying souvenirs. Spinoff: Grey Panthers; senior citizens combat age discrimination.

Snow and ice in your county in the long ago. Slant: How the inhabitants regarded snow as a blessing instead of a nuisance. It is automobile transportation and pollution that make snow such a mess today. How the snow-lovers of the distant past would move snow, even from the woods, to the roads and pack it down to produce smooth highways; care of the bridges. How people of that time would preserve ice for later use, in the absence of ice-manufacturing plants.

Order in the house! How the sergeant-at-arms of the state senate—and his counterpart in the legislature—take care of unruliness when the tempers of the lawmakers reach the boiling point. Kinds of legislation that generate the most arguments; the hottest encounters. Eruption of fisticuffs, and ejections.

A youngster of your city who is a bird trainer. Feats with such pets as parakeets, canaries, lovebirds, cockatoos, or exotic birds. Do males or females master tricks quicker? Does the trainer raise birds as a money-making hobby?

23

A local patent attorney. Slant: How a lawyer has an influential part in the nation's progress through his work with inventors. His association with inventions that have been of unusual benefit; marketing the products abroad. New inventions from which the lawyer expects dramatic results.

The largest writer's club in your state. The founders and highlights of its existence; the current officers; the "sellingest" members; latest sales to national magazines and book publishers. The youngest selling author. A typical meeting; prominent writers as speakers.

A minister of your section who is a collector of rare Bibles. The oldest of the volumes and their values; how they were obtained; the original owners. How the collection is displayed at churches, civic events, and other places. Spinoff: Recent improvements in Bible translation and reactions to the changes.

Midget automobile racing in your state. Leading drivers and their records. Their most thrilling races and near-fatal mishaps. What does it cost to construct a midget racer? This form of racing as a drawing card. Spinoff: Motorcycle racing; dune buggies.

24

A widely known judge of art exhibits in your state. Judging exhibits from the county fair to competitions at arts centers. The judge as an artist; works that have received praise from other art authorities. Present trends in art and the most promising artists of today.

Does stamp collecting still rate as "the hobby of kings and the king of hobbies"? Let's have the answer from leaders of a local philatelic society. The largest stamp collections among the members, and the most valuable stamps. Stamp design trends over the years: Changes in stamp-making. How the United States Postal Service promotes stamp collecting; the sale of collecting kits.

The trees of your state that provide the best lumber. The kinds of timber that are in the greatest demand at local lumber companies. The most expensive; calls for unusual kinds of wood; species of trees on the decline in the state. Is "tree-napping" prevalent?

The magic cry of gold! Gold mania struck the United States on this day in 1848 when James Wilson Marshall spotted the precious metal at Sutter's Mill in California. Gold fields in your state that have excited the mining fever. The most profitable of the mines. Operators who made themselves wealthy overnight. Panning streams for gold today.

25

An insight into the university press of your state. The editorial director and the assistants. The first books and their authors. Number of volumes published annually; the variety of subjects. Some university books on unlikely subjects have had a good market in recent years. Books that have experienced the most sales. Slant: How university presses make possible the publication of books of special significance to their states.

A veteran court stenographer of your section. How many miles does he or she travel annually in the performance of duty? The number of words taken during his or her career; the trials with the longest testimony; number of trials witnessed; the most colorful. Has he or she witnessed executions?

Hunting historical secrets. How historians of the state historical society search through documents for information that will shed light on persons or events. Historical mysteries that are arousing the most attention. The latest historical discoveries that have rewarded researchers.

A star of an ice skating show in your section who captivates audiences with his or her juggling skill. What are the most difficult objects to juggle? Special problems of juggling on ice versus dry land. The time the skater spends with juggling rehearsals a day. Spinoff: Other skating stars; clowns on ice.

26

What would the wife of the governor propose as the state dish? The governor's favorites in food; banquets for notables and the menus. Recipes of the First Lady that are most requested by friends.

The latest advances in dental equipment, as described by the president of the dental association of your county. Anniversary angle: George F. Green was given a patent on an electric dental drill on January 26, 1875. Other milestones in the dental profession, especially the introduction of anesthetics for painless dentistry; William Morton as a pioneer in using ether in tooth extraction.

A leading geologist who holds a state position. Different kinds of surveys and the results. Providing basic aerial geologic mapping and mineral resource investigations. How state agencies, private industry, and the general public receive geologic advice.

Members of the local police and fire departments as musicians and singers. Do any of them belong to bands? How about the chiefs? Members who belong to singing groups. The cop or fireman who plays the most instruments.

27

The winter life of a baseball league president in your state. Preparing for the approaching season, including the playing schedule and putting the park in order. Is he a onetime team manager? His close friendships with diamond stars; discovery and development of noted players; his collection of autographed balls. His foremost cases as president.

Vietnam Day, which commemorates the official signing of the peace agreements ending the Vietnam War on this day in 1973. The battle deaths to that date amounted to 46,498, as compared with 6,824 in the Revolutionary War. Servicemen of your county who made the supreme sacrifice.

Beware of freeloaders. The problem at local theaters and sports events in detecting persons seeking free entrance. Tricks that failed; the cleverest stunts attempted. Slipping under the tent at the circus. Spinoffs: Fraudulent ticket sales; scalping.

The founders and first presidents of the state universities in your state and nearby states. Note that the University of Georgia, the first state university, received its charter on this day in 1785. How the pioneer educators have been honored.

28

An interview with a carillonneur of your state. Slant: The love for the concert stage high above the ground. Number of recitals per week; the carillonneur's favorite songs; his or her own compositions. The number of carillons in the state.

Creatures down on the farm—and their prices. What would the county agent consider bargain prices for a package of bees with a queen, or a mule or a horse, or a cow, or a goat or sheep, or a hog, or a duck?

A veteran physician's large collection of medical journals. Slant: The contrast between the old and the new in the medical world as revealed by the magazines. Stories announcing major discoveries and new treatments over the years. The importance of journals in the enormous task of staying current. Medical humor found in the periodicals.

The serious side of a comedian of your state. Strains imposed on family life. Problems in the marriage and how they have been worked out. Give-and-take situations. Long stays on the road filling engagements. The joy of children.

29

The chemist versus the criminal. Actual cases in which the work of the chemist in a police laboratory in your state led to convictions. The equipment and conducting tests. The detective mind of the chemist!

A woman's press club of your state. The most prominent members and their experiences; those who have been foreign correspondents. Winners of the club's annual awards. The biggest scoops, or exclusives, by members. Veteran editors of women's pages on newspapers; travel editors who hardly stop going.

Diamond stars associated with your state and adjoining states who are represented in the Baseball Hall of Fame at Cooperstown, New York. Anniversary angle: On January 29, 1936, the first five men were elected—Ty Cobb, Walter Johnson, Christy Mathewson, Babe Ruth, and Honus Wagner. The records established by the stars; the highest annual salaries.

The oldest dance teacher in your city in length of career. An estimate of the total number of students. Former pupils who have made a name for themselves, dancing or otherwise. Dance crazes of bygone years. The activities of a dance teaching society. What does the teacher plan to do on retirement?

30

The manufacture of artificial flowers. How a local resident derives a good income from their sale. How the flowers are made; the materials. The best months and occasions for the sale of the flowers. The most popular flowers and colors; methods of cleaning. Pros and cons of artificial flowers: esthetics versus practicality.

Thomas Jefferson, the third president, as a bookworm (his library developed into the nucleus of the Library of Congress). Anniversary angle: On this day in 1815 Congress authorized the purchase of his library as the central part of the Library of Congress. How his more than 6,400 volumes replaced the books that met destruction when the British burned the capitol.

Practical jokes on apprentices. What rookie cops and firemen learned too late! How cub reporters and printer's devils in newspaper offices fell hook, line, and sinker. Tricks played upon college freshmen by upper classmen in bygone years. Hazing that bordered on the danger line.

An aviator of your section who is a star of air shows. Is he a war veteran? His most dangerous stunts; scares during performances. Risking his life for benefit shows. His reputation as a daredevil pilot. Spinoff: Barnstormers and the age of aviation before CAB and FAA controls.

<h1 style="text-align:center">31</h1>

An amateur astronomer of your section. How he or she built a telescope; the cost of it. What have been his most fascinating experiences as a stargazer? His studies and deductions; his comments on the latest discoveries concerning stars. The astronomer's interest in astrology, also related to the heavenly bodies. Is he a horoscope fan?

Left-handed blues among local citizens—and meeting the challenge. How left-handedness can produce psychological problems. Tactical problems posed to the left-handed person, unrealized by the general right-handed populace. How lefties adapt themselves to situations and even band together. The activities of the League of Lefthanders of New Milford, New Jersey, and its publication.

An interpreter of your section as a lifesaver in communications barriers. Is he or she a language professor or a native of a foreign country familiar with a number of languages? Quick calls for the interpreter's services, as in cases of emergency—illness or in court.

The most difficult languages. Spinoff: A linguist of the state who engages in translation, perhaps for a publishing company.

Screen monsters who live in the memory of local motion picture and TV fans. Movie and video buffs' selection of the five most unforgettable monster films of all time. Remakes of monster movies. Modern techniques in horror films versus the subtlety and conventions of the past.

FEBRUARY

Month of History and Romance

Although February ranks as "Shorty," you will find it action-packed from start to finish and deserving of the title History Month. As examples, there are the anniversaries of the births of Presidents George Washington, William Henry Harrison, and Abraham Lincoln, as well as an array of other notables.

On the list are Thomas A. Edison, Henry Wadsworth Longfellow, Victor Herbert, Horace Greeley, Aaron Burr, Cyrus Hall McCormick, Susan B. Anthony, Mary Garden, Enrico Caruso, Victor Herbert, James Joyce, Jules Verne, Elizabeth Blackwell, Solomon R. Guggenheim, Charles A. Lindbergh, Gertrude Stein, Sinclair Lewis, John Foster Dulles, Adlai E. Stevenson, and William F. Cody ("Buffalo Bill").

You can hitch your typewriter to a string of historical events for February: 1. The Supreme Court held its first meeting, 1790; 2. National League organized in professional baseball, 1867; 4. Confederate States of America created at Montgomery, Alabama, 1861; 4. United Service Organizations (USO) founded, 1941; 8. The College of William and Mary, the second oldest college in the United States, received charter, 1693; 10. France surrendered Canada to Great Britain by the Treaty of Paris, 1763; 15. U.S.S. *Maine* exploded in Havana Harbor, 1898; 21. Washington Monument in Washington, D.C., dedicated, 1885; 22. The United States purchased the Florida Territory from Spain, 1819; 24. William S. Otis patented the steam shovel, 1839; and 26. Napoleon fled from the island of Elba, 1815.

One day of the year leaves no doubt that "the world loves a lover." St. Valentine's Day, a festival of love on February 14 when countless lovers express their amorous sentiments with flowers, candy and cards.

Every four years another day in this month is given over to Cupid—February 29 in Leap Year. On this day, heralded as Bachelor's Day, the fairer sex can turn the tables and sally forth without inhibition in quest of male game. Writers can content themselves with reporting the custom that has lasted for centuries.

Special days run fast and furious: February 2. Ground Hog Day; 3. The Four Chaplains Memorial Day; 5. Roger Williams Day; 11. National Inventors Day; 12. Nancy Hanks Lincoln Memorial Day in Booneville, Indiana; 20. John Glenn Day; and 23. Iwo Jima Day.

Special months and weeks spell out good news for writers— American Heart Month, National Cherry Month, Boy Scouts of America Scouting Anniversary Week, National Children's Dental Health Week, and National Crime Prevention Week. And, just between us, why not a Be-Kind-to-Writers Week?

1

What a scientist of your state says about spirits. Investigations into ghost stories and other supernatural matters. Haunted house tales that have lingered for generations. Seances, strange goings-on; hoaxes that have been exposed. Local Haunted Places?

Do twins work alike? Instances in your city in which twins follow the same occupation. Are some even partners in business? The ultimate ambitions of the pairs and their preparation. Do the twins dress alike in adulthood?

Bulletins distributed by the office of the county farm agent or the extension service of an agricultural college. The person in charge of the mailing duties. Slant: How the publications form an ever growing library of information that enriches the lives of farmers and gardeners, both literally and figuratively. The number of pamphlets available; the most popular subjects; amount of literature kept on hand at all times.

An interview with a junior golf champion. His or her greatest shots; the match that won the crown. Trophies belonging to the champ. Number one thrills in tourneys. Any holes in one? Skill in other sports; greatest ambitions; college plans. Do Dad and Mom play golf?

2

Ground Hog Day. The opinion of the oldest farmers in your county about the ground hog's supposed skill in weather prognostication. The coldest springs in their memory. Ground hog fanciers keep the animal as pets and await its return from the burrow after a winter of hiberation. Slant: The farmer's all-consuming interest in weather because it spells success or failure for his operations.

The professor of meteorology at a local or a nearby college. The number of students the classes attract; the feminine members; opportunities in the Weather Bureau as well as in commercial fields, as airlines and industry. The professor's observations about long-range forecasting.

The dietitian at the city jail. Arranging the menu from day to day; preparing the food; cost of the meals. Feasts on holidays. Any food strikes by prisoners? Slant: The uncertain number of "guests" each day.

Testing eyesight at the driver's license bureau. Applicants for driving licenses who are surprised to find they have defective vision. The percentage of applicants who need glasses. The equipment used.

3

The largest artists' colony in the state. Husband and wife artists; young artists who show great promise; artists with a national repuation. Colonists who have been art teachers the longest. Changes in styles over the years. Art auctions by the colony.

The dean of alteration tailors at local department stores. Does he or she alter more women's clothes than men's? Are men easier to please than women? Impatient customers who want alterations in a jiffy. Busiest days. Changes in styles down the years.

The local high school course in automobile mechanics. The instructor and the facilities; practical experience; graduates of past years who have gained more than ordinary success. Spinoffs: Are vocational courses in high school on the increase? Adult education courses in practical matters.

Coupon clippers. The pulling power of coupons in newspapers and magazines, explained by store managers. Today four out of five

United States households take advantage of coupons. Kinds of coupons that are most effective. Are men just as enthusiastic as women over coupons? The strangest coupon stories; coupon cheaters and coupon hogs.

4

Weekend fever. "R and R" for local residents. Getting away from it all or getting with it. Slant: The wide range of activities available; different strokes for different folks; where they go and what they do and why. Dancing and prancing at a discotheque; sporting events, fishing and boating, hiking and camping, concerts and art exhibits. Spinoff: The views of an industrial psychologist on "long weekends."

Roller skating as part of the recreational activities in your area. Slant: The varied benefits of skating for both sexes, including preschool kids. Speed and also figure skating; skating to music. Winners of skating trophies; coaches' tips on this year-round sport.

A local citizen who has built his own airplane. How the build-it-yourself theme holds special appeal for aviators. The designing of the aircraft; the materials and the cost; safety features; testing. The safety margin of homemade planes. Does the owner have any trouble assuring passengers? Naming the craft.

The birth of the Winter Olympics and the first champions in the competition. The organization of the first such games on February 4, 1932, and the supporters. Choosing Olympic athletes; candidates from your state; meeting the expense.

5

A day with a baggageman of an airline, bus company or a railroad serving your city. How many pieces of luggage does he take care of each day? The busiest days and months. The strangest pieces of luggage; lost or damaged luggage. Instances of mistaken identity. Does the baggageman get letters from passengers? Are women more insistent on baggage care than men?

An interview with a wholesale florist of your section. The wide area served by the company; the routes each day. An insight into refrigerated transports. The flowers most in demand; those gaining in popularity. The main problems of a wholesale florist. Floral designers.

The college hostess and housemother for women at a college in your area. Slant: How she is well known and loved for her motherly advice and comforting words. How she can be hard-boiled at times. What to do with homesick coeds. Spinoff: The development of coed dorms. Pro and con; views of students and educators.

Feats of a trick marksman of your state. Slant: Producing magic—not death—with guns. How the marksman hits his target in various ways, as with the aid of mirrors; shooting a cigarette in assistant's mouth; the performer's repertoire; the most difficult shots. Amount of practice necessary.

6

What happens to used books? The answer is found in the business of used-book stores. A local example. How customers can trade in books. The wide range of subjects. Hardcovers versus paperbacks. How nonfiction compares with fiction in popularity. Special problems of a used-book dealer. Spinoff: The fate of old books at the public library in your city. The librarian's account of what happens when a volume grows too shopworn or out-of-date. Retiring old reference books and encyclopedias from service; the rebinding of books to lengthen their life span.

The oldest creator of collage in your city. Slant: How this form of art offers a challenge to senior citizens and gives them an outlet for their creative talents. What objects the man or woman uses in making collages; the technique. Collages that have amazed the most viewers; prize-winning exhibits.

A veteran typewriter repairman in your city. A rough estimate of the number of typewriters he has fixed; the leading troubles. The task of repairing typewriters used by the students in typing classes at school. Typewriter improvements in recent years. Are electric typewriters the sales leaders? Exotic typewriters. The repairman's ten tips for taking care of a typewriter.

7

The chaplain of the legislature or senate in your state. The spiritual leadership that the lawmakers as well as the general population find in the chaplain. His career in the ministry; largest churches he has pastored; number of converts. The chaplain's interest in law-making. Any pieces of legislation he would suggest?

What does the devil look like? Query local members of the clergy. How the devil has been depicted by Bible illustrators. How in the Middle Ages he was drawn with horns, cloven hoofs, and a tail. The influence of recent popular movies and books on Satanic themes, or on the physical concept of the devil.

The family tree of the state historian. Slant: How the history specialist has used all the resources at his command to "dig up the bones" in his clan. How far back does he trace his roots? How he keeps the family history up to date. The coat of arms; ancient let-ters; preserving family portraits. The oldest living members of the family.

The five greatest headaches of the manager of a leading opera house. Emergencies that give him or her fits. Sickness that poses problems; singers with throat trouble. Last-minute replacements and transportation difficulties.

8

The catalogue goes on and on and on. The growing number of or-ders through the catalogue departments of local stores and also from catalogues mailed directly to the home. Are more and more working women resorting to catalogue orders? What consumer research reveals about the future of catalogue ordering.

The beauty parlor comes to the hospital. A local hospital that sup-plies such things as manicure, shampoo and hair set. Slant: Beauty treatments as a morale builder for the women patients. Observa-tions by the head of the hospital's beauty shop; number of licensed beauticians.

The local champion of pocket billiards. His reputation as a trick shooter; his most exciting matches in championship play; his toughest opponents. Does he play daily? Advice that he offers begin-ners; his early mentors.

Car troubles at local drive-ins. Begin with automobile woes at bank drive-ins; lengthy delays with amateur mechanics coming to the rescue. How about cars that break down at movie drive-ins? Fast-food drive-ins are not exempt from the curse. Cars that break down in the midst of drive-through zoos.

9

True or false: The image of newspapermen and women in movies. What do real newspaper people of your city think of reel reporters and editors who have graced screens through the years? What they pronounce the most realistic movies of the newsroom. Actors and actresses they would prefer to play their part in a movie.

The weather service more than a century ago and the scope of its duties. Anniversary angle: The United States National Weather Service was established as a unit of the United States Army on February 9, 1870. How twenty years later the setup was transformed into a civilian organization called the Weather Bureau. How accurate were forecasts at that time?

The activities of a dog club of your city. Fund-raising projects, such as puppy matches; points about showing dogs. Awarding ribbons and trophies; the leading winners in recent years. Officials of the kennel club. Obedience training classes. The chief breeds of dogs; current champions; the highest priced canines. Speaking of dogs, you might describe the luxuries of dogdom's accessories, or focus on so-called talking dogs.

Favorite Bible characters of Sunday school children. Slant: Why certain characters of the Old and the New Testaments have made the deepest impression on the boys and the girls. Qualities that the children admire in their favorite characters.

10

A veteran ballet teacher of your section. A typical beginner's class; developing the basic skills through the months; teaching the positions of the body, head, and arms. Feats of the advanced pupils. The daily practice followed by persons who decide to make ballet a career. The most successful ballet dancers produced by the teacher.

The operator of a rag laundry in your city. Slant: How he or she puts hopes in the old phrase of rags to riches. How the laundry supplies and launders rags that are used in industry. Does the company launder rags used for other purposes? Sources of the rags; the size of the area served by the laundry.

To the rescue of camera users who may be stumped about what to photograph! Tips from a professional photographer of your city for camera fans in search of more meaningful pictures. What would the pro recommend as twenty-five topnotch subjects for the shutterbugs? Winter gems.

The attraction of basketmaking. Slant: The survival of this art that was practiced among primitive people. An insight into a craft with perennial tourist lure. The basic appeal of baskets. Various designs in baskets. Materials and their sources. The oldest basketmakers and their output.

11

The world of skiing. Ski resorts have added a new dimension to the sports industry and each winter gain countless converts. How machines create artificial snow; the daily cost. The height of the greatest slopes; how the mechanical lifts transport the skiers to the top. Ski fashions; the items worn for safety; coping with crowding. The leading skiers at your nearest resort. Romance on the ski slopes! A day in the life of a ski instructor.

The cymbal player in a local or a nearby symphony orchestra. Slant: Cymbals are mentioned in the Old Testament. The size of the cymbals and their attraction; points about mastering this form of music. Spinoff: Origins of other musical instruments.

The breeding of dwarf animals, as explained by the director of the animal husbandry department of an agricultural college in your state. The great curiosity the dwarf creatures arouse. The normal occurrence of these animals. What animals commonly generate dwarfs? The price of the dwarfs.

National Inventors Day, in honor of all inventors. How societies of inventors observe this special day. The organization of inventors in your state and its get-togethers. Predictions of inventions by the twenty-first century.

12

Abraham Lincoln's birthday. Five women in the life of the sixteenth president, beginning with his mother, Nancy Hanks Lincoln, and his stepmother, Sarah Bush Johnston Lincoln. His sweethearts Ann Rutledge and Mary Owens, and his wife, the former Mary Todd, whom he met at a dance. His wedding on November 4, 1842—the marriage produced no daughters.

A specialist of your state who is noted for correcting clubfeet. Are most cases present at birth? Injuries or diseases that sometimes cause this condition. How the foot is reshaped and repositioned; surgical treatment; special exercises to strengthen the muscles.

The oldest courthouse in your state. Who built the historic structure? Laying the cornerstone; the speakers. Has the building been remodeled extensively? Noted trials there. The first sentence of death imposed by a court there.

School letters presented athletes of a local high school. The sport that leads in the number of monogram awards; winners of the most letters. The number of girls who won letters the past year, compared to the male wearers. Letters awarded for achievement other than athletic.

13

Poultry research. Activities at an experimental station in your state. Feeding experiments; increasing egg production. The station's director and his predictions about poultry in the next decade. Slant: How the poultry industry is meeting the challenge in food requirements as the nation's population rises.

The advent of the magazine industry in the United States. It happened on this day in 1741 when the *American Magazine,* published by Andrew Bradford in Philadelphia, first appeared. Philadelphia as a publishing center through the years. The Curtis Publishing Company and the *Saturday Evening Post.*

The life of a fence builder, in both the city and in rural areas. A local fence builder or installer, and the amount he and his assistants do in an average week. Kinds of fences, and the most elaborate. Extent of electrical fencing. Is barbed wire in much demand?

Physical education program for physically handicapped persons, as designed by both teachers and physicians. The benefits of the exercises, and the enjoyment by the students. Special equipment to suit the needs of the youngsters. Spinoff: Programs for the rehabilitation of stroke and accident victims.

14

St. Valentine's Day. Top honeymoon trips today, as related by the operator of a travel agency in your city. The longest travels of local newlyweds; the longest stays. Foreign countries and cities preferred by honeymooners; the leading attractions there, winter and summer. Favorite places in the United States for the new Mr. and Mrs. Is Niagara Falls still in the running? Travel tips for honeymooners.

The Champion singer for weddings in your city. Average number of singing appearances per month; carrying on despite sickness, because the wedding—like show business—must go on. Traveling considerable distances to take part in ceremonies. Observations about weddings, as on the bride, and relatives. You might want to concentrate on humor at weddings.

The courtship and marriage of the first family of your city. Was it love at first sight for the mayor and his wife? The first date. Did true love run smoothly? Recollections of the big day of the wedding and the honeymoon trip. The couple's advice to lovers of today. You may go statewide in scope and give the treatment to the governor and his Juliet.

The use of voting machines in your state. Anniversary angle: On February 14, 1899, Congress authorized the use of voting machines in national elections. The first city in your state to install voting machines; the number of such cities at present. The cost of a machine and the operation. Have the machines eliminated voting fraud?

15

"My first coaching job." The reminiscences of the top athletic coach, high school and college, in your section. Unforgettable lessons from the first positions. Stars he developed; the most thrilling plays during his career. Scrapbooks and trophies.

Spanish-American War Memorial Day and *Maine* Memorial Day. Number of troops from your county who served in the war; descendants can furnish details. Reunions of the veterans over the years.

Spinoff: Oddities about the war. Its origin, and consequences.

Postage meters in your city. Slant: The convenience of these machines that print the amount of postage on the envelope and also give adhesive strips with the proper denomination. Manufacturers of the machines; details of the operation. The number of firms in your city that use them. Spinoff: Local businesses hurt the most by rising postal rates.

Putting white elephants in the black. How local citizens accomplish this. They hold garage sales, try their luck at a jockey lot, or trek to a swap shop for a happy solution. Stores with white elephants on their hands chop prices for quick disposal and even stage white elephant sales. Managers can confess their biggest white elephants.

16

February as the anniversary month of a number of organizations. They include the Benevolent Protective Order of Elks, established in New York City on this day in 1868. February 18, 1864, witnessed the founding of the Knights of Pythias in Washington, D.C., and the Rotary Club came into existence in Chicago on February 23, 1905. The advent of these clubs in your city and the first officers.

Running away from home. Data from the head of the county shelter. Do girl runaways outnumber boys? Romantic reasons. The drastic changes in youth motivation in running away. Spinoff: Husbands or wives who are runaways. The most effective methods of tracing.

Young exponents of judo, karate, and other martial arts in your city. Classes where youngsters learn the art of self-defense; the coach. Body conditioning; promotion of students; title holders among the pupils; amazing feats by girls. Taking part in tournaments. Special costumes and rituals.

A clergyman who serves at a school for the deaf. How he works actively with the students; religious services at the institution, with the use of sign language. Students who would like to enter the ministry.

17

Histories of your state. How many histories have been published?

The earliest historians and their accuracy. Slant: The love of the state displayed by the historians over the years. State histories used as textbooks. Best sellers among the histories; the latest on the market. The number of histories in the local library. Authors of the histories.

The pattern departments of local stores. What does the volume of pattern sales indicate about the popularity of sewing? Any radical changes in patterns in the past decade? How customers seek the advice of clerks in selecting a pattern. Do many people buy the wrong size? Keeping a good supply of patterns; watching the seasons. Are most of the pattern clerks sewing devotees themselves?

The birth of the National Congress of Mothers, now the National Congress of Parents and Teachers, on February 17, 1897. When the movement spread to your state; the current president of the state organization and the goals this year. Long-time leaders in the state. How the range of the organization's activities has changed over the years.

The manager of an airline serving your city. His main duties; the least known of them; improving airline service, both passenger and freight. The manager as an aviator; the safety of aviation, as stressed by the subject. Efforts to make the entire family aviation conscious.

18

— Trying to prevent dead-on-arrivals at the hospital through CPR— cardiopulmonary resuscitation. Instructions given to local citizens about how to save persons whose hearts have stopped beating. Practicing the techniques on lifelike mannequins. CPR instructors who speak before businesses, churches, and clubs. Spinoff: Heimlich maneuver to prevent choking.

The bigger and brighter, the better. The sign wizard of your city says so. Slant: How the competition between sign makers has spurred designers to greater efforts in imagination and skill. The most spectacular sign the local expert has created. Attention-getting effects, such as movements that dramatize the sign's message.

An interview with a food broker of your city. A typical day at his brokerage house. Changes in food tastes; emphasis on frozen foods. Slant: The variety of today's foods combined with quick preparation for the cook's convenience. How the manager of the establishment keeps his fingers on the pulse of the food industry.

Memories of covered bridges in your section. Your fact-giver is the president of the county historical society. Slant: The covered bridge as a revered institution, a refuge from storms and a romantic spot for lovers. The number of covered bridges in the area in bygone years; builders of the bridges; kinds of timber used in the construction. Do any covered bridges remain in the state?

19

Welcome, truck drivers—you are the kings of the road. A super-large truck stop in your section where the drivers relax and obtain meals, fuel, lodging and mechanics if needed. The comradeship of the drivers and stories of experiences. The array of truckers' souvenirs and sundries. Fighting against undesirable elements, such as prostitution.

Dial-a-prayer. The wide popularity of a prayer phone in your city. Details of the operation; ministers who give the prayers. Comments by pastors about the twenty-four-hour service. Number of calls per week; the length of the prayers. Spinoff: Other dial-a-lines.

Early recording stars, such as Enrico Caruso, Medea Figner, and Nikolay Figner. Thomas A. Edison was issued a patent on the phonograph on February 19, 1878. How the voices of such notables as P. T. Barnum, Robert Browning, and William Gladstone were preserved by the early talking machine. *Disappearing Records due to CDs*

Helping hands for the retarded adults of your city. The head of your county's association for retarded citizens can tell of the progress the workers have achieved with their efforts and patience. Easing the day-by-day burdens of the individuals. The trend away from institutionalization of retarded adults.

20

Guided tours in your city. How the Welcome sign is out at numerous places, including industrial plants and newspaper offices. The children who get a bang out of visiting the post office and the police and fire departments—mixing learning with fun. Tours of a dam and power house, the gas plant, an ice company, and the bakery.

The queen of shot givers in your county. The nurse who gives the most shots at the county health department. Slant: How she is the children's best friend despite their fear of the needle. How to calm kids—and adults—when "shooting." Kinds of injections; free clinics. Statistics about reduction in cases of diseases. Worst epidemics in bygone years. Resurgence of some diseases due to immunization apathy.

John Glenn Day, in recognition of the Marine test pilot who made the first orbit of the earth by a United States astronaut. Tributes to the native of Cambridge, Ohio, for his historic feat in *Friendship 7* by local citizens. The modesty of Glenn, who, like the aviation hero of another era, Charles A. Lindbergh, preferred the use of "we" to "I." Glenn's switch to a political career.

The children's section of the local library. Slant: Boys and girls have their bestsellers in fiction and nonfiction just like their parents. The current bestsellers and the librarian's opinion of the stories. The number of children's volumes; the amount of nonfiction. Magazines for kids. The vacation reading program in the summer.

21

The survival of the waterwheel in your section as a means of grinding grain. The oldest one and its operator; the amount of trade the business enjoys today. Tourists' fascination with the waterwheel and the operation.

Old buses. The disposal of the buses in your city when new ones are bought, and the prices. Unusual uses for second-hand buses; buyers, such as entertainers, churches that transport members to services and outings, and privately owned bus lines.

The dedication of the Washington Monument in Washington, D.C., on this day in 1885. How political arguments and lack of money delayed the completion of the monument until 1884, although it had been started in 1848. The memorial stones from states and foreign countries in the all-stone structure.

A church theater group of your city. The director and assistants. The most outstanding performances. Is a rotating casting system used? The ages most interested in dramatics. How many adult players have joined youngsters in the productions? The matter of costumes; make-up; stage workers.

22

George Washington's birthday. The first real job of the Father of His Country—helping Lord Fairfax survey his buildings for more than a year. The pay for the work and young Washington's satisfaction with it. How as commander of the Army he wanted no pay beyond his actual expenses; his salary as president of the new nation.

The battle to save Mount Vernon. The heroine, Ann Pamela Cunningham, founded the movement to preserve George Washington's home. Slant: How, despite many discouragements and a severe spinal affliction, the South Carolinian managed to raise $200,000 to purchase Mount Vernon on February 22, 1859, so that speculators might not acquire the place. How she resided at Mount Vernon from 1868 until 1874 and supervised the estate.

Salaries of mayors in your state. How does your city compare with others in this respect? Cities that pay the most. Any women who serve as chief executives? The dean of the mayors.

The portable laboratory of a large police department. Slant: Combatting criminals by carrying police equipment to the scene of the crime. The extensive amount of equipment, including a darkroom, fingerprint and other specialized cameras, and plaster-casting kit. The newest gadgets. Solving the almost perfect crime.

23

Customs that foreign-born residents of your section still follow as in their native lands. Special days: Songs that stir memories. Natives of abroad who have been transferred to the United States by industrial companies. Mixed marriages by military personnel. Countries with the largest number of natives in your state. Such a feature suggests one based on favorite cooking recipes from "back home."

A visit to a fertilizer factory in your county. Slant: The extensive preparation for the spring season of planting, with the fertilizer plant as the forerunner. The ingredients of fertilizers; the process of manufacture; the daily output. Spinoff: Trend back to natural fertilizers as petrochemical costs rise.

Sex education in schools of your state. How the teachers present the subject; reaction of parents, pro and con. Textbooks and other material. The views of the state superintendent of education. The pioneers in such courses. Spinoff: Planned Parenthood and other organizations disseminating birth control information to young people.

Clowns and animals. Slant: The devotion that exists between the laugh-makers and the animals. Ply amateur and professional clowns with questions. Animals easiest to train, according to the clowns; the most difficult tricks to teach. Temper of the animal performers.

24

Mr. Country Fiddler of your county. The oldest fiddler at dances and entertainments, and his skill. Number of tunes in his repertoire; his favorites. Slant: The subject's efforts to preserve country fiddling despite other fads in music. How many fiddles does he have? Are any of his grandchildren humdinger fiddlers?

The switchboard operator at a local hospital. Estimate of the number of daily calls; paging in the hospital. Giving out information on the condition of patients. The number of room telephones in the hospital. Spinoffs: Hospital public relations director. Importance of volunteers.

The introduction of the income tax law in the United States. Mark down today as the anniversary of the Sixteenth Amendment to the Constitution. Local reaction, as found in newspaper files. The amount of the bite in the beginning; the extent of violations.

A local collector of whips. The wide variety of whips, ranging from the buggy whip to the bull whip. The longest whip in the collection and its history; whips that were acquired overseas; total value of the collection.

25

Wanted: Information on any and all subjects. The challenges faced by the writer of an Action Line-type column for a large newspaper in your state. How readers phone in or mail their questions. The principal types of questions that descend upon the columnist every day; the most difficult of them to answer. The heavy research and the amount of correspondence in search of the requested information.

Lost and found balls on a local golf course. Retrieving balls from the waters of a lake, in the woods, or on the fairway; the largest number recovered at one time. The experiences of the retriever in such recovery. Is he or she an ardent golfer?

Your city's seal. People, animals, and plants depicted in it; the emblems and colors, and what they denote. The city motto as an inscription. The designer of the seal.

A saddle club of your county. The activities of the club. Horse shows; prize winners; the ringmaster and the judges. Unusual names for horses of the club's members; teaching horses—young and old—new tricks. Bridle paths.

26

A home for retired and elderly people maintained by a religious denomination in your state. Slant: How the church members' concern for the elderly is a prime example of their Christian faith. Operation of the project, and the monthly expense. The superintendent of the home and ministering to the occupants' needs with compassion. Worthwhile work by some of the residents.

A commercial mushroom grower. Growing mushrooms under the proper conditions of darkness, temperature, and humidity. The processing plant where the mushrooms are graded. Size of the nation's annual crop. Spinoff: Wild mushroom hunting. Truffles.

Sisters of government officials in your city, county, and state. Are some of the women in government working themselves? Interests shared by brothers and sisters. How sisters, especially big sisters, have aided the officials in their careers. Hobbies, literary preferences, and other favorites of the sisters.

A male resident of your city who has made people sit up and take notice because of his feats with needlework. How and why he became interested in such work. His most elaborate creations. Knitting and macrame were originally male pursuits.

27

Conquering unruly rivers with flood control in your state. How dams and reservoirs have been constructed to prevent flooding once common along rivers. Worst floods, especially in the spring, on record. How some of the dams also produce hydroelectric power. Organizations fighting new dams because of the contention that some dams do more harm than good.

A veteran meat inspector of the public health service of your state. Slant: Protecting your health by making certain meat is of high quality and sanitary. Are rejections frequent? Improvements in sanitary conditions during the past quarter of a century. Number of meat inspectors in the state.

The six worst problems encountered by campus police. The experiences of security guards at a college in your state in preventing disorders and rounding up lawbreakers. The most common types of thefts. Pranks that get out of hand. Changing nature of campus problems over the years.

An agent who has a long list of models on his string. What he or she names as must qualities, such as excellent posture, poise, and grace in movements. Did most of the models attend modeling schools? The ages of models in their prime. Children who model. Any animal models?

28

An interview with a daredevil driver appearing in your section. Slant: The stunt man's car crashing exploits answer the demand for greater thrills at stock car races. Obtaining automobiles to be wrecked on purpose; the most sensational acts; unscheduled thrills. Serious injuries and long hospital stays.

Of what are men's hats made today? Slant: Guess what is on your head! Search out the city's number one sellers of male headgear for the answers. Beaver fur is used as the best felts, and factories also produce felts from the fur of muskrat, nutria, and rabbit. Manufacture of panama hats from toquilla and jipijapa. Throw light on the high silk hat, the derby, the homburg—and last but not least, the Stetson of cowboy glory. Has hat wearing declined over the years?

The voyage of the *California* to the West Coast in the gold rush beginning in 1848. The vessel—the first ship to carry gold-seekers to California—arrived at San Francisco on this day in 1849. The departure from New York City on October 8, 1848, and the journey around Cape Horn. The variety of the passengers, and the chaotic conditions aboard.

The movie preview. How local theater managers give sneak previews to obtain reactions. Do the managers consider themselves hard-boiled critics? Recent movies that have lived up to the greatest expectations. Managers' selection of the ten best pictures of the past year.

29

Leap Year. Watch out, bachelors! Boy-chasing by fair maidens in Leap Year, à la Sadie Hawkins Day. A psychologist's views on Leap Year, when girls traditionally have the opportunity to pursue males to their hearts' content.

The busy life of a bridal consultant of your city, Leap Year or not. The steps in planning a wedding; making preparations. Selection of wedding gown and accessories; the attendants' attire; deciding upon the music; the rehearsal and reception plans. The diversity of wedding ceremonies and the degree of formality in recent years.

Marriage laws of your state. Does the state ban the marriage of first cousins? Legal age limits; blood tests; waiting periods. Comparison with regulations in other states.

Shortchanged! The birthday-celebration fate of persons born on February 29—Leap Year babies. Local citizens who will have the thrill of celebrating a birthday today; parties to whoop things up. Presents for this out-of-the-ordinary occasion. When and how does a Leap Year person celebrate his or her birthday in an off year?

MARCH

Spring Stirrings

March traditionally enters with a blustery display, but as the days grow mild, nature responds with a gradual awakening. The change of seasons comes on March 21, and signals an increase in seasonal activities.

St. Patrick's Day on March 17 lends an added touch of green. The Irish observe the date in honor of their patron saint, and in the United States the celebration takes the form of parades and the wearing of the shamrock in cities and communities across the continent. The observance is part of a fat calendar of events that makes the month a favorite with the nonfiction fraternity.

Writers can welcome an enticing list of special days: 1. Admission Day in Nebraska and Ohio; 2. Texas Independence Day; 3. Admission Day in Florida; 3. National Anthem Day; 4. Admission Day in Vermont; 6. Alamo Day; 7. Burbank Day; 9. Amerigo Vespucci Day; 11. Johnny Appleseed Day; 16. Docking Day, honoring Neil Armstrong and David Scott for the first inspace docking spacecraft on March 14, 1966; 21. Earth Day, which stresses the importance of preserving the earth's resources; 25. Maryland Day, commemorating the arrival of Lord Baltimore's first settlers in Maryland in 1634; and 30. Seward's Day in Alaska.

March also offers Girl Scout Week, Camp Fire Girls Birthday Week, American Camping Week, Save Your Vision Week, National Wildlife Week, and National Poison Prevention Week, not to mention Red Cross Month.

Writers can capitalize upon the birth anniversaries of such leaders as Presidents James Madison, Grover Cleveland, John

Tyler, and Andrew Jackson; Vice President John C. Calhoun, Albert Einstein, Sam Houston, David Livingstone, Robert Frost, Harry Houdini, Wilhelm Roentgen, Frederic Chopin, Elizabeth Barrett Browning, Alexander Graham Bell, Knute Rockne, Oliver Wendell Holmes, and Rudolf Diesel.

Anniversaries of historical occasions beg for attention: 3. The Missouri Compromise adopted, 1820; 7. Alexander Graham Bell patented the telephone, 1876; 14. Cotton gin was patented by Eli Whitney, 1794; 15. The American Legion was founded, 1919; 16. United States Military Academy was established at West Point, New York, 1802; 30. United States bought Alaska from Russia, 1867; and 31. Commodore Matthew C. Perry negotiated the first treaty between the United States and Japan, 1854, and the Roosevelt administration introduced the Civilian Conservation Corps, 1933.

Whatever the subject, whatever the distance down the corridors of time, your mission is to make truth stranger than fiction.

1

Batter up! The crack of baseball leather against bat means the arrival of March—and action on the diamond. The rise in the popularity of college baseball in your state. One significant trend: How the colleges have taken much of the spotlight from the minor leagues. How major league scouts hover over college stars. Former college players of your state now in the majors.

How superstitious are owners of hotels, motels, apartments, and even houses in your city? Do any of them avoid the number 13 on rooms, floors, or homes because they do not wish to take a chance with bad luck? Do many patrons object to number 13 quarters? Spinoff: Other superstitions.

Flowers and plants in the hospital. Interview nurses about experiences both pleasant and unpleasant. Keeping flowers as fresh as possible. Favorite flowers of the patients. Is there any flower switching or swiping in hospitals?

How the state archaeologist enjoys living in the past. His or her duties in locating, recording, and excavating prehistoric and historic campsites and villages. Relics from Indian mounds, river banks, and fields in your section, and their preservation. The most interesting finds. How the archaeologist advises the archaeological society of your state, museums, and historical organizations.

2

Photography as a hobby with local aviators. Slant: Discovering your city and countryside, and its most inpressive features from the air. The best time for aerial photography. the types of cameras; striking pictures taken from the sky. The business uses of aerial photography.

The Fountain of Youth county in your state. That is, the county with the most centenarians. Their combined ages. To what do they attribute their longevity? The most amazing things about each centenarian. Their earliest memories; the greatest leaders during their lifetime, in their estimation. Their impressions of the scientific progress of today. *when the Sleepin Wakes*

Food where and when you want it. The leading mobile caterer of your section. How he or she regularly feeds hundreds and often thousands at one time; the largest conventions served; the hours spent in preparation of mammoth meals. The special problems of preparing food in such large quantities, and for transport. The facilities and organization; the number of helpers and mobile stoves; the subject's favorite recipes.

Theater marquees in your city. The task of changing signs whenever the program changes. Lighting effects. Mistakes in spelling, which stand out more than "typo-gremlins" in newspapers. What the manager considers the most effective types of ballyhoo in front of a theater.

3

Kite-flying fever in your city. Kites dancing in the breeze greet the arrival of March, the Windy Month. How the sport has won more respectability and devotees within recent years. The interest of the local YMCA leader in kites. Local youths' excitement in building kites; the various styles of kites and flying methods. Tournaments and girl participants.

The battle of the sexes in newspaper comic strips. The observations of a professor of psychology in a local or a nearby college. How husbands and wives—as Dagwood and Blondie, the Wizard of Id and his wife, and the Andy Capps—are pitted against each other by cartoonists. Wives as dominant characters. Other types of male-female relationship as evidenced in the comics.

The secrets of creating heads, as revealed by a sculptor of your state. Different methods and materials. How to fashion traits into head sculpture. The time consumed in sculpturing a head, and the price hanging over the head. The sculptor's most noted works, exhibits, and highest honors.

Bomb squad! The unacclaimed heroes of a demolition squad in your state. How they disarm explosives and even bombs that pose danger to human life and property; equipment and techniques; longest distances traveled in their life-and-death mission. The greatest risks the squad has faced.

4

Western wear. Horace Greeley advised, "Go West, young man, go West!" but the West is always moving east—in clothes. How Americans in all regions have adopted Western duds with zeal. The various kinds of Western garb and accessories that can be bought in your city. Styles at dude ranches. Spinoff: Western styles that have gained international acceptance.

The quarantine laws of your state as well as those of nearby states. Slant: Maintaining quarantines to protect vital crops from plant and animal diseases and insects. Diseases that have caused the most damage in recent years; enforcement of the laws. Quarantine evaders and smugglers.

"Say Cheese." A school picture photographer. His or her most amusing experiences. Best methods of insuring appealing poses; dealing with "muggers."

Winston Churchill as a phrase coiner. Anniversary angle: On this day in 1946 he originated the famous phrase the Iron Curtain for Russian censorship in a speech at Westminster College in Fulton, Missouri; "From Stettin in the Baltic to Trieste in the Adriatic an iron curtain has descended over the Continent."

5

Local bird lovers who welcome the purple martins and other birds in the spring. Bird enthusiasts who make housing for the purple martins—elaborate, decorated, and human-style apartments. Ornate quarters for other species. Local members of the National Audubon Society and their comments on why the purple martin is so special to bird lovers.

Nationality organizations in the capital of your state. Slant: How the clubs enable the members to preserve the customs, traditions, and celebrations of their native lands. The largest groups and their principal activities. Natives of foreign lands who have made considerable wealth—a rags-to-riches saga; their donations to charity.

Notables of your state and adjoining states who are represented in the Hall of Fame in New York City. Anniversary angle: The Hall of Fame was born on this day in 1900 with Henry Mitchell, a former chancellor of New York University, as the founder. The bronze busts; their sculptors and the ceremonies at the unveilings. The quotations on the memorial tablets beneath the busts.

The county sheriff's better half. Lift the curtain on the officer's home life. His wife's domestic accomplishments, as in cooking, and also her work in organizations, as the law officers' auxiliary. Does she have a law enforcement job? Does she like the drama found in her husband's position? The wife's likes and dislikes; favorites in reading, television, and movies.

6

The champion clogging team of your state, The trophies that have been won by these dancers. The group's director and the time the cloggers devote to practice each week. The oldest dancers and their agility; the costumes of the entertainers and their designers. Television appearances and longest tours.

Battleground of science and superstition—the common cold. See local physicians for the latest and most effective treatments. The number and variety of cold remedies sold over the counter in your city. Old time cures that still claim a following. The Food and Drug Administration has tested over 50,000 cold medicines.

Grand gestures that went unclaimed. Have any local institutions (orphanages, schools, churches, old folk's homes) been the recipients of anonymous gifts or bequests? Query private citizens and especially the older generation about the invisible helping hand in times of need. Any such stories from the great depression? Slant: Attempts to track down the benefactors. Any successes or good guesses? Spinoff: People who take credit for crimes they did not commit. Go to the police for examples of this odd phenomenon and obtain a psychologist's views.

It's marble-shooting time! Slant: How the appearance of marble shooters heralds the coming of spring. Marble sales in local stores. The variety and evolution of marbles over the years. Girl disciples. Marble language. The annual marble tournament, the champion of which may go to the national competition. Regional and state winners.

7

The farmer and explosives. Slant: Explosions are all in a day's work down on the farm. Purposes of the earth-shattering events, such as the use of explosives to fell trees, blow out stumps, or loosen soil for deep cultivation. The county agent can lead you to the right people and places.

Burbank Day, in honor of Luther Burbank, the Plant Wizard, who was born on a farm near Lancaster, Massachusetts, on March 7, 1849. How he always conducted at least 1,000 experiments at one time on his grounds in Santa Rosa, California, and originated more than 600 varieties of plants, including over forty types of plums. A local horticulturist's observations about Burbank. Arboretum / Huntington

The business office of a local railroad station. Slant: The behind-the-scenes work that makes the engineer, conductor, and brakeman possible. Business office duties that enable a railroad to tick, e.g., soliciting passenger and freight business.

The introduction of the telephone into your city and the reaction of citizens to the marvel. The patenting of Alexander Graham Bell's invention on this day in 1876. The first telephone office locally, the charges, the equipment and the manager. What the older residents of the city can reveal.

8

The Number One booster of sewing machines in your city—none

other than the dean of sewing machine demonstrators. The years he or she has spent in this role, and the progress in the machines during this period. The main points in demonstrating a machine and answering all the questions of prospective customers. Is there a seasonal sales boom?

Art on wheels in your state. How the state art association or department of education sponsors a mobile art exhibit. The chief promoter of the traveling art gallery and the cities on the circuit; places that draw the largest crowds. The most popular types of exhibit. Artists who accompany the moving gallery and serve as guides to visitors.

An armored car service in your city. Who custom builds such cars and what is the price? Special devices in the vehicle. Precautions taken in making the collection of money. Any holdup attempts? How does reality compare with television and movie dramatizations? Spinoff: Private security guards for hire.

The highest county seat in your state. The altitude of the city. Is the city situated on an elevation? Slant: How the government seat stands high in scenic attractions and civic distinctions. Officials of the city and the county. Do they include women?

9

The latest college in your state or nearby state to add water polo to its sports program. Slant: How the sport combines swimming ability and endurance with the thrills of polo. How colleges and athletic clubs on the West Coast have led the other parts of the nation. Competition in the Olympic Games.

The manager of the local country club. Slant: The business side of the operation of the club. The most popular attractions, including the golf course. The golf pro and his record on the links. Expansion of the club's activities within the past year. Top events for the women; social highlights. Membership campaigns. The effects of inflation on private clubs.

Prevention of dam disasters. This duty falls upon the shoulders of an engineer who puts into practice the saying, A stitch in time saves nine—a dam inspector with the state's land resources commission or the U.S. Corps of Engineers. The most common faults, such as seepage, inadequate spillway capacity, structural troubles, and tree growth on the dam. The most troublesome or dangerous dams in your area. Correction of defects.

Amerigo Vespucci Day, paying tribute to the Italian merchant-explorer whose name is carried by North and South America. His voyage to the American continent in 1499, seven years after Christopher Columbus discovered the Western Hemisphere but assumed the territory was part of the Indies. A local historian's list of the five most important voyages in the history of mankind. Examples of misjustice of names. Cost of pioneer expeditions.

10

Colleges as newsmakers. How news bureaus of the various colleges in the state generate publicity. Directors and their assistants; the photographers. Types of stories that draw the greatest attention. Annual events and their coverage. Slant: Colleges, like business concerns, need publicity to keep them in the public eye.

Opening locked cars. Absentminded drivers who lock the keys inside. Solving the predicament, including the old coat hanger technique, without smashing a window. Calling locksmiths. Any small children or animals accidentally locked in automobiles? How recent changes in car design make opening a locked automobile more difficult.

Wonders with spools. A local craftsman who makes pieces of furniture and novel items, as corner whatnots, fruit baskets, and doll beds. Slant: How he has mixed pleasure and skill for a moneymaking hobby. How today wooden spools are rare, having been widely replaced by plastic and styrofoam.

The operator of a clip joint—that is, a newspaper clipping service in your state. How the clipping bureau cuts stories out of newspapers and sells them to the subjects; number of newspapers used. The alertness of the clippers; how they have to cross-reference or just watch for mentions. How often do they miss a story or an item? The charge of clippings. Famous clients. Selling wedding announcements and stories.

11

A horse trainer need not take a back seat to the lion tamer or any other animal expert. The practice and patience needed in developing performing horses that star in a circus playing in your section or are featured in local horse shows. The commands used by the master; the most difficult tricks for horses. The IQ of a horse; the old routine of a horse "counting" with his foot. The animals' eagerness to please the trainer.

Battlefield visits by a local resident. Is this a hobby, involving the love of history? Mementoes from the sites; photographs taken by the visitor. Battles with the highest casualties; conflicts in which both sides claimed victory.

The tallest buildings in your state. Signs or slogans atop the skyscrapers. Have any of the structures been struck by lightning? Bird-bumping and maintenance problems. Cost of the buildings. Any problems in renting the office space? Unusual businesses; the highest occupant; sightseeing from the top. Any suicides?

Historic gavels used by judges in your state. Ones made out of wood from famous houses; donors of them; oldest gavels in use. Gavels with the most sentimental value to the jurists. Making certain that prized gavels will not disappear all of a sudden. How long does a gavel last, in actual use?

12

The county agent in the role of photographer. Slant: His worthwhile efforts in preserving in pictorial form the results of his office's work in improving farm methods and products. Before and after photographs; pictures of champion crops; the most beautiful of the county agent's rural scenes.

The chief occupational diseases in your state and the safety measures. How precautions must be taken by painters, chemical workers, textile employees, and glass workers, among others. Passage of laws and the legislators who sponsored them.

The oldest Sunday School class in your city. The teacher and his or her length of service. Organizers of the class. Any charter members still living? Members with the best attendance records; the class musicians; current officers.

The head of the state highway department's information desk. Slant: How the calls are seasonal, but increase during bad weather, as snowstorms. The blizzards of complaints. Telling callers about the best routes. The voluminous data kept at the information desk.

13

Teenage members of a coin club in your section. The largest collection; rare coins in the youngster's possession. The most popular type of coins. The teenager's parents as numismatists. Is coin collecting making a close race with stamp collecting? The family with the most members in the club; how they got started in the hobby. Spinoff: Young children who collect coins.

The speed of various animals and birds, as reported by owners of your section. The speed of a horse, as described by a horse trainer, and the speed of farm animals, as related by a large-scale farmer. A zookeeper or other informed overall observers can contribute their knowledge.

Care of equipment at the local police department. Slant: The need for perfectly operating equipment in combatting crime day and night. The total number of pistols and other firearms; the oldest and the newest models. Need for good car conditions; extraordinary demands upon the automobiles. Crowd control devices, such as tear gas and riot control equipment; bulletproof vests, shields, and helmets. And officers must keep their pencils sharpened.

Dye-making in pioneer times. The recollections of your county's oldest citizens about producing dyes with natural materials, as oak galls, roots, and berries. By way of contrast, the modern processes in the manufacture of dyes.

14

A boat factory of your state. Kinds of material, as wood and fiberglass; steps in the manufacture; weekly output. The designers of the crafts; the largest and the smallest boats turned out by the company. The most successful promotion efforts. Slant: How boat making is just as vigorous in the winter as in the summer.

Volunteer firemen of your county as unsung heroes. How the members of the volunteer fire departments report to the fire station from wherever they are as soon as possible after an alarm and face danger in fighting the blaze. The ages and occupations of the members; the degree of ostentation they use in identifying their cars. The fire trucks and equipment; training of the volunteers.

Record filibusters in the General Assembly of your state, Legislators who tried to stop a measure by prolonged debate. The basic techniques of filibustering. Some of the bills that have been talked to death.

Cities of your state with Indian names. Who suggested the names? How accurate or close to the originals are they? Indian names that have achieved nationwide and even literary fame. How the chambers of commerce of the cities publicize the Indian name connection. Tribes that once inhabited the area, and treaties that ceded land to the settlers.

15

An author who is widely known for his or her articles or short stories in a church weekly in your state. Drawing upon actual experiences for some of the stories. Fan mail from readers and suggestions for future contributions. Does the writer plan to write a book?

The Battle of the Carolinas—birthplace of President Andrew Jackson, who was born on March 15, 1767. South Carolina claims his birth occurred on an uncle's farm near the Waxhaw settlement in that state, and Old Hickory concurred. North Carolinians' contend the seventh president was born in their state.

Weddings in the minister's home. Is this practice decreasing? Arousing the clergymen at late hours. Forgetting the marriage licenses. Rounding up witnesses—even the minister's wife. Elderly men and women who speak the vows at the parsonage. Any elopements?

A hospital for alcoholics in your state. The steps in ridding persons of the John Barleycorn influence, and the time—and cost—required for this transformation. Have the steps changed drastically over the years? The percentage of arrested alcoholism; also the percentage of men and women patients. The operator of the hospital and his background; the number of staff members. Results of latest research on alcoholism.

16

Horoscopes are here to stay! Millions of newspaper readers are avid fans and daily consult what the "stars" hold in store for them. Horoscope columnists who have the greatest readership; their training in astrology. Local citizens who turn to their horoscopes even before breakfast. The increasing prominence of the horoscope in matters of romance and compatibility.

Posters as safety promoters. Local industrial plants that make extensive use of posters. How posters feature graphic drawings and are changed at least once a month. Reduction of accidents in the places; safety records and awards. Spinoff: Poster designers; political posters. Posters as art.

— The life of a control engineer at a local radio or television station. The duties of the control man. Amusing incidents in his career, his favorite programs and entertainers. Latest improvements in equipment.

Black Press Day and how it is being observed. Anniversary angle: The first black newspaper in the United States—*Freedom's Journal* on Varick Street in New York City—was established on March 16, 1827. The black newspaper that tops the nation in circulation; the black publications in your city and their publishers; editorial objectives.

17

St. Patrick's Day. The legends about Saint Patrick, including his driving snakes into the sea, as recounted by a native of Ireland who resides in your city. How he or she and not only the authentic Irish but the would-be, pseudo, and part-descended Irish in the city proudly wear the shamrock today.

Old Irish jokes never die—they just fade away until St. Patrick's Day. A local citizen who is a native of Ireland can supply examples of genuine Irish wit and humor, as opposed to American Irish jokes.

The conservatory of a college in your section. The most interesting of the flowers and the plants on display there; the rarest; the amount of care and time needed. The head horticulturist and also development of the conservatory into a showplace of the campus. Latest results of plant breeding.

The mayor of your city as a club joiner. Organizations to which he has belonged the longest time; offices he has held. The value of the groups, in the mayor's estimation; the most unusual clubs of which he has been a member. Slant: The chief executive's qualities of leadership make him a sought-after figure in other circles.

18

Factory outlets in your city. The wide variety of types of products sold; the advantages and drawbacks of this form of shopping. Customers who travel hundreds of miles to take advantage of the savings.

Memorable dates in the history of your state. What dates hold the most significance—the red-letter days on the historical calendar? The state historian's opinions and his narration of the events. Dates that are observed by schools and by public ceremonies.

The "mom" of a high school's athletic teams—the wife of the coach. Has she attended every game year after year? Slant: "Mom" as the Number One rooter for the squads. Her greatest thrills, particularly in championship games. Any sons or daughters on a team?

Old rackets in new garb. See local law enforcement officials about rackets that have been reported or broken up in recent months. Are men or women more susceptible? Warnings to the public, especially retired persons. Slant: the constant campaign to protect the sucker who, according to Barnum, is born every minute.

19

Unique water towers in your part of the state. The highest one; the largest; the oldest; the most decorated. Are some brightly painted or made to simulate something else, as a smiling face or a giant baseball? Chief builders of water towers today and the cost. Youthful daredevils who scale water towers, as to paint the score of a sports event their school has won.

Maps at your fingertips. How many maps are in the local library? Who uses the maps? How school children make use of the maps. The leading atlases; map changes. Special maps available such as maps of parks, bicycle and bus routes.

A leading shell collector of your city. The profuse variety of shapes and designs; specimens from the longest distances. The shells considered the most beautiful. World travelers who have added to the collection; shells brought back by servicemen. Shells that have remarkable stories behind them.

Airplanes for rent. A flying service of your city that provides rentals. How businessmen and athletes take advantage of the opportunity for timesaving and comfort. Tourists and thrill-seekers who rent. Longest flights by renters. Emergencies.

20

The technological revolution on newspapers in your state. Thanks to computerized operations every step in the process of getting out the news has been speeded up and simplified. From the writing of the story to the typesetting there are radical departures from the way things used to be. The boon of this printing miracle to the advertising department as well as the newsroom. Query veteran newsmen for their views (pro and con) on the impact of the computer on newspapers.

The origin of the Farm Bureau, which opened the first office in Binghamton, New York, on March 20, 1911. The Bureau's beginning in your state and early officers; the size of the present membership and the programs the organization sponsors for boys and girls in addition to adults. Raising living standards on the farm.

Help for the spiritual needs of travelers in your area. Men and women who act as chaplains at hotels and motels. How counseling training qualified them to deal with the burdens of strangers in the community and perhaps prevent suicide. Dealing with marital, job, and alcoholic problems.

A look at the operation of a fruit company in your city. Where does the company obtain its large variety of fruits and nuts—from what states and foreign countries? The best-selling items locally. Cold storage facilities and their sanitation requirements.

21

Advent of spring—with fishing devotees seeking out their favorite lakes and rivers. The largest fishing club in your county. The champion angler; his or her fishing secrets and greatest catch. The most popular varieties of fish among the members. Prizes for the biggest catches. Izaak Waltons in their 80's, male and female. Fish stories that would have taxed the imagination of Baron von Munchausen.

Spring fashions displayed by a local model. New fashion trends and comments by the models. The mood of Paris designers this year. Wardrobe accessories. Classic fashions versus yearly changes.

Early United States senators from your state. Their part in important legislation. How long did they serve in the Senate? Their
greatest political campaigns and highest honors. Any monuments
to their memory? Descendants and their interest, or participation,
in politics.

Traffic officer from the air in your state. How large cities use heli-
copters to control traffic. Slant: How the mobility of the aircraft
enables the pilot to comprehend and untangle any jam with only a
microphone. Summoning police cars and ambulances when needed.
Superhighway speed-gauging from the air.

22

The dean of gunsmiths in your county. The most common repairs;
the rarest guns. The oldest ones the subject has repaired. Do some
owners fail to call for their guns? Is the gunsmith a gun collector? If
so, the most interesting guns in his collection. The gunsmith as a
gun swapper. Spinoff: Engraving and customizing guns.

The secrets of seeking valuable minerals. How a geologist of your
state, employed by private industry, conducts his search. His most
successful discoveries. Instruments used by the geologist. Does
hunch ever play a part?

Pulling strings—not in politics but in the art of puppetry. An entertainer of your section who carries special delight to children. How
puppets are made; the materials; the most popular characters; giving them names. Writing the scripts. Touring with the puppet show.

Firsts in agricultural products in your state. The superintendent of
an experimental station that specializes in farming research. The
most notable experiments; breeding procedures for variety development; methods of testing. Insect and disease control.

23

Bees as villains, and add to the list other insects as hornets, wasps,
and fire ants. Their stings can prove fatal. How some persons are
highly allergic to such bites and carry emergency sting kits for injections of epinephrine. A local allergist's warning about insect stings,
and his figures of fatalities in the United States annually.

The printing company that produces the high school yearbooks of your city. How many schools does the concern service in this capacity? The most unusual or most difficult design to print; award-winning yearbooks. The company's latest equipment, in both printing and engraving. The total number of annuals published yearly.

Liberty Day. Where statesmen have made famous declarations. Anniversary angle: Patrick Henry uttered "Give me liberty or give me death" before the Virginia Provincial Convention on this day in 1775. His oratory against the Stamp Act in 1765, ending with "If *this* be treason, make the most of it." President Abraham Lincoln's Gettysburg Address of less than three minutes when the battlefield was dedicated as a national cemetery. How the chief executive considered his speech a failure.

A veteran wedding decorator of your city. Approximate number of weddings he or she has decorated; the most in one day. Have there been any notable changes in wedding decor over the years? Problems that suddenly arise. Weddings cancelled at the last minute. Nuptial humor. Payment generally prompt?

24

A well-known bird painter of your state. How he or she has made a thorough study of bird habits. Visits to wildlife refuges; the rarest birds painted; what he or she thinks of as the most beautiful—or hard to paint—bird; selling the paintings. The painter's description of the most interesting habits of birds. Any birds as pets?

The county registrar of deeds. Oldest deeds on file, and the price of land at that time. An average day with the registrar. Microfilming records to conserve space. Visitors to the office in search of information.

The newspaper and magazine section at the local library. The number of newspapers and periodicals on the subscription list; the extent of their popularity; types of magazines that attract the most patrons. Researchers who use the back numbers.

Railroads in your state that exist no longer. Slant: How bus and airplane travel spelled the loss of revenue for some trains, just as the advent of railroads came as a blow to river transportation. The presidents of the railroads and the heyday of operation; the main junctions; the fares; excursions. The romantic names of railroad lines and passenger cars. The worst wrecks and the toll in human life.

25

Friendships via balloons. How local children have made friends by releasing balloons with attached invitations for the finders to be pen pals. The adult leader of the youths. The children's enjoyment of the project. The farthest distances the balloons have flown.

Mountain memorials. The achievements of Gutzon Borglum, born on this day in 1867, who is remembered for the sculpturing of the heads of four presidents on Mount Rushmore in South Dakota—the largest statues in the world. How Borglum started work on the Confederate Memorial on Stone Mountain near Atlanta, Georgia, but gave up after a quarrel with the sponsors. Spinoff: Human resemblances as part of mountains, such as Caesar's Head in South Carolina and the Old Man of the Mountains in New Hampshire, about which Nathaniel Hawthorne wrote in his story, "The Great Stone Face." Legends about the profiles.

A taxidermic school. Number of present students; most common and uncommon animals stuffed. Where most of the animals are obtained; main points of training; the most difficult phases of the technique to master. Is the owner or operator of the school an enthusiastic hunter? Do any local institutions use stuffed animals as decor? Advances in taxidermic technology.

Brothers and/or sisters of your section who are widely known acrobatic dancers. How they keep on the go with constant performances; stunts that make the biggest hit with audiences. Daily practice; perfecting new stunts. Hobbies that claim their spare time.

26

When Easter falls in place on the calendar, it means the rabbit boom of the year. The foremost rabbit raiser of your section. The sales leap at this time of year; the different sizes and types of rabbits. Does the rabbit's temperament suit the animal well as an Easter symbol? Rabbit sales to stores in a wide area. Strict supervision of baby animal sales in recent years. Facts about the commercial raising of rabbits, both for pets and for meat.

Easter egg trees and their addition to the observance of Easter. Parents and grandparents, along with neighbors, who decorate trees in the yard for Easter enjoyment. How the eggs are prepared; different styles of tree decorations. The pleasure the trees provide for local neighborhoods and passing motorists.

A shoe repair shop in your city. Is it a husband and wife operation? Does the wife perform part of the work? Pride in the materials and appearance of shoes as the secret of success. Sale of shoes that are never picked up. Is shoe repair as active today as in the past? Do they repair luggage or do tack and harness work?

School days for local, county, and state law enforcement officers. Taking law enforcement and criminology courses at colleges and special training schools. The instruction given at the FBI National Academy in Washington, D.C. Pistol practice at an outdoor range; the best shots. Learning to analyze evidence and examining materials under a microscope. mary miller

27

The mechanical department of the local bus company. The number of mechanics, and their work in keeping the buses in running condition. Going to the rescue of broken-down buses. Keeping an ample supply of parts—just in case. How often are new buses acquired?

Amusing experiences of triplets in your section. Cases of mistaken identity, as in classrooms; pranks played by the triplets; problems posed by the trio. The matter of identical clothes. Do all wear the same sizes? Instances in which three heads are far, far better than one.

The history of a battleship named after your state. Anniversary angle: President George Washington signed the act that established the United States Navy on this day in 1794, the year Congress agreed to construct six frigates to combat piracy. The christening of the battleship, and highlights of its service. Cruisers in the Navy that received their names from cities in your state and adjoining states. Has a battleship's name ever had any relation to its success or failure?

Anybody for calendar reform? Do most local citizens feel the Gregorian calendar serves us satisfactorily despite some defects? Reaction to proposals for the International Fixed Calendar, which would consist of thirteen months of twenty-eight days each, and the World Calendar, a subject before the United Nations in 1954. Resistance to calendar changes over the years.

28

Minor league baseball teams in your state that are part of the American and National league's farm systems. How the parent club sends young players of great promise to the minors for seasoning. What percentage of the athletes make the climb to the majors? The salaries in the minors and the hardships. Players that return to the minors.

The life of a sandblaster. The operator of a company in your area that cleans brick and stone buildings by sandblasting. The highest structures treated; city halls, jails, and courthouses that have been "face-lifted"; the extensive scaffolding and safety measures. Other purposes of sandblasting.

A law enforcement officer of your section who is well known for his lectures. What he stresses in his crime prevention addresses; longest trips to make appearances. Does he prefer talking to young people or to adults? His views on juvenile maladjustment. Latest statistics about crime in the state.

The woes of complaint departments in your city, as telephone and public utilities. What do the departments themselves complain about? Worst kinds of griping; efforts to soothe the ire of customers. Comments on the old saw that the customer is always right.

29

A sportsman of your section who has been on safari in Africa or to exotic locations elsewhere. Taking along a camera as well as a gun. Experiences with big game that were too close for comfort. Largest animals bagged; mounting heads. The guides and the worst territory. What the sportsman learned about animal habits and lifestyle differences.

The popularity of trade journals. How owners and managers of local establishments are ardent subscribers of magazines devoted to their trades in order to obtain news and suggestions to improve their business. The variety of professions and industries covered by trade journals, as in the drug, jewelry, optical, ice cream, medical, plumbing, printing, and writing fields. Slant: The comradeship of business and professional leaders in the exchange of profitable ideas.

The historian of the local chapter of the Daughters of the American Revolution. Her research and new light she has cast on Revolutionary War events; turning up documents. Preparing pamphlets and even books concerning the war. Correspondence with DAR historians in other states; visits to museums and battlefields.

Descendants of the founders of your city. Do any of them reside in the city? Relics of the founders; trials and tribulations of the pioneers; the founders' foremost adventures; the price of land in the settlers' time. PASADENA

30

The manufacture and erection of church steeples. Interview the pastors of local churches that have installed new steeples in the past year or two. The demand for steeples, as described by a steeple company representative; the materials, the tallest spires, and the prices. Conventional designs as well as radical new ones. Installing a steeple.

Seward's Day, a legal holiday which Alaskans observe in commemoration of Secretary of State William Henry Seward's purchase of Alaska from Russia on this day in 1867. The cost: About four cents an acre—among the greatest bargains in history. How the move met ridicule and promoted critics to call Alaska "Seward's Ice Box" and "Seward's Folly." Importance of Alaska, then and now.

A woman of your section who is a prominent cattle raiser. How she performs a "man's job" at her farm or ranch; the largest herd of cattle she has had at one time. Her skill on a horse. Does she use a jeep to supervise her operations or tend to chores? Her most extraordinary experiences; coping with rustling, sickness, and attacks by wild packs of animals, as dogs.

The care of flowers and shrubbery in the state parks. The most predominant plants; points about their cultivation; flowers that bloom the earliest. Park patrons who capture the beauty with their cameras. Any trouble with plant theft? Slant: How the state park system develops the beauty in addition to the recreational facilities.

31

The operator of an auctioneering school in your state. His background; what he enumerates as the most helpful attributes for successful auctioneering; the financial rewards in this field. The length of the course and the price; the range of enrollees. The tricks of the auctioneer's famed chant.

The investment counselor for the government of your city. How the finance committee of the city council arranged his services to determine the method of investing funds, as in connection with the city employee pension plan. The counselor's position with a firm of financial management; the growing demand for such counseling. Examples of wise investments.

Moviemakers in a school of your state. Slant: Students are learning about motion picture production firsthand. Has the state's art commission provided the school with a movie authority to guide their efforts? Preparing the script, selecting the director, and casting the roles; the camera crew and equipment; shooting the scenes. Film criticism in the classroom.

A faith healer of your city who has a wide reputation for cures. Local services in which numerous persons came with physical problems, including diseases, and reported themselves healed. Claims of cancer and deafness cures. The appeal of faith healing today. How the healer explains his powers.

APRIL

Month of Youthful Spirit

Lovers of the spring season share the feelings of the incomparable William Shakespeare, who observed: "When proud-pied April, dressed in all his trim/Has put a spirit of youth in everything." It is the change from a snow white winter mantle to a coat of floral colors that makes April a favorite month.

Ironically, writers who turn back the calendar in American history can look upon April as the war month, beginning with the outbreak of the American Revolution on April 19, 1775. The Civil War erupted on April 12, 1861; the Spanish-American War on April 21, 1898, and the United States declared war against Germany on April 6, 1917. Paul Revere carried out his famous midnight ride on April 18, 1775, while General Robert E. Lee surrendered to General Ulysses S. Grant on April 9, 1865.

Other special days in April based upon warfare: Patriot's Day as the anniversary of the first battle of the American Revolution, San Jacinto Day in Texas, Fort Sumter Day commemorating the opening engagement of the Civil War and Bataan Day.

April also gives writers an uncommonly good opportunity to show how things started. The United States Mint was established on April 2, 1792; the Pony Express was born on April 3, 1860; Joseph C. Smith founded the Mormon Church on April 6, 1830; the Book-of-the-Month Club originated on April 6, 1926; a motion picture was shown for the first time, in New York City, on April 23, 1896, and the first public television broadcast was made from the Empire State Building on April 30, 1939.

Additional events with April anniversaries are: 3. Robert Ford killed bandit Jesse James, 1882; 6. Robert Peary reached the North Pole, 1909; 14. Actor John Wilkes Booth shot President Abraham Lincoln, 1865; 15. The ocean liner *Titanic* perished, 1912, and 28. Mutiny descended upon the British ship *Bounty,* 1789.

April brings the observance of Cancer Control Month as well as National Library Week, Pan American Week, Earth Week, National Coin Week, Bike Safety Week, and National YWCA Week. Writers can also use American Creed Day, National Arbor Day, Commodore Perry Day, Pan American Day, Oklahoma Day, Maryland Admission Day, and Lei Day in Hawaii.

The birth anniversaries of four United States presidents occur in April: Thomas Jefferson, James Buchanan, Ulysses S. Grant, and James Monroe. Other noted personalities born in the month have been Booker T. Washington, Joseph Pulitzer, Adolf Hitler, Mary Pickford, Edward Everett Hale, Stephen A. Douglas, J. Robert Oppenheimer, Henry Houdini, Henry Clay, Washington Irving, John J. McGraw, Samuel F.B. Morse, John Burroughs, Guglielmo Marconi, and Queen Juliana of the Netherlands.

April has a festive touch when Easter falls during the month, as it generally does. Gardeners and farmers look forward to planting on Good Friday, and flower growers keep in mind the venerable saying that April showers bring May flowers. Although April may be fickle about the weather, it is far from that when it comes to article writers.

1

April Fools' Day—a feast of fun observed since 1564. Poll local students about their favorite trick on teachers, parents, and others. The middle generation can remember the gag about the pocketbook with a string, and the oldest residents of the city can recall April Fool pranks of long ago, when buggies were put on top of barns and Chic Sale houses were overturned.

Pranks of college athletes on this day and on other occasions. Freshmen hazing. Acts that backfired. How members of a team have played pranks on rival squads prior to an important game; retaliation; fierce rivalry.

"My favorite practical jokes." Funny and unfunny experiences of a humorist or jokester of your section, including instances when the victim failed to appreciate the joke. Can women take a joke better than men? Kinds of pranks that go over best of all; the newest routine of the humorist/jokester. Slant: How fun is the best medicine for the spectators and also the fun-maker himself.

— Hoaxes played upon various services in your city, as police and fire departments and ambulance drivers. Slant: Being victims of potentially dangerous pranks is a year-round affair. Epidemics of false alarms; ambulances sent long distances by pranksters. Acts of spite; catching culprits.

2

The culinary expert of a local radio or television station. The number of recipes she receives weekly; testing them; her favorites. Old-time recipes that still ring the bell. Recipes of meat dishes and seafood; the "Cook of the Airlanes" prizes; casserole dishes in big favor; kinds of cakes and pies the listeners seem to prefer.

The sale of sheet music in your city. Do sheet music sales follow the record hit list? Best sellers during past months. Instruments that lead in sheet music popularity. Movie and TV musicals that create a demand for sheet music. Are young people the top buyers of sheet music? The most popular composers. What is the market for jazz and classical?

Best sellers in garden sculpture. The report of a resident of your county who specializes in making the products, as bird baths. Other items, as cherubs, fountains, and animal sculpture. The processes of manufacture. How materials and tastes have changed.

Pascua Florida Day, marking the anniversary of Juan Ponce de Leon's discovery of Florida in 1513. How Pascua Florida means "flowery feast" and is the Spanish term for Easter Sunday, on which day the Spanish soldier and explorer spotted the coast and called the land La Florida. His search for the fabled Fountain of Youth; legends about youth-restoring fountains, springs, and waters since medieval times.

3

A local member of the Ninety-Nines, Inc., an international organization of licensed women pilots. Her most thrilling experiences during her flying career; her most nervous moments. Her longest flights. The activities of the state chapter of the Ninety-Nines; the number of fliers, and the dean of them. How the local ladybird encourages other women to enter aviation.

The nemesis of Robert Ford, who shot Jesse James on this day in 1882. Slant: The assassin, who lacked the courage to be a full-fledged bandit, was destined to die by violence ten years after he murdered James. Ford, driven out of the state, was shot down in a quarrel. How his brother Charley committed suicide in a weed patch near his home at Richmond, Missouri.

Girl Scouts of your city who have foreign pen pals. Slant: Across-the-ocean friendships are strengthened by the exchange of gifts as well as letters—and perhaps tapes. Depicting customs and manners in letters; sending photographs abroad. Chief interests in teenagers overseas. Have any of the local Scouts been visited by their pen pals?

The Meals-On-Wheels program for elderly citizens of your city. How the meals are prepared daily except Saturday and Sunday and delivered by volunteers. The menu variety and nutritive value of the food. Number of meals served and how they are financed. The morale building of the program because it shows the oldsters that someone cares. Spinoff: Private wheeled catering services; feeding construction workers.

4

The cherry tree as a symbol of spring. Ask a nursery operator of your section about the popularity of cherry trees and their care. The varieties of cherries best suited to your area. States that lead in the number of cherry trees and output. The sale of purely decorative trees with no edible fruit. The best known of cherry blossom festivals.

The photographer of a local or a nearby college. Slant: The uses of still and motion picture photography in the academic and administrative branches of the institution. The various kinds of photos he is called upon to make; photographing school activities; making a pictorial record of athletic events. The photographer's most unusual pictures.

Local and state chapters of Civil War organizations, as the United Daughters of the Confederacy. Officers of the chapters. A typical meeting; outstanding speakers during the past several months; qualifications for membership; descendants of war heroes. War relics in the possession of members; letters from soldiers.

A local expert of hand lace-making. How she has been making lace for years, probably carrying on the art of her grandmother. Is needlework, as tatting, declining? How the subject puts her skill to use on linens and clothes. Other decorative purposes.

5

A look at the sweet tooth of the local population. The persistent appetite for candy, as shown by the purchases at supermarkets or a candy specialty store. Have candy sales increased during the past few years? Rise in prices. Best-selling kinds of candy. Old-time candies versus newer species. The snack bar at local theaters.

Writers of your state who have written autobiographies. The most recent and the extent of their success. These authors in the role of lecturers; autograph parties. The advantages and disadvantages of doing a personal history. Slant: The truth of Goethe's observation: "Every author in some degree portrays himself in his works, even if it be against his will."

The romance and marriage of Pocahontas. Anniversary angle: The Indian princess, the daughter of Powhatan, was married to John Rolfe on April 5, 1614. How she later traveled to London as an American princess and found herself welcomed by royalty. Her sickness and death in 1617; her tomb in Virginia. Pocahontas' son Thomas and descendants, including the second wife of President Woodrow Wilson.

Dancing half a century ago. A retired professional dancer of your area can recount the biggest names in the dancing world in that period. Has he or she taught dancing? Trophies won in contests; favorite partners on the dance floor. Theatrical appearances.

6

Would-be record-breakers in your section. Attempts to break records listed in the *Guinness Book of World Records*. Groups and individuals who seek world laurels. Their practice for the attempts. The rewards for winning championships, both in personal satisfaction and in honors.

Soil testing. Samples sent to the experimental agricultural stations in your state for analysis. The method of the testers. Slant: How advice on fertilizers will increase the crop yields of the farmers and gardeners. The enormous number of home and suburban gardeners who submit their soil for diagnosis. Kinds of soil best suited for various crops.

The first men of your county to give up their lives in different wars. Anniversary angle: The anniversary of Uncle Sam's declaration of war upon Germany falls on this day. Were the bodies of all the victims returned home? Other members of the families who distinguished themselves in that war and other conflicts; medals.

The hobby of telepathy followed by a local resident. How he or she became interested in extrasensory perception, and experiments in ESP. Correspondence with other devotees of telepathy. Results of latest research. Writing articles on the subject.

7

The executive director of the state board of medical examiners. The number of members and an insight into a meeting. Frequency of hearings and examinations; the number of physicians admitted to practice last year. Counties that suffer from a shortage of doctors.

What is the proper age to marry? Go to local Wearers of the Cloth—and their wives. Do most of them agree on the age? Do most officiating persons give advice to the couples? Counseling sessions before marriage. Opinions about "May-December" marriages.

People who gave Samuel F.B. Morse a helping hand in the development of the telegraph. Anniversary angle: This native of Charleston, Massachusetts, applied for his first patent on the telegraph on this day in 1838. Partners in Morse's telegraph rights were: Leonard Gale, Alfred Vail, and Congressman F.O.J. Smith. Slant: How his partners and rival inventors fired legal claims at Morse.

Qualifications to join local clubs. The word from the presidents themselves. Organizations with the most difficult qualifications. Average number of persons joining the clubs annually; the oldest members; fund-raising projects. Spinoff: Unusual national and international clubs such as the Explorer's Club.

8

Tagged fish. Slant: How these marked denizens of the rivers and lakes in your section add excitement to the sport of fishing. How the fish and wildlife department applies tags to the fish to keep track of their migration. Varieties of fish tagged. Largest tagged fish caught; sums of money given the catchers. Tagged fish contests sponsored by newspapers.

The municipal reference library of your city. Slant: The importance of the volumes to members of the departments of the city government who want to know as much as possible about their work. Volumes that receive the most attention; legal books; the city code. Newest additions to the library.

The unfading interest in tattoos. A veteran sailor or industrial worker can describe the common and uncommon designs and emblems over the years. What is the leading tattoo—the heart? Military emblems and religious symbols. Colors used in the patterns. The range of positions for tattoos, other than the arms and chest; the back and even a bald head. Changes in tattoo technology and the latest wrinkles. The highest prices. Annual conventions of the North American Tattoo Club.

What is average in your city? First, check a shoe store for the average size; then take in a hat firm. Follow with shirts, pants, dresses, overcoats, gloves, and other things. Slant: The reader will gain a new perspective on his or her size.

9

Cost of various animals, given by a zookeeper in the area. The prices paid for the zoo's animals, ranging from elephants, jaguars, and bears to lions, camels, and monkeys. The most exotic animal. From where did most of the present zoo occupants come? The longevity of the animals, and the oldest; the happiest in captivity.

General Robert E. Lee's Waterloo. His surrender of the Confederate Army to General Ulysses S. Grant on this day in 1865. How the Virginian, with a force of only 25,000 and Grant in close pursuit, gave up and after the war urged Southerners to join in national unity. A local history buff who has visited the National Historical Park near Appomattox and his description of the main attractions.

"My worst scares." A steeplejack of your section who has had a few frightening moments. The highest steeples and smokestacks he has painted or repaired; safety precautions. Is he fascinated by great heights, and does he harbor any superstitions? Number of steeplejacks in the county.

The admittance office of a local hospital. What information is necessary before admitting the patients? How some husbands and wives know so little about the background of their mates. Financial questions. Barely beating the delivery time in maternity cases. Discharge planning; any attempted "escapes"?

10

Have camera—will travel. The hither and yon adventures of a TV cameraman of your section who covers sports events over a wide area. The most colorful athletes, in his opinion, and story-book finishes to championship games. Coaches he admires the most. Meeting deadlines at the TV station. Spinoff: Cameramen who cover other events.

The birth of the United States patent system. How Congress established a patent commission on this day in 1790 with the secretaries of war and state, and the attorney general as members. Samuel Hopkins of Vermont obtained the first patent on July 11, 1790, for a process of treating wood ashes to make lye for soap manufacture. How almost 10,000 patents were granted between 1790 and 1838.

The dean of tombstone salesmen in your county. How he finds countless persons who do not wish to discuss death. Types of tombstones and kinds of material, as marble and granite, in greatest demand now; inscriptions preferred. Any trend toward decoration. Use of scripture.

Salvation Army Founder's Day. How local SA workers carry out services in honor of William Booth, the founder, who was born at Nottingham, England, on this day in 1829. The problems overcome by the onetime Methodist minister and his wife in developing an organization devoted to helping poor people. The local sale of *the War Cry,* a weekly founded by Booth.

11

—Toy departments of local stores. Slant: Toy selling is not restricted to the Christmas season. The effect of toy advertising on children's programs on television. Perennial favorites in the toy line; new toys that promise to sell like wildfire. The safety-mindedness of toy manufacturers. OLDEST TOYS & SALES; 10 TOP OLD TOYS,

Beautification along the highways. How the state highway department wages war on weeds and overgrowth; spraying. Planting and cutting grass; ornamentals; choosing highway-proof plantings. The practical side of certain plantings. From the motorist's standpoint, what kinds of beautification are most admired and appreciated?

The probation officer of your district. Number of persons on probation; the percentage of women. How the official checks on the probationers; probationers who make unusually good readjustment with new jobs. Slant: Instilling respect and ambition in probationers to restore them to the status of good citizens.

The largest gymnastic team in your state. Slant: How the sensational performances of the members form a tribute to the efficiency of the coach. The most amazing stunts presented by the acrobats; wire walking and trapeze wizards. The absolute necessity of split-second timing and teamwork. Does gymnastic training have any career applications?

12

Dogwood, the queen of spring. The dogwood center of your state as a leader in outdoor beauty. Dogwood planting campaigns within recent years. Dogwood trails that are features of tours. Is there a dogwood festival? Both Virginia and North Carolina have the dogwood as the state flower.

Fort Sumter Day, designated because the Civil War started at Fort Sumter in South Carolina on this day in 1861. The firing of the first shot and the drama of the engagement. The Fort Sumter National Monument, consisting of two acres, in the Charleston Harbor, and the number of visitors it attracts annually.

Donation of clothing locally. Churches and organizations that welcome and distribute garments for needy families and disaster victims. Kinds of clothing needed most of all; distribution of the items. Resale shops and second-hand clothing stores.

Disposal of chemical wastes in your county. Current government regulations regarding disposal of waste products by manufacturing plants. Keeping air and water from becoming polluted. The expense of these processes.

13

The regional office of the United States Postal Service in your section. The director and his typical day. The most pressing problems at present; recent improvements. The director's assistants and their duties; the number of cities under the regional headquarters.

The wife of a leading evangelist of your state. Is she associated with her husband in the work? Problems in raising a family and schooling the children. Longest trips to conduct revivals; meetings that have drawn the largest attendance. How the ministry has given the husband and wife close friendships over the nation.

Want a private detective? Wide range of duties they perform, such as private investigations in domestic troubles. Local businesses, as stores, banks, and hotels, who employ private detectives to solve thefts. Former police officers working for a detective agency.

Rag dolls as the all-time favorite of homemade dolls. A local woman who makes rag dolls both for sale and as gifts. The materials and artistry used in her doll production. Is the maker a doll collector?

14

The leading authority on Indian relics of your state. The most valuable; the hardest to acquire; the largest collection in the state. Places in the state that still yield relics. Slant: The term Indian relics takes in a large number of items in addition to the arrowhead.

A duck raiser in your county. His favorite breed. The size of his pond; the operation of a duck farm; and the farthest markets. The sale of ducklings. Any use for duck feathers? Duck recipes. Ducks as pets.

The champion sky diver of your section. How the addict developed an interest in the sport; his reactions on his first jump. The number of leaps and the highest one; the most tricky and involved routines while jumping. Have the subject and his companions formed a club of sky divers? The jumping equipment and the cost; parachute technology.

The most frightening witch stories on record. What the state historian looks upon as the most shocking behavior attributed to witches. The execution of persons accused of witchcraft in colonial America; the ducking stool as a form of punishment. The last trials for acts of witchcraft. The renewed interest in the "black arts" in recent years, and the forming of covens.

15

The ambulance of the local fire department. Dramatic examples of how it has helped save lives. The vehicle's equipment; administering oxygen to smoke inhalation victims. Longest trips to give aid.

A fashion buyer for the largest department store of your city. Slant: How the buyer keeps his or her pulse on the style picture at all times. Making buying trips to market centers; selecting merchandise. Judging what is right for the store; any drastically wrong guesses? What to expect in fashions in the coming season.

Your state constitution. Framers of the original state constitution and its features. Amendments from time to time. The latest constitutional convention. Do local lawyers think changes are due?

Be a good sport—buy a ticket. The headaches encountered by local organizations, churches, schools, and Scouts in selling tickets to moneymaking events such as banquets, beauty contests, raffles, plays, and circuses. Do men, women, or children make the most effective ticket sellers? Making the sales pitch. Most common evasions.

16

A community that straddles the state line. Homes and stores in two states; the matter of taxes. Attractions of the community and their appeal to tourists; the industrial progress within recent years. Slant: Two states, like two heads, are better than one. The post office and other well-known places.

Tree trimming by telephone and power companies in your city. The number of workers required per year. Any accidents? Discomfort during extremes of hot and cold weather. Disposal of limbs and cuttings. How some citizens try to induce the trimmers to do more than necessary and even cut down trees. Encountering opposition by tree owners; experiences with birds or animals.

A visiting nurse of the county health department. The number of miles she travels monthly paying visits to sick persons in their homes. Imparting cheer to the patients, especially senior citizens. Do many patients bring up spiritual matters or seek the nurse's advice on personal and business problems?

Making the bus service as accommodating as possible. It is all in a day's work for the traffic manager of a local bus company. Slant: The dependence of a large segment of the city's population upon the bus system. Arranging the best routes; keeping the buses running on schedule.

17

Entertainers of the 4-H organization in your county. Contest winners within the past year; the variety of entertainment, from dancing and singing to piano playing and puppet shows. Do any of the players hope for a career in entertaining? Television appearances.

What's for dessert? The five top desserts as revealed by the managers of restaurants and hotels in your city. Does ice cream rank higher than pie and cake? Kinds of puddings that are favorites; flaming desserts. Preferences of men, women, and children; seasonal shifts in patterns.

The sport of river raft racing. The exciting experiences of a champion, and his major victories. Rivers that give the most spills and thrills. Danger on the rapids. The great number of participants in races, and the time of the winners. Spinoffs: Whitewater canoeing and kayaking.

Flag Day in American Samoa, which territory is supervised by the United States Department of the Interior. How the residents observe this public holiday with parades, dancing, and singing in remembrance of the first raising of the American flag there on April 17, 1900. Strategic importance of Samoa. Spinoff: Other American territories.

18

Success secrets via cassettes. A local or area booster of the wide range of instructions and techniques given on tape, featuring both career help and self-improvement. Some programs consist of leading names in professions describing their path to success. Other educational programs available on tape.

Making a record a hit. Much depends upon the record distributor in your area. The activities designed to popularize singers and their new discs. Putting fast-breaking hits into the hands of dealers pronto; various ways in which records are promoted. Record celebrities who pay visits to radio and television stations; stars of/from your state.

The San Francisco holocaust. The earthquake and fire struck the City at the Golden Gate on this day in 1906. How fires raged for three days and approximately 500 persons lost their lives. The destruction of more than 490 blocks of buildings. The rapid rebuilding. Other famous earthquakes in the United States. How present-day engineers design houses and buildings for better protection against earthquakes.

The state forests in your state. Their area and how they are sites for research and demonstration in forest tree planting as well as forest management practices. The major projects now underway; methods developed in state forests that are used in the state and elsewhere.

19

Speakers before women's organization of your city. Interview the chairwoman of the program committees of such clubs. Speakers who have come the longest distances; favorite topics of talks.

The president of the gem and mineral society of your state. The society's progress under his leadership; growth of membership. A typical meeting; nationally known authorities on programs. Rockhounding as a hobby. Explorations; trips to other states; exhibits by the society and exhibit winners.

Non-duty chores performed by local postmen. Slant: Variety is the spice of life for Uncle Sam's mail carriers, Acting in times of emergency, as extinguishing a fire. Doing kind deeds for the elderly. Have any of the postmen been decorated for service beyond the call of duty?

The new crop of farmers who will graduate from an agricultural college in your state shortly. Will the class set any records? Number and type of agricultural degrees to be awarded. The professors' report on agribusiness careers. Will jobs go begging?

20

Activities of your city's First Lady. Slant: How she represents the city at functions and conventions, both as a guest and as a speaker. Engagements per week; largest organizations she has addressed. Clubs in which she holds memberships and has filled offices. Deciding upon what clothes to wear. Attending conventions with her husband.

An amateur herpetologist of your section. Little-known facts and debunking of some snake superstitions by the collector. His collection: The number of occupants and species; the most unusual and the longest reptiles. The subject's travels to collect various kinds of snakes. Meals for the serpents.

Sunday school and church literature in your city. The sources of the magazines and an insight into the publishing houses. The persons in charge of the reading material; the distribution. The weekly cost; the Sunday school departments that receive the most publications. Providing shut-in members with periodicals.

The undying interest in Adolf Hitler. Anniversary angle: The dictator of Nazi Germany was born on this day in 1889. Any calls at the library for material concerning him? Is a copy of *Mein Kampf* in the library? The most popular books dealing with Der Fuhrer's personal life, especially his relationship with Eva Braun. Local residents' feelings about Nazi displays in the United States.

21

Recreactional therapy for psychologically handicapped persons. Facts from the director of the mental health clinic in your section or the superintendent of the state hospital. Slant: How the activities help to restore confidence besides providing physical improvements. Kinds of recreation; the facilities.

The fate of understudies in the Little Theater of your city. The emotions of the understudy as he or she awaits the big break. How the illness of a star has thrust an understudy to stardom. The most notable performances by local understudies, told by the director of the local Little Theater.

Want to buy a church? The fate of churches that are replaced by new buildings. Highest prices brought by old houses of worship in your county. Are there any rites necessary to secularize an old church? Disposal of the church furnishings, including the pews and pulpit. Remodeling the edifices for homes or other uses.

The story behind wedding invitations. Stories by the proprietor or manager of a local printing company that does a large business in invitations. Months in which the most are printed; the least. New trends and styles. The excitement of the future brides and their parents over the preparations; the largest orders for invitations; rush printing; misprints. Weddings that are delayed or called off after invitations have been printed.

22

Women criminals as escape artists? To what extent are the inmates of the women's prison in your state escape-minded? Clever plots that failed; escapees who have not been caught. Special escape precautions taken by the guards at the prison.

Arbor Day, a legal holiday in Nebraska, where the day was first observed in 1872. The founding of Arbor Day by J. Sterling Morton, governor of Nebraska. How the custom spread to other states. Part of the observance is planting trees and shrubs at schools and colleges, hospitals, and churches.

Religion on the drawing board. An artist of your state who specializes in religious cartoons. His Sunday school and church activities. Slant: How he puts his artistic talents to the task of promoting religion. The present number of newspapers and magazines that publish his religious art. His cartoons that have been republished the most times.

The woman's touch in barbering. How many barbershops employ women? Slant: How these women prefer serving men than their own sex in beauty emporiums. How they feel at home cutting children's hair. Tips from the lady barbers and observations about male vanity. The percentage of women students at a barbering school in the state.

23

The publisher of a poetry magazine in your state. Both the headaches and the pleasures of the enterprise. The best-known contributors; the youngest and the oldest poets. Number of states in which the periodical has its circulation. Poems that have produced the most fan mail. The publisher's reputation as a poet. Any state association of poets?

Really sick or playing tricks? The problems of absenteeism in local stores, industrial plants, and offices. Managers' estimates of the extent of play sickness by employees and the number of hours lost by the practice. Varying amounts of sick leave granted workers; attempts to authenticate illnesses and methods of evasion. What are the symptoms or patterns of play sickness?

Epitaphs in the oldest church cemetery in your county. The longest inscriptions and the use of scripture. The oldest tombstones and their dates; the largest family plots. Is a caretaker employed for the cemetery or do the church members do the cleaning? Slant: The pride and reverence the congregation manifests in the ancient cemetery which contains the remains of the early members. MISSION; VALLEY BLVD; ALTADENA.

Love and William Shakespeare, supposedly born on this day in 1564. A Shakespearean buff of your state can describe love's part in the personal life of the Bard of Avon. When he married a farmer's daughter, Anne Hathaway, in 1582, his age stood at 18 and Anne's at 26. How he created the most famous literary lovers of all time, Romeo and Juliet. "The course of true love never did run smooth," Shakespeare wrote in *A Midsummer Night's Dream*.

24

Children of former beauty queens of your state. Contest winners with the most children; those who have had twins. Slant: How title holders gave up dreams of glamorous careers, even stage and perhaps screen stardom, for a mother's role in real life. Scrapbooks of the mothers. Do not overlook the husbands of the beauties.

The fastest girl in the county! To be exact, the best runner on the girls' track team. Are any of her sisters or brothers cinder stars? The coach and the training. Records set by the girl speedsters; trophies on her mantel; state competition. Her participation in other sports.

Home-made cars of youngsters in your city. Special features; races and the winners. Sponsors of the competition. Do any girls join in the hobby? The All-American Soapbox Derby is held in Akron, Ohio, the soapbox racing capital.

Revelations of an industrial psychologist of your state. Methods of screening and working with employees; the foremost causes of tension. Determining how efficiently a worker can perform his or her duties and whether he or she will find full enjoyment. Five rules for harmony between the boss and the employee. The subject's suggestions for people being interviewed or tested by an industrial psychologist.

25

The highest waterfall in your state. Its development as a tourist attraction and the facilities for picnic lovers. How the falls were named; fatal mishaps. Any change in the waterfall over the years? Its different aspects, in different seasons. Tips on how to take good photos of the waterfall.

The secretary-treasurer of the highway department of your state. Slant: Keeping up with the financial status of the huge operation of the department, and how it equals the task of the head of the state's largest corporation. The number of employees and the volume of the budget. Largest projects at present. What kinds of projects are given the greatest priority?

Tracking down typo-gremlins, the job of proofreaders on newspapers and at commercial printing establishments. On the local scene, do women outnumber men as gremlin hunters? Do any proofreaders have collections of embarrassing lines? Notable typos that have slipped through, into print.

The largest church nurseries locally. The heads of the nurseries; the facilities and the hours. Operation of nurseries through the week as an aid to working mothers. The knack of entertaining children; teaching kids togetherness; instruction in simple arts.

26

Old boxcars of a railroad serving your city. The average life of boxcars; their uses after they have been retired. Does the railroad donate any of them to worthy causes, such as a youth organization, to be used as sleeping quarters? How some of the boxcars have been renovated; the most unusual ones.

The top grower of tulips or other spring bulbs in your county. How tulips and other flowers are part of spring magic. The number of acres devoted to cultivation. The sale of tulips or other spring flowers to the public and florists. Favorite varieties. Shipment of bulbs to distant places.

Songs that hold a tender spot in the hearts of local citizens of various nationalities. Composers of these selections; the oldest of the numbers. Songs handed down from one generation to another. Children's tunes.

Do pipe smokers seldom change their smoking habit? Local citizens who would not look familiar without a pipe. Addicts who have nursed a pipe the longest. The smoker with the most extensive collection of pipes. Doctor's opinion on risks of pipe smoking.

27

Picnicking as the Great American Custom. The picnic facilities of state parks in your state as well as roadside rests and city parks, and how they are filled to capacity in spring and summer. The parks that lure the most picnickers, particularly on holidays. Outdoor cooking facilities. Size up the most popular picnic menus. Coping with litterbugging.

The largest professional sorority among women in your city. Special projects sponsored by the chapter; social activities. Officers for the current year. How many professions locally have fraternities or sororities?

Renting of uniforms to industrial plants in your section. Supplying the right sizes; adding the workers' and companies' names. The total number of uniforms rented by the foremost industrial laundry. Other rental items. The designer of a company's or an industry's uniform. How long does a uniform last?

Do's and don'ts for expectant mothers. What local doctors recommend during pregnancy, as in food and exercise. The worst and the best things the future mother can do. Avoidance of miscarriages. Vital imprtance of prenatal care.

28

The operator of a stock car track in your section. Slant: How the races hold as much excitement for the operator as for the customers. Keeping the track in excellent condition; lining up topflight drivers; the prizes; the leading prize-winners; speed records. The most colorful participants. The worst accidents on the speedway.

Science and wood. A company of your section that increases the durability and the strength of wood by the use of certain chemicals. Chemicals that make lumber safe against fire, water, and termites. Demand for such wood; fence posts, telephone poles, and housing.

Street games in your city. The competitive spirit that prevails in these games that abound in the streets and also on public playgrounds. The constant variety of games; old and new—hopscotch, crack the whip, skipping rope, dodge ball, guarding the treasure. Favorite games of children of different ages.

Speech restoration for cancer patients. Examples of local persons who have developed esophageal speech after losing their larynx. The latest developments in voice restoration, including a vibrator pressed against the neck and an electronic voice box implanted in the patient. Comments by a professor of otolaryngology at a university medical school.

29

Take a walk; a hiking club of your city. Slant: How the middle-aged generation does not play second fiddle to the younger set in hiking. The longest and the most fascinating hikes, equipment, and the time required; social events of the club. Health aspects of walking versus jogging.

Wax museums; going strong at tourist centers. The fairs of old featured notorious criminals, but now wax museums exhibit lifelike figures of presidents and their wives, world headliners, and other notables. The cost of a wax figure today. Josephine Tussaud as the master creator of figures.

What is the most stubborn animal? The opinion of longtime farmers of your county, and the experiences upon which they base their judgment. Is the mule a much slandered animal in this respect? The easiest animals to direct. How acts of kindness and understanding in animal handling have paid off for the farmers.

The local librarian as etiquette authority. The deluge of calls about this and that in the social whirl. Consulting etiquette books in the library; settling arguments. Visits by brides-to-be and clearing up points about weddings. Spinoff: Changing manners over the years.

30

Festival fever—and queens. Cities and communities in your state that will stage a wide variety of festivals during the year. Festivals may pay tribute to almost anything from Shakespeare to strawberries. Fair maidens who reigned as festival queens last year.

The first presidential inauguration. Anniversary angle: George Washington took the oath of office on this day in 1789. He and his family never lived in the White House, because it was not completed until after his term, and he was sworn in in New York City. The most urgent problems Washington faced.

Success as a green-eyed monster in marriage. The views of a psychiatrist of your section about the effects of a highly successful career upon a couple. Lifestyle changes and new sets of friends. Examples of entertainers who fell victim. Five ways to save such tottering marriages.

Hobos come to life again in the spring. Has the number dwindled in your section in recent years? A typical day, including the type of meal, for a hobo; his garb. A railroad detective's encounters with Knights of the Road who still ride the rods. The annual National Hobo Convention at Britt, Iowa, and the highlight, the election of the king and the queen.

MAY

Month of Flowers

May's beauty marks the fifth month as Beauty Queen. Spring reaches its height of charm with the flowers and wild plants in bloom. The outdoors forms a natural stage for May Day and the Maypole, a custom as old as the Middle Ages.

May also brings the Month of Mary, in which Roman Catholics throughout the world offer special devotionals to the Blessed Virgin. And members of all faiths join in the activities of National Family Week in the United States.

Other special weeks are National Be Kind to Animals Week, National Goodwill Week, National Music Week, National Nursing Home Week, National Transportation Week, Police Week, and World Trade Week. Mental Health Month, National Tavern Month, Steelmark Month, and Radio Month are among the special ways this month has been singled out.

Among special days are V-E Day, American Indian Day, Mother's Day, Armed Forces Day, National Maritime Day, Dewey Day in honor of Admiral George Dewey, Law Day under the sponsorship of the American Bar Association, World Red Cross Day, North Pole Flight Day, Jamestown Day, Lafayette Day, Lindbergh Flight Day, and Memorial Day.

Two presidents—Harry S. Truman and John Fitzgerald Kennedy—were born in May. So were Karl Marx, Sigmund Freud, Robert E. Peary, Robert Browning, Sir James M. Barrie, Ottmar Mergenthaler, Irving Berlin, Bob Hope, Gene Tunney, Gabriel D. Fahrenheit, Pierre Curie, William H. Seward, Rudolph Valentino, Dolly Madison, Richard Wagner, Sir Arthur Conan Doyle, Patrick

Henry, and Walt Whitman.

These anniversaries occur in May: 2. Hudson's Bay Company chartered, 1670; 4. Haymarket Riot raged in Chicago, 1886; 6. United States forces capitulated on Corregidor to Japan, 1942; 7. German sub torpedoed the *Lusitania,* 1915; 9. Mother's Day first observed, 1914; 12. Roald Amundsen carried out flight over the North Pole, 1926; 14. First permanent English settlement in America, at Jamestown, Virginia, 1607; 15. First regular airmail service inaugurated in United States, 1918; 18. Selective Service Act adopted, 1917; 20. Amelia Earhart departed on first solo flight across Atlantic Ocean by a woman, 1932; 21. Democrats held their first national convention, 1832; and Charles A. Lindbergh completed first transatlantic solo flight, 1927; 28. Birth of Dionne quintuplets, 1934; 31. Johntown, Pennsylvania, flood, 1889; and United States copyright law passed, 1790.

May, as Beauty Queen, witnesses numerous festivals—salutes ranging from apple blossom time to choral music. For instance, the city of Holland, Michigan, lives up to its name with a nationally known tulip festival. All states have their share of festivals, and the folks who man the state tourist bureaus stand ready to oblige writers.

1

May Day, with memories of the traditional Maypole. Yesteryear's festivities at schools of your city and county and the recollections of the older generation, especially retired teachers. The chief ambitions of the May Queens at the colleges in your section of the state could form a second article.

An installer and repairman of newspaper presses. Slant: He is a vital cog, both literally and figuratively, in the dissemination of the news. His reputation as a machinery expert; at home with the smallest and the largest presses. Answering emergency calls at any time. Press improvements.

The problem of antique thefts. The disappearance of rare antiques from antique shops and historical homes in your state, as discussed by law enforcement officers. How the thieves dispose of their loot in distant places; arrests and breaking up rings. The difficulty of tracing stolen antiques. Steps to prevent thefts. How museums protect relics.

The cost of city recreation, as given by the director. How many of the recreational programs have a monthly fee for city and non-city residents for participation in a sport or activity? Sums realized from baseball and softball leagues as well as tennis and football playing. Special programs: Craft workshops; concerts and plays.

2

Keeping the State House spick and span. A typical day with the custodian and his assistants. The most difficult of the cleaning duties. Finding objects; the most valuable of them. Slant: The capitol ranks as one of the showplaces of the state. Average number of visitors daily; barrages of questions; the leading points of attractions in the State House.

Secretary of the manager of the local airport. The scope of his or her duties. The thrill of meeting celebrities. The extent of the secretary's airmindedness; his or her longest flights. Is she a pilot herself? You could make a series out of other secretaries, including those of the police and fire departments.

The most unusual barns in your county today. Slant: How mechanization and specialization by farmers have reduced the number of barns. The county agent's comments about the latest word in barn design. Comparison of the cost of barns and homes. Spinoff: Conversion of old barns to homes.

The curiosity of radio and television devotees. Questions they telephone or mail to the stations. The most common; the oddest. Queries about the personal life of performers, as age, birthplace, and marital status. Requests for autographs.

3

The leading quarry in your state. Slant: Although quarrying once was an exceedingly dangerous occupation, improvements in methods and machinery have reduced the number of accidents among workers. The equipment and the processes in quarrying. Quarry products of your state. Safety precautions. Disused quarries as recreational facilities.

The reservation manager of a local hotel or motel. Reservations from the farthest states; reserving honeymoon suites. Are many reservations cancelled? Busiest seasons, as for conventions.

Athletic teams that put in their reservations for overnight.

A liars' club or, in more polite language, a tall tale roundtable. A group in your region or state that awards prizes for the most outlandish stories. Imitators of the Burlington Liars Club. Are weather yarns frequently "the greatest?" Fishing and hunting tales that have been winners. Tall tales in American folklore; Paul Bunyan, Pecos Bill, Mike Fink.

The first medical school in your state. Its import in providing physicians for communities, large and small. The professors and the first graduates; the worst epidemics of that period and the forms of treatment. Anniversary angle: The opening of the first American medical school in Philadelphia on this day in 1765.

4

A silhouette artist of your section who is carrying on this art with distinction. Slant: How he or she performs "black magic," transforming a sheet of paper into a subject's profile. Development of the talent; the number of years spent as a silhouette wizard; exhibitions. Prominent persons who have posed.

Educational reforms brought about by Horace Mann, "Father of the Public School System," who was born on this day in 1795. Tribute to this native of Franklin, Massachusetts, by a college president of your section. Mann's founding of the first state normal school in the United States at Lexington, Massachusetts. His election to New York University's Hall of Fame in 1900.

An arson expert of your city. The methods used to determine whether a blaze was set. Searching the ruins for vital clues. Number of arson arrests and convictions during the past year. Is arson more rampant in the city or in rural areas?

Students' Memorial Day. How it honors the memory of the four students who lost their lives during anti-war demonstrations at Kent State University in Ohio on this day in 1970. Students martyred elsewhere also receive tribute. Current sentiment on campus.

5

A scholar or researcher of your state well known for the study of dialects. Most unusual dialects in the state. Regional customs associated with dialect. How radio and TV have reduced the differences in dialect.

Discovery of Jamaica by Christopher Columbus. Anniversary angle: The event took place on this day in 1494 during his second voyage. Spaniards settled the island fifteen years later. How Columbus delighted in the place, with the Indian name Xaymaca, meaning "island of fountains." The island as a favorite resort today.

A local resident who models papier-maché into figures. How he or she prepares the material and creates figures large and small. The artistic talent shown in the decoration of products. How the output is marketed.

Tape correspondence. Exchange of tapes through mail, even overseas. Slant: How pen pals are transformed into tape pals. Making a file of tape letters. Tape letters as part of school or club projects.

6

The top photographer of the state's wildlife and marine resources department. Slant: How the photographer receives his hunting thrills shooting with a camera instead of a gun. Counties with the largest abundance of wildlife and marine species. The numerous uses of the still and movie pictures; the most difficult photographs taken. Advice on wildlife photography.

Cheapness of land in your county in pioneer days. Anniversary angle: Manhattan Island was purchased from the Indians on this day in 1625 for $24 worth of trinkets. First settlers in your county and the amount they paid for property; in contrast, the land prices in the county today.

A local church member who has not missed services for a quarter of a century or longer. Highlights of his or her religious endeavors during this period; taking part in expansion of the church quarters and fund-raising campaigns. Honors that have been bestowed. Other members of the family as church attenders. Observations on changing religious attitudes over the years. Importance of spiritual fellowship.

The adventures of Robert E. Peary and his wife in the Arctic. Anniversary angle: Peary was born on this day in 1856. Mrs. Peary, the former Josephine Diebitech, of Washington, became the first white woman to winter with an Arctic expedition. The Pearys' first child, Marie Ahnighito, was born farther north than any other child in the world.

7

Artisans and craftsmen in your area. Which individuals or companies are creating products that can't come off an assembly line or be programmed by a computer? Are many of these persons second and third generations of families in the same trade? Spinoffs: Young people and crafts; craft co-ops and communes.

Preserving the deer in your state. Maintaining the deer population in balance with the food supply. Setting aside an open season for hunters; the bag limits. What deer eat. Game refuges for deer in the state. Number of deer killed by drivers. Spinoff: Same treatment can apply to other game animals.

Objects left on school buses by students. Experiences of bus drivers. The articles generally forgotten; finding of money. Phone calls to the drivers in order to relieve anxiety. Slant: Don't poke fun at the absent-minded professor!

The champion anesthetist in your city. His years of service giving anesthetics during operations, and the hospitals where he has served. An estimate of the number of his patients; the progress of anesthetics in recent years. Pioneers in anesthesiology.

8

V-E (Victory in Europe) Day, commemorating the end of World War Two in Europe in 1945. Recollections of the first V-E Day by members of local veterans organizations. The most ferocious battles in which these veterans' participated, and their experiences. Spinoff: Foreign brides taken by servicemen and the wives' participation in community affairs today.

Renewed interest in wine making at home. Who are the persons of your area most interested in this today, buying the ingredients and supplies from shops? Persons who may have been making dandelion wine for years. Grape and blackberry varieties; honey wine or mead; parsnip wine. Spinoff: Beer and ale making.

A music lover of your section who prides himself or herself on violin making. Slant: How he or she finds such craftsmanship an expression of the fascination of music. Step-by-step construction of violins; the kinds of wood, forming the instrument, and the polishing. The various instruments the musician-craftsman plays.

Illness on airplanes, buses, and trains. Recollections of pilots, conductors, and bus drivers. Most common sicknesses. Do many persons suffer from motion sickness? Has the stork paid visits on planes? Worst emergency cases. Are stewardesses, conductors, and bus drivers given any medical or first aid training?

9

Fascination with the rainbow. The belief of ancient Greeks that a rainbow meant the outbreak of war or torrential rains. Noah's sighting of the rainbow after the flood. American Indian rainbow legends. The source of the rainbow's brilliant colors. The rainbow in art and literature.

An honest-to-goodness "village" in your state as a hobby or a commercial enterprise. Some tourist centers have "villages" as attractions. How the founder has created the replica for his enjoyment and that of the general public. The components—likely a general store, post office, bank, church or chapel, saloon, and craft or trade shops. The creator's designing of the project and his investment.

The largest college choir in your state. The director and his or her methods. The amount of practice per week. Longest tours; songs that go over best; awards. How many of the members are from out of state?

An organization of farm women in your community. The president and her discussion of the principal accomplishments in the past year and this year's objectives. The dedication of a farm wife as a partner in the farming enterprise and as a homemaker. One estimate is that a farm wife deserves $17,000 in annual wages.

10

Guiding a dinner theater in your section to success. Slant: How the operator fills the need for quality and variety in both plays and meals. The progress of the enterprise since its opening; its most successful production; the director of the plays and his or her techniques. The most experienced actors and actresses with the group.

A visit to a balloon factory. The balloon vendor at parades and other places, as amusement parks and fairs. Kinds of specialty balloons. Larges balloons manufactured; the daily output; consumer preferences.

Microfilming records in your city. Slant: The growing popularity of this method to preserve records and as an aid to storage space. Local government offices and institutions, as banks and public utilities, that avail themselves of microfilming. The amount of historical material put on film by a historical society in your city or state.

Golden Spike Day, full of meaning for railroad buffs. The day commemorates the meeting of the Union Pacific and the Central Pacific railroads in Utah on May 10, 1869—the first transcontinental railway. Leland Stanford, president of the Central Pacific, drove a golden spike linking East and West. What happened to the golden spike?

11

The research laboratory of an industrial organization or plant in your section. The lab's leading researchers, and the numerous products or improvements they have produced in recent years. The emphasis on safety. The scientific apparatus with which new products are created and tested. Giving approval to products.

Mother's Day (whenever the date of observance). The mother with the largest number of adopted children in your city, not including foster homes. Reasons for the adoptions. Any twins or refugees? Special interests and talents of the boys and the girls; hobbies. Tribute on Mother's Day.

Suggestion boxes pay off. Leading businesses and plants of your city that engage in this practice. Awarding prizes. The best of the ideas and the amount of saving in both time and expense. Any patents resulting from suggestions? Adoption of ideas on a national scale.

The local and regional use of male telephone operators. Reactions to men operators; curious callers who inquire about the switch from women to men operators. How in early days high school youths served as operators but gave way to women with their pleasant voices.

12

The publication activities of the local high schools, climaxed by the appearance of yearbooks near graduation. Faculty advisors for the student newspapers and yearbooks; eager-beaver photographers and cartoonists; editors meeting deadlines.

The feats of Roald Amundsen, the flying explorer, and the excitement he created in comparison with space heroes. Anniversary angle: He flew over the North Pole on May 12, 1926. How the newspapers of your city treated this milestone in exploration; editorials, if any. How Amundsen and his plane disappeared in the Arctic while rushing to the relief of Colonel Umberto Nobile.

The livestock king of your county. The leading breed; improving the stock. The size of the ranch; number of workers; marketing. Is the story a rags-to-riches saga?

National Hospital Day, an annual observance since 1921. Programs honoring Florence Nightingale, a nurse in the Crimean War who as a nursing authority spent her life in hospital improvement. Number of different jobs found in a local hospital; the education and training needed for such work. The daily operating expense of the hospital.

13

Mountains of pictures available—for a price. The seller: The operator of a photo agency in your state. Number of pictures in stock, and the range of fees. How magazines, book publishers, billboard companies, and calendar makers are among heavy buyers. Subjects in most demand. How the pictures are obtained.

Wild and wooly driving tests! Unforgettable experiences of a Motor Vehicle Bureau official in testing applicants for driving licenses. Losing control of the car and winding up in a ditch, or worse. The most difficult driving tasks for the beginner. How many applicants take repeated tests before making the grade?

When eating like a hog pays off—champions in food consumption in your section. Contests in which the participants vie with each other in eating the most pancakes, hot dogs, pizzas, biscuits, doughnuts, bananas, and such. Stomach aches afterwards. Do contestants forego food for a few days in order to whet their appetites? The techniques of winners.

Local post office box stories. The number of boxes, the sizes, and the charge for their use. The rush of the postal workers to put up the box mail every morning; the time of completion. Any attempts of mail theft? Keys absentmindedly left in boxes. Do any patrons prefer specific numbers? Do many renters fall behind in payment? Box patrons who move from the city without notifying the post office. Any waiting list for boxes?

14

What's in a brand name? How leading manufacturers in your state have selected names for their products. Latest in brand names, and sales campaigns. Brand names considered the most valuable.

Keeping the diapers off the clothesline. A diaper service of your city that picks 'em up and brings 'em back. The miles covered by the company daily; locating prospective clients. The number of washers and dryers that do their duty. How disposable diapers have created competition.

Painting traffic lines on highways in your county and nearby counties. The use of paint machines to repaint worn-out lines or paint lines on newly resurfaced areas. Amount of painting that can be accomplished in a day. Keeping motorists off the wet paint. How long do painted lines last? Facts given by a state highway engineer. Spinoff: New ideas in highway marking; reflective wands and bumps.

A chainstore magnate of your section. Did he or she have a humble beginning as a merchant? Were there early partners? Rules the business leader has followed in building the chainstore empire. Acts of philanthropy.

15

The debating team of a local or a nearby college. The coach and his or her opinion of what makes a winning debating team. Topics of discussion. The matter of judging. The results of debates with other colleges.

A local transporter of mobile homes. The average number he transports during a month; the highway regulations and safety precautions. The long trips that the driver makes in carrying the mobile homes from factories to dealers and home sites. The principal factories of such housing. How many homes are made in a day? Spinoff: Advances in mobile home technology: modular homes.

Peace Officers Memorial Day. The observance of this day by Presidential proclamation since 1963; highlights of events in your section today. Peace officers who have lost their lives in the line of duty during the past year. Changing attitudes of and toward the police.

Covering the news front of Washington, D. C. What is it like for a Washington correspondent who reports news affecting your city and state? A typical day for the Washington reporter of the local newspaper. The sources of his news, including congressmen and senators from your state; exclusives scored by the correspondent.

16

Rental movies from a public library in your section. The lending time of the films; how they are for both entertainment and education. The size of the movie collection, and the various topics. Do groups and organizations borrow the movies?

Lingo at a power plant in your county, as explained by a veteran employee. Newest additions to the slanguage. The most confusing terms to a layman. You might expand into a series about lingos in various occupations and industries.

The advent of the nickel. The appearance of the five-cent coin on May 16, 1866, and its reception. Rare nickels in the collection of a veteran coin collector in your city. The varied designs of the nickel and its changing physical composition over the years. The fame of the buffalo nickel.

Wanted: Conventions. Your interview: The manager of the convention bureau in your city or elsewhere in the state. His or her efforts to attract groups to the city for conventions; contacting local bodies and also using direct mailings to organizations far and near. Slant: How chamber of commerce gives full support because conventions play an important role in its economic development program.

17

The playroom of the pediatric unit at a local hospital. The experiences of the recreational therapist and how he or she encourages the children to indulge in group projects. Planning the recreational sessions to suit the patients, some of whom are on stretchers or in wheelchairs. The tables with a variety of games, toys and books for different ages. How patients welcome the sessions.

An interview with the head of the state arts commission. How the commission is stimulating interest in cultural activities, including the theater, art, and poetry reading, by subsidies. Government grants for the performing arts. Performers brought to the state by the arts commission; aid to community theaters; development of local talent.

The Number One Kentucky Derby family in your city. The number of years they have witnessed the horse racing classic, rain or shine; their choice of the most thrilling finishes. The colorful ceremonies before the actual race. Other racing events the family would not miss.

Favorites of an orchestra leader in your state. Not only favorite tunes and entertainment figures, but also authors, athletes, and food. Meeting favorites. Does he collect autographs?

18

The work of a postal inspector in your state. His record of catching violators. Methods employed to trap persons removing money from letters or using the mails to defraud. The slickest operators; the latest frauds.

A long-time bricklayer in your county. His first job and the rate of pay; largest and most unusual projects on which he has worked. Accidents and stays in the hospital. Any significant changes in brickwork styles or brick technology during the past decade? The popularity of used bricks in new buildings. Has the bricklayer been employed in many parts of the nation?

The state association of industrial nurses. The reduction of industrial accidents through safety programs. The most common types of injuries. The president and other officers of the association; the group's activities. Their feelings about OSHA.

Nicknames of political leaders and their origin, such as the Rail Splitter for Abraham Lincoln. Anniversary angle: The native Kentuckian was nominated for the presidency for the first time on May 18, 1860. How his nickname came as an outgrowth of the Illinois State Republican Convention, which was held at Decatur a week before the National Convention in Chicago. How John Hanks carried two rails, which he and Lincoln had made in 1830, to the national convention and made a hit.

19

A resident of your county who makes windmills as a hobby. The most elaborate, and the largest; sale of them as novelties. Slant: The renewal of commercial interest in windmills as a source of energy. Farms in your county that used windmills in the past.

The organization for the support of the athletic programs of a local or a nearby college. How funds are collected for scholarships and intercollegiate sports. The quotas of the counties in the state and elsewhere; contribution increases during the past few years. The officers and directors. Speeches by coaches before members.

If you do not succeed at first. . . . Failures of business leaders in your state before they made it big. First ventures that flopped but left important lessons. The turning point in the careers. Formulas for success.

A sand man of your city. Slant: This is not the man who sends children to the Land of Nod. This sandman supplies sand for sandboxes and other uses. How he obtains the sand and has built a thriving business upon a foundation of sand! Largest orders the operator has filled; unique uses of sand.

20

Expeditions of a well-known naturalist of your state. Were the expeditions made into sparsely-populated areas, as forests, swamplands, mountains, or islands? The naturalist's reports on the animals and birds. The discovery of unusual or odd plants. Are they of any medical or industrial value?

An egg market in your section. The economic importance of the facility to farmers, as it provides a ready market for eggs. The machinery for processing and packaging of eggs. Daily posting of egg prices. The trend toward large scale commercial egg production.

The writing career of Amelia Earhart, the first woman to make a solo flight across the Atlantic Ocean. Anniversary angle: The native of Atchison, Kansas, began her flight on this day in 1932. The aviatrix wrote *20 Hrs. 40 Min., 1928, The Fun of It,* and *Last Flight,* while her husband, publisher George Palmer Putnam, authored her biography, *Soaring Wings.*

Billboard spoilers. Complaints by the operator of a billboard company of your city. Damage to signs, as by bullets and rocks. How often are posters changed? The worst maintenance problems. Any destruction by radical environmental groups?

21

A sculptor of your section who has attracted wide attention with his scrap metal art. Sources of material; steps in the process; use of welding equipment. His most ambitious piece of sculpture so far; sale and location of some of his work.

A local repairman of cash registers. Quick service in emergencies; the problem of parts. The oldest registers he still repairs; the most ornate or valuable. History of the register since its invention by James Ritty of Dayton, Ohio, in 1879. Electronic registers which also provide inventory control. Scanners for electronic price codes.

The practice of some banks, service stations, doctors, dentists, and drug stores in your city of passing along suckers and other edibles to the small fry. The amount of freebies given in a day. The handouts as business builders.

—Activities of the local chapter of the Junior Red Cross. Your anniversary peg is the organization of the American Red Cross on May 21, 1881, by Clara Barton. How the children perform worthwhile duties, as working in the chapter office, canteens, and blood centers. Service to hospital patients and also helping with the water safety program.

22

The popularity of campsites at the state park nearest your city. Are the majority of the campers fugitives from the hectic pace of metropolitan life? Amusements for the campers and other park users—swimming, boating, fishing, skiing, hiking, horseback riding. The number of states represented by the campers.

A collection of antique pianos in your section. The oldest and the rarest piano in the collection and its value; self-player pianos with their rolls of music. Is the collector a piano dealer or teacher? Does he or she collect old organs?

Maritime Day. It commemorates the beginning of the voyage of the *Savannah,* the first transatlantic steamship, from Savannah, Georgia, on this day in 1819. A local model shipbuilder who has specialized in replicas of history-making ships. The builder as an authority on the history of early ships.

How profitable are private parking lots in your city? Private operators who rent parking facilities by the week or month. Keeping alert for car accessory thieves. Spinoff: Municipal parking taxes to encourage alternate forms of transportation.

23

An outdoors enthusiast of your state who specializes in mountain climbing. How he spends his vacations and spare time matching his endurance against mountain peaks. His training regimen. His favorite states for mountain climbing; mountains that offer the greatest challenge. Mishaps that almost spelled disaster.

The leading makers of costumes for country music singers in your section. How the increase in the popularity of country music, in concerts and over radio and television, has swamped the costume expert with orders. Top performers as patrons; the most unique costumes. The latest styles for male and female vocalists. Spinoff: Local makers of any type of costumes.

The oldest church building in your city. The founders of the church and the first pastor; the most treasured relics in the house of worship. Is the original pulpit still in use? Early dignitaries of the city who worshipped there; the adjoining cemetery and the oldest graves. The present pastor's deep interest in the structure's history.

The extent of artificial insemination among your state's population. The estimated number of such births in the state—and also in

the nation—the past year. Sperm banks, and the cost of the procedure. Have any single women turned to this method of mother-
hood? The psychological implications for the husband and the wife
in a typical case.

24

The business manager of an orphanage in your section. Slant: How
problems have multiplied for this official because of that demon inflation. How the children help out in work, such as gardening. The
support of the orphanage, as by religious denominations. Expansion
programs. Have orphanage "populations" changed over the years?

The champion woman trapshooter in your state. How she became
interested in the sport, and her early instructors. The trophies she
has earned in trapshooting, in which the saucer-shaped targets are
known as clay pigeons. The champion's record score. Spinoff:
Women archers and "marksmen."

The evolution of bridge construction. Anniversary angle: The
Brooklyn Bridge was opened to traffic on this day in 1883. Bridges
now in the process of construction; in your state; the costliest; latest
innovations. Interview a bridge engineer on bridges of the future.
Spinoff: Testing the safety and strength of a bridge after it has been
standing for decades.

Uniforms of the local high schools. Where are the athletic and other
kinds of uniforms kept? The task of keeping them clean. Replacement of uniform due to wear and tear; total value of uniforms.
Uniforms and numbers of celebrated athletes.

25

"My favorite river." The choices of the most extensive travelers in
your city. Songs associated with rivers. Spinoff: How the rivers in
your state received their names, as by Indian origin.

Who plays the piccolo? The director of a local orchestra or band
can lead you to such a musician. The player's preference for this instrument. Are piccolo players few and far between? Spinoff: Players
of other unusual instruments in your city.

Dan Cupid on tape. A local resident who records weddings. Slant:
How the bride and groom want to preserve the sound of their wed-

ding in addition to the photographs. The demand for wedding tapes; orders by members of the wedding parties. Filming the ceremony.

A woman of your section who sells agricultural and industrial machinery. Slant: How she adds to her sales accomplishments with her ability to demonstrate tractors and other machinery. How her job is a profitable outlet for her interest in farm machines. Her attire for the job.

26

The Bureau of Vital Statistics of the state board of health. How the purpose is to keep an accurate record of all births, deaths, and causes of death in the state. The means used; the state registrar and assistants. The formation of the bureau and the first registrar; an examination of early versus recent statistics.

The boarding of animals and even pet birds in your city by a veterinarian. The wisdom of making early reservations for your pet when you are leaving on a visit or on vacation. How the vet may have air-conditioned cages and runs for the boarders; unusual boarders, as pet wildlife; prices for the service.

Fraternal twins in your city. The youngest and the oldest of the pairs. Their likes and dislikes; similarity in names; nicknames. Twins at graduation time. Twins with different hobbies. Palling around with twins.

Tips for landscape improvement from a veteran landscape gardener of your section. Advice on how to harmonize the grounds with the buildings. Enrichment of the soil; deciding on the kinds of flowers, shrubs, and trees to suit the structures. The choice of fences and gardens and their locations.

27

The superintendent of the riding attractions at a leading amusement center in your state. Slant: How such centers and county and state fairs have depended upon rides to thrill their patrons. Both children and adults as excitement-seekers.The most popular, the newest rides. Safety of rides.

Local firemen and policemen as blood donors. The long-time practice of fire and police departments providing blood for transfusions. Slant: How they help to save lives outside of their official duties.

Sites of one-time Indian villages in your section of the state. Mounds and relics dug up there. Slant: How the relics are fascinating physical evidences of the life that existed before the coming of the white man. Observations by a leading historian of your state. Relics from the villages in museums.

Dirt is not dirt cheap. The sale of dirt by firms in your county; the price of a truckload of topsoil. The demand for dirt; how it is obtained and processed.

28

A gift shop in your city that handles items made by local artists and craftsmen. Slant: How selling these items on consignment benefits both parties. The wide variety of gift items and the best-sellers; the busiest times, as during the Christmas season.

A look at the dairy association of your state through the president. Major activities of the association; promotion of milk and ice cream consumption. Oldest dairymen in point of age as well as years of service. Contrasts between the old and the new. The president's predictions about the industry.

How to give away a fortune. An in-depth study of the foremost philanthropist of your state. The largest gifts. The annual total of donations. How he has been recognized for his contributions. How the philanthropist's wealth was made. Spinoff: A local woman widely known for her gifts to charity. Latest donations; events she has sponsored. Slant: How she has used her wealth to make dreams of her youth come true.

An aged furniture caner of your city. How many chairs has he caned during his life? Years that brought him his best business. The oldest pieces of furniture bottomed by him. Where does he obtain his materials?

29

Means of livelihood for shut-ins in your section. Are any of them newspaper or magazine writers? Do any operate a magazine subscription service, a saw sharpening service or a telephone answering service? Did any persons run a business before becoming a shut-in? Slant: Like the proverbial inventor of a better mouse trap, they have caused the public to beat a path to their door.

Special privileges of the retired people of your city. Men and women over 65 gain favors, such as discounts at drug stores and other places of business; discounts on travel and entertainment breaks for the elderly. Medicare and other government sponsored programs. Is there a tuition discount at a local college?

The patriotic heritage of Rhode Island, the smallest state. Anniversary angle: It was on this day in 1790 that Little Rhody, the first American colony to proclaim independence from England in 1776, became the last of the thirteen original states to ratify the federal Constitution. How Esek Hopkins, a native of Rhode Island, served as the first commander of the Navy.

A chalkboard artist of your city who performs for young people. Use of the chalkboard in emphasizing points during a talk; story-telling with chalk. Entertaining adults as effectively as youngsters; invitations to entertain in distant states. Teaching this form of art to young admirers.

30

Scales large and small. The largest in local use, in contrast with tiny laboratory scales. Show the numerous types of scales, including platform scales, grocery store scales and weighing machines that furnish weight-and-fortune cards for the coin-droppers. How the state government checks scales for accuracy. Scales for home use, such as bathroom and kitchen scales. What about the metric system and scales?

A clergyman of your section who holds services at campsites or vacation resorts. Slant: How most of his audience are campers and vacationers and therefore strangers who form new friendships at the services. The average length of his sermons; the number of converts during his unusual ministry; baptisms. His belief in bringing the Gospel to the people.

Crusades of a television editorialist. Campaigns that the editorial broadcaster considers his greatest successes; the wide range of his subjects. The amount of fan mail, pro and con, he draws during a campaign; giving opponents of his views rebuttal time. Hottest issues, past and present. Is he a former editorial writer for a newspaper? Spinoff: TV as the new home of the investigative reporter and muckraker.

The first observance of Memorial Day in your state. How during the Civil War some Southern women decorated the graves of Confederate and Union soldiers. The introduction of ceremonies in your city, and the instigators. Modern-day observances and customs of Memorial Day.

31

Safety first! The safety engineer of a building company in your section as the construction worker's best friend. Safety regulations the engineer has initiated; awards the company has won for the number of hours without an accident. Is common sense about safety not so common? National conferences on safety in the construction industry and the results.

The oldest rural mail carrier of a post office in your area in point of service. The number of vehicles he has worn out in his duties along all kinds of roads. How he overcame rural obstacles so the mail could go through. Lasting friendships with patrons who have greeted him at the mailboxes. The kindness of patrons who favor him with country produce.

More food for your money. More and more families are saving on the grocery bill by buying through cooperatives. The expansion of food co-ops in your state; the warehouses of supplies and their operation. The nearest co-op information center. Spinoff: Some areas have co-ops whereby members can purchase appliances and other household goods at discount. Fees for membership.

The largest nationality communities, as in California where a high number of residents of Japanese and Chinese ancestry have settled in San Francisco and Los Angeles. The customs of Chinatown in San Francisco, and the celebration of holidays. The popularity of Chinese restaurants in your state and elsewhere over the nation.

JUNE

Month of Brides and Roses

Besides introducing the summer season, June plays an important role in the affairs of the heart; Dan Cupid has cast a spell on June since the days of the early Romans. Authorities believe the Romans named the month for Juno, patron goddess of marriage.

June still reigns as the month of brides, and composers of romantic songs have shown a fondness for linking June and the moon. June is called National Rose Month, honoring a flower that is often linked to romance.

On Father's Day, which is observed on the third Sunday of the month, the rose is the official flower. June also offers Flag Day, Senior Citizens Day in Oklahoma, D-Day, Teachers' Day in Massachusetts, Bunker Hill Day, Watergate Day, Federal Union Day, Custer Day, Magna Carta Day, and United Nations Charter Day. Residents of Kentucky, Tennessee, Arkansas, and West Virginia celebrate Admission Days in June. Other observances of the month are Flag Week, Amateur Radio Week, National Fraternal Week, and National Little League Baseball Week.

Writers can work up articles on these June anniversaries: 3. De Soto staked out Spain's claim for Florida, 1539; 4. Rome surrendered to Allies, 1944; 5. Public balloon made first ascent, in France, 1783; 6. YMCA founded in London, 1844; 10. German soldiers destroyed Lidice in Czechoslovakia, 1942; 14. Continental Congress adopted the stars and stripes design for the American flag, 1777; and Hawaii formed as territory, 1900; 15. Charles Goodyear received patent for rubber vulcanization, 1844; 21. Cyrus McCormick awarded patent for reaper, 1834; 23. William Penn and Indians signed treaty, 1683; 28. German delegates signed Treaty of Versailles, 1919; and 30. United States Fish and Wildlife Service created, 1940.

June has been the birthday month of Mormon founder Brigham Young, Cole Porter, railway pioneer George Stephenson, General Winfield Scott, Harriet Beecher Stowe, Helen Keller, Jack Dempsey, Lou Gehrig, William James Mayo, John McCormack, Frank Lloyd Wright, Jefferson Davis, Nathan Hale, Anthony Eden, John Hersey, Irvin S. Cobb, Peter Paul Reubens, William Edgar Borah, Marilyn Monroe, and Edward, Duke of Windsor, who gave up the British throne for "the woman I love."

1

All eyes on the wedding cake! Behind the scenes with a veteran caterer of your city who has prepared more cakes and refreshments for wedding festivities than any other local person. The most elaborate receptions the caterer has served; estimating the amount of refreshments needed. Most weddings served in a single day.

A sailboat club of your county. Women who show themselves expert at the helm. The excitement of sailboat racing: The champion. The largest and the smallest of the sailboats and the cost. A professional boatbuilder of your area who designs and builds sailboats.

The reign of the strawberry in your state. The foremost strawberry growers and shippers; varieties and the most prolific of them; favorites of the producers. Height of the season and the picking. Is there a Pick-Ur-Own system? Any strawberry festivals? The county with the Number One output. Recipes for strawberry concoctions, as ice cream, cakes, and pies.

Statehood Day in Kentucky and Tennessee. Programs commemorating the admissions and tribute to early leaders. The birthplace of Abraham Lincoln near Hodgenville, Kentucky, and two presidents—Andrew Jackson and James Polk—as residents of Tennessee. First governor of each state.

2

Who throws his weight around the most locally? The champion weight lifter, of course. The use of barbells and dumbbells; the three standard lifts—the press, the clean and jerk, and the snatch. The best lifts by the champ. His training program; features of his meals; his equipment. His participation in other sports, as tennis or golf. The subject's early instructors in weight lifting. Tips on body-building.

A large hotel of your city that provides a tourist bureau. Slant: How the bureau serves as a ready and dependable guide for tourists and makes their vacations more enjoyable. The director and his knowledge of geography and the leading attractions of the area. Travel literature and road maps he dispenses.

Marriages in the White House. Anniversary angle: Grover Cleveland became the first president to be married there, in a ceremony on this day in 1886. How Mrs. Cleveland was one of the youngest First Ladies and proved herself a delightful hostess. Spinoff: Role of the First Lady over the years.

—Journeys into the future—time capsules. How cities in your section of the state have deposited capsules of material in safe places, as in downtown parks, for opening half a century or a full century later. The items, as a history of the city and the county, newspapers, photographs, and records, including statistics. Dedications of the capsules. Have any from the last century been opened?

3

Roses are red, and white, pink, yellow, blue, even black. This is National Rose Month in recognition of the flower that has ruled as a favorite since time immemorial. The far-out new color varieties. How roses thrive in every climate and are grown in all fifty states. The largest rose gardens in your city and the varieties represented there. Local members of the American Rose Society. Rose festivals, notably in Portland, Oregon.

Animal portraits. Slant: How a local commercial photographer combines the love for animals and for photography. The surprisingly large number of assignments for pictures of household pets. Are cats harder to pose than dogs? The props for an animal photograph; striving for the right expression. What the photographer considers his or her animal photo masterpieces.

De Soto National Memorial Park near Bradenton, Florida. It occupies the site of Hernando De Soto's landing in that state. Anniversary angle: The explorer claimed Florida for Spain on this day in 1539. Attractions at the twenty-four-acre park. De Soto County and the city of De Soto in Florida were named in honor of De Soto, who made an expedition through Florida and into Georgia, the Carolinas, and Alabama in a fruitless search for gold.

The millionaire county of your state. Which county leads in the number of millionaires? How the wealthiest made their money. From rags to riches. The youngest millionaires and their hobbies. Business mottoes and advice.

4

Part-time farming in your county. Persons who hold regular jobs and farm on the side to produce much of their food and meat. How family members help with the chores on small farms.

A day with a mobile history museum. Slant: The museum's service as a traveling history book for children and adults alike. How the trailer is outfitted, and the exhibits that draw the most interest. Photographs along with the relics; the director of the project. Tours of the state, and the number of visitors.

The bands of local fraternal or service organizations. For instance, how many persons are in the band of the American Legion post? Leaders of the groups; frequency of practice sessions; the variety of instruments. The matter of uniforms; parades in which the bands take part; winning prizes.

Take a card—a business card! The most unusual business cards printed or used in your city. Contact printing companies as well as star salesmen. Do any use humor on a card? Types of businesses that make the greatest use of business cards. Bilingual cards used by foreign-traveling businessmen.

5

A smoke jumper in the United States Forest Service as hero. Slant: How he is able to reach fires in practically inaccessible places. His training for such a career. The kinds of plane and parachute used; dropping equipment by parachute. Longest flights to combat blazes; using hand pumps and chemicals.

A peacock raiser of your section. Slant: How he or she is as proud as a peacock about this operation. Are the peacocks extremely tame? Human qualities of the birds; examples of vanity. The gay colors of the peacock; the time it takes for the tails to grow full length. How peacocks molt in the summer. What peacocks eat; the buyers of the fowls and their feathers.

The superintendent of your city's park. The mixture of beauty and recreational facilities. The recreational director and assistants. Competition in baseball and softball. Swimming lessons. Group activities in nature study, arts, and handicrafts.

World Environment Day, which is observed by the members of the United Nations. How people everywhere can work for preservation of the environment. An interview with president of an environmental group in your state that has waged effective campaigns against neglect and destruction of the environment.

6

"My recollections of D-day." Flashbacks to the beginning of the invasion of France in World War Two on the anniversary of the event. The most vivid memories of those who took part in the invasion. Winning medals for heroism.

The state chapter of the Little People of America, Inc. Story of the growth of the chapter by the state coordinator. The qualifications to join—people not over four feet, eleven inches are eligible. How the dwarfs and midgets make the most of their smallness; common and uncommon occupations for them. An insight into their homes and family lives. Highlights of district meetings.

A veteran railroad flagman serving your city. Has he worked for the same railroad during his entire career? Performing his duties in the worst kinds of weather, especially in winter. Is the flagman a model railroad addict? His feelings about today's railway system.

The funny bone of a cartoon and joke editor of a magazine in your state. Does his or her work show that humor can be found in practically everything? The main ingredients of a cartoon; different styles of artists. Gentle humor versus slapstick. Most popular types of jokes; old humor with new twists.

7

The Number One "hat lady" of your city. The owner of a hat shop or the woman clerk in a local store who has sold more hats than any other salesladies in the city. Seasons of greatest hat sales, as Easter; making buying trips to New York City and elsewhere. How hair styles affect hat sales. The changing styles of hats over the years.

Crop predicting in your state. The director of the State Crop Reporting Service can "spill the beans." Conditions that enter into the predictions; the frequency and effect of forecasts.

Royalty in your city—by name only. What the city telephone directory reveals in the way of citizens named King, Queen, and Prince. The largest families of them; family reunions. The oldest Kings, Queens, Princes, and probably Dukes, and the number of their descendants. Spinoff: The most colorful names of local residents, Brown, Green, White, Gray, and Black. To go further, round up persons with the same names as celebrities, some of whom they may have met.

Summer jobs for high school and college athletes of your city. The most unusual kinds of work; the best muscle-building ones. Working in a sporting goods store or in the sports department of a newspaper. Jobs with construction companies. Recreation programs and children's sports camps. Any positions with professional teams?

8

The ceremony of Bar Mitzvah, a Jewish ritual conducted when a boy is initiated into the religious community. The festivities following Bar Mitzvahs held in your city, and also those after the Bas, or Bat, Mitzvah conducted for girls.

How cheap—or dear—is talk? Statistics by the local telephone company, including the growth in the number of calls, locally and long distance, monthly. The number of business and residence phones. Is the practice of unlisted numbers increasing? Spinoff: Decline in personal letter writing due to telephone calls.

A belly dancing teacher. Slant: How it is one of the oldest dances; it originated in the Middle East during Biblical times. What organizations and institutions offer or sponsor the classes? The physical exercise and the benefits, as cited by the instructor. The time a student generally needs to master this form of dancing.

Delivery of wedding gifts. The excitement of the bride-to-be and her family in receiving the presents. Selection of china, glassware, and silver patterns by the future bride; keeping records of what pieces have been bought. The chore of wrapping the presents and sometimes mailing them. Which month leads in the volume of nuptial gifts—June?

9

How to take up a hobby. Local hobbyists can give advice on how to select a suitable hobby and obtain the fullest enjoyment from it. Indoor and outdoor hobbies; those with financial profit; major collecting hobbies.

A salesman of a church supply company who sells locally. The various products, as bulletin boards, stained glass windows, clocks, chairs, altars and pews, organs, pulpits, and choir robes. The states covered by the salesman. Meeting the demands of the modern as well as the traditional church.

Cities in your state that are home to well-known actors. Anniversary angle: John Howard Payne, an actor and the author of the song, "Home, Sweet Home," was born on this day in 1791. Did any of the stars receive their start in their hometowns? Visits back home. Did some of the performers marry hometown sweethearts?

A rural electric system of your section owned by the consumers. The number of farms served by the system, and the number of ways electricity serves the farmer. The expansion of rural electricity service since the advent of the REA.

10

Bells and music on the street mean the ice cream vendor is on the way—a magnet for children, not to mention adults. Kinds of ice cream and other frozen delights. The cost of an ice cream truck and its upkeep. The routes, and the number of miles covered daily; the days with the most sales. How the driver practices safety measures.

The popularity of the horse in the Space Age. Slant: How increased leisure time has caused people to turn to horses, riding or watching them. Breeders of pleasure horses in your section; how members of 4-H clubs manifest interest in horses; the growth of horse shows in the state.

Local churches that provide for hard-of-hearing people. The houses of worship with the most "plug-ins" for hearing aids. Also, how many blind persons attend church services in your city? Sightless members who are among the most ardent workers. Braille Bibles.

The perennial appeal of Shakespeare. A Shakespearean festival staged annually in your state. Productions in outdoor settings; plays that draw the largest audiences. The director's reputation as a Shakespearean authority. The background of the players. Spinoff: A Shakespearean scholar of your city. Favorite quotations from the Bard of Avon that are established in everyday speech. Lectures he or she makes to groups in and out of the state.

11

Photocopying machines. Where they are and who uses them. Is the service a success? The conveniences for the users, ranging from students to business and professional people. Cost of the machines; the different types.

The leading coin dealer in the state. How his transactions are national in scope and necessitate heavy correspondence. The steady flow of visitors to his place of business; activities at a coin auction. The most valuable coins the dealer has owned or sold.

Kamehameha Day—a time of celebration in Hawaii with a parade and pageantry. How the islanders honor King Kamehameha I, who in 1782 began a ten-year war that gave him control of Hawaii Island. Progress of the islands under his rule. Spinoff: Hawaii today; cost of living; vacation and retirement haven.

The foremost electrical contractor in your section. Slant: How he amounts to a live wire in the area or a number of states. His beginning, probably on a modest scale. The safety mindedness of the company. Latest innovations in the electrical world.

12

A young bark collector of your city. How he or she removes sections of bark from trees and mounts them on cardboard. The trees represented; unusual formations on the bark; specimens from the longest distances. Spinoff: Other types of nature collecting hobbies, as collecting leaves, seed, and cones.

Physically handicapped children as swimmers. Slant: How such a program in your section offers therapy as well as social interaction for the boys and the girls. The instructor and the size of the swimming classes. The remarkable results. How the children have a splashing good time even if they do not swim. Spinoff: Swimming as a top fitness activity. 1,000-mile clubs at local YMCA.

Top sellers in plug-cut tobacco in local stores. Has the use of chewing tobacco decreased in recent years? The oldest manufacturing companies in existence. The gradual disappearance of spittoons. Baseball players as traditional chewers.

The diary that made Anne Frank a world figure. Anniversary angle: The German-Dutch adolescent who kept a diary while hiding from the Nazis was born on June 12, 1929. The success of her diary in book form, *The Diary of a Young Girl,* as a play and also a motion picture.

13

A large company of your city built on distrust of humanity—a seller of safes. What kind of sales talk does a safe salesman make? Safes for various purposes. The largest safes; the smallest. Features of the latest models. Installing safes. Calls to the company for a safe opener.

The leadership of General Winfield Scott in the Mexican campaign of 1847 when he led the invading expedition. Old Fuss and Feathers was born on this day in 1786. The Virginian's victories at Vera Cruz, Cerro Gordo, Contreras-Churubusco, Molino del Ray, and Chapultepec; his capture of the Mexican capital on September 14. His defeat for the presidency in the 1852 election.

The butcher and the baker in one of the largest restaurants in your city. Their preparation of the meat and the bread; daily output. The variety of meats, and the amount kept on hand. Their respective specialities and favorites.

Interviewing famous personalities. Experiences of a veteran radio or television newsman of your section in covering memorable events. Quotes of celebrities that left deep impressions in the newsman's memory. Mingling with movie stars; exclusives with political leaders.

14

A juvenile aid bureau of your section. Providing recreational facilities to combat juvenile delinquency; what underprivileged children need most of all, according to the bureau's director. Taking care of abandoned children. Runaway boys and girls from other cities who become stranded.

Flag Day. The heroism of Sergeant William Jasper in rescuing the flag at Fort Sullivan, now Fort Moultrie, in the harbor at Charleston, South Carolina, on June 28, 1776. His famous words, "Don't let us fight without a flag," as he rushed to the flag despite the shower of bullets and restored it during the ten-hour battle lost by the British. Fort Moultrie as a tourist attraction today.

The most versatile hunter of your county. How the outdoorsman engages in numerous kinds of hunts. The most cagey animals to bag. Tactics for different animals. His dogs and his pride—and confidence—in them. His most challenging pursuits. Hunts in distant states and even in foreign countries.

Women who serve in a detective agency in your state. Slant: The women behind the scenes tracking down mysteries. Have any of them run into unusual or dangerous situations? Instances in which a woman catches a woman. How detective stories rate with the women on the staff.

15

Producing the city directory. Number of persons conducting the census; the time, and the cost. Do many residents object to giving full information? The most difficult duties of making the directory. A typical schedule, from the beginning to the date of publication.

Magna Carta Day. King John's signing of the Magna Carta, a document known as the cornerstone of English liberty, took place on this day in 1215. It granted his subjects certain rights and developed into the basis of all English-speaking nations' constitutions. The ruler's bitterness over the act.

The stage manager of the local Little Theater. The indispensible work of the technical staff backstage. Problems of scenery; operation of the lighting; things that might mar the smoothness of the production. Does the stage manager sometimes appear in roles?

The largest collection of Indian pottery in your state. Is it in a museum, and who found and preserved this aboriginal handiwork? The tribe who made the pottery. The most interesting or decorative pieces in the exhibit. Estimated age of the pottery and the value.

16

Bringing outdoor beauty indoors. Advice from a well-known indoor gardener of your city—how to make an indoor garden, what plants to choose, and how to care for them. Plants that provide the most interior decoration; the use of hanging baskets to display plants; exotic plants.

An old-time cider maker of your county. Does he have a hand-operated cider press? Grinding or crushing apples to make the beverage; the annual output. Kinds of apples he uses. Does he prefer sweet or hard cider? Promoting apple brandy, called applejack. Sale of cider at roadside stands.

The activities of the National Guard in your area. Armories and storage facilities. The drills and the training periods. The annual field training. How the governor can put the Guard members on active duty in cases of emergency. Worst disasters in which members have helped. Origins of the National Guard and its role in War. Spinoff: Universal military service in some countries.

Local hosts to foreign visitors. Slant: The boom in foreign tourists in the United States. Conversing in foreign languages. What places in your state impressed the tourists the most, and why?

17

Strides by "women of the cloth"—women ministers. How many denominations permit women to be ordained into the ministry? Women pastors with the largest congregations. Where the women received their ministerial training. Women students in a seminary. Women evangelists and record crusades.

Exploration of the Mississippi River, the Father of Waters. Anniversary angle: Father Jacques Marquette and Louis Joliet began their exploration of the river on this day in 1673 and advanced as far as the mouth of the Arkansas River. How Hernando de Soto, regarded as the river's discoverer, died on the river's banks and his companions deposited his body with his armor in the waters.

Giving a helping hand. A well-known citizen of your state who makes a practice of giving college scholarships to worthy boys and girls. Slant: How he has been honored for his generosity in making dreams come true. Did the donor of the scholarships have difficulty in receiving his own education? Total number of scholarships he has given; reunions and achievements of the recipients.

A long-time button sewer at a dry cleaning establishment in your city. Any idea how many buttons he or she sews on weekly? Assortment of buttons on hand; cuff links left on shirts. Alterations performed on clothes; the most frequent repairs. Spinoff: Items left in clothing at dry cleaning establishments.

18

What is the bravest breed of dog? Opinions of veterinarians, kennel keepers, and dog raisers or trainers in your city. Slant: How the saying, "A dog is man's best friend," has been proved by outstanding instances of bravery on the part of canines. Dogs that have been honored for saving people's lives.

A woodworking hobbyist of your county who makes his own furniture. The products in which he takes the greatest pride. Designing the furniture; the materials and the time required to produce it. Offers that admirers have made him for the furniture.

Waterloo Day, which commemorates the anniversary of Napoleon's final defeat in the Battle of Waterloo waged in 1815. His death as an exile on the island of St. Helena, and the burial of his remains under the Hotel des Invalides' dome in Paris. How other famous generals "met their Waterloo."

Granddads and grandmoms as newspaper carriers. Slant: The traditional newsboy delivering papers on a bicycle has lost ground to a growing number of middle-aged or older carriers. Delivery by automobile. How the newsgirl has made inroads.

19

Father's Day, held on the third Sunday of this month, was first observed on June 19 in 1910. The observance was first suggested by a woman, Mrs. John B. Dodd. A centenarian of your section can unfold memories of a father's life a century ago. His or her recollections of how Father reared his family and drilled the ingredients of success into the minds of the children.

Wedding customs in your city. Features of the ceremonies and festivities with different nationalities. The attire and music; the range of flowers, and the refreshments.

The daily barrage of questions at the local post office. Anxious inquiries about the arrival and departure time of the mail. Callers who insist upon talking with the postmaster; complaints and bouquets. Seasons of the most questions, as Christmas.

The busy life of a tent salesman. Slant: How the camping craze and the proliferation of campgrounds have increased demand. The zooming popularity of weekend and vacation camping. Deluxe and specialized tents; largest and smallest sizes in tents and the demand for them.

20

A day on a cattle ranch in your section. The breeds and the reasons they are preferred. Are the cattle branded? Are ranch workers hard to hire in view of the competition from high-paying industrial jobs. Traces of the Old West. Going to market with cattle—a cattle auction.

The largest gun club in your section. How the gun and pistol owners meet regularly for practice and fellowship. The target range, and the best marksmen. The most unusual firearms; the oldest. The member with the biggest gun collection.

The editor of the monthly magazine of the ETV operation in your state. Slant: How the publication is distributed free of charge to citizens of the state interested in educational television activities and programming. The editor's work in compiling the program listings as well as articles. The art director and his or her cover designs. ETV programming versus that of commercial stations. Spinoff: Educational or public radio.

Your state's society in Washington, D.C. The regular meetings and the highlights of the year; chief social events. The president and other officers. Senators and congressmen from your state as participants in the proceedings. Greeting and entertaining visitors from the state.

21

Beginning of summer. A day with the owner-promoter of a resort in your state. His revelations about how he has built a flourishing resort with appeal for the entire family. Attracting both local pleasure-seekers and tourists from afar. The most successful promotions.

Cyrus McCormick as a gold miner. McCormick was granted a patent for the reaping machine on June 21, 1834. His purchase of gold mines in McCormick, South Carolina, and also his acquisition of several thousand acres of land. He found no profit in the venture, but donated land for the town and also property for worthwhile institutions.

Church athletic teams. Slant: How churches emphasize recreation and physical development along with spiritual growth. The sports in which the churches organize teams; playing facilities. The coaches and championship squads. Do local teams compete with those of churches over the county or the state?

Record days. Check with various county offices, as the probate judge's office, the tax office, and the like. Highest figures in land sales, weddings, divorces, etc.

22

The director of the state parks in your state as a keen observer of park systems in other states. Slant: How he exchanges ideas with park directors elsewhere and keeps his state park abreast of the newest developments. The state with the most parks; the variety of activity at state parks.

The first automobile salesman in your city. Slant: How a large part of the citizenry looked upon the dealer as something of a daredevil who might go broke. The initial purchasers of the horseless carriage locally; the cost of the vehicle and the need to possess mechanical know-how. The speed of the first cars; early speed laws enacted by the city council.

The grape king of your section. The acreage and the number of workers; improving the vineyard. The task of pruning and spraying against insects and diseases. Harvesting; where the grapes are sold.

Favorite varieties. Grape cultivation as one of the largest fruit industries worldwide.

An organization of your city that aids an orphanage. Regular contributions as well as donation of gifts on special occasions, as Thanksgiving and Christmas. Donors who spent their childhood in orphanages. Paying visits to the orphanage and forming close friendships. Finding jobs for orphans after their schooling.

23

The writer's stepping stones—a writer's conference in your state or a neighboring state. The director and the number of students. Slant: How the conference enables authors to discover their greatest weaknesses and be directed into the most likely markets. A typical day, beginning with breakfast. Reading and criticizing manuscripts; lectures by editors and literary agents. Social activities.

Unmatched summers in your county. Round-up summers that have made the greatest news from the weather standpoint. Summers with the most rainfall and the highest temperature, in contrast with the least precipitation and the lowest mercury reading. The effects on crops and also on the lives of city dwellers.

Say it with postcards. Local stores that offer postcards with local and area scenes and even the foldup kind. Typical pictures and the ones with the most appeal to tourists. A photographer who specializes in taking postcard photos. Humorous postcards; postcard collectors. Photographic-paper cards for making your own.

William Penn's success as a peacemaker with the Indians. He signed the Great Treaty of Shackamaxon on the banks of the Delaware River on this day in 1683, proclaiming that the Indians and the colonists would "live in love as long as the sun gave light." The peace between the Quakers and the Indians for almost seventy years.

24

The division of maternal and child health of the state department of health. The director and his or her discussion of both problems and progress. Teaching maternal care; the reduction in infant mortality. The nutrition consultant.

Have a pretzel? A visit to a bakery that produces pretzels and an interview with the owner. The ingredients and the preparation; the shapes, sizes, and flavors of pretzels and the distribution.

The lure of perfumes. Stores in your city that lead in perfume sales. The highest price of perfume locally. The popularity of perfume as birthday, wedding anniversary, and holiday gifts. Are most men hesitant about buying perfume? Ingredients of the perfumes. Ask a salesperson about the most effective use of perfumes; perfume storage.

The grounds keeper at a large airport in your section. Slant: The beautification of the grounds as a daily advertisement for the state as passengers come and go. The kinds of flowers and shrubbery; the time devoted to trimming the shrubbery; the years of experience behind the keeper's green thumb; fountains and pools that add to the beauty.

25

The art of making artificial eyes in your city. The steps in providing a person with an artificial eye. Growing accustomed to its use. A local eye specialist noted for such work; the average cost. Producing artificial eyes and the emphasis on making them look natural.

Places named in honor of General George A. Custer, known as "Yellow Hair" by the Indians. Indians ended the life of General Custer in the Battle of Little Big Horn in Montana on this day in 1876. Many states contain places named Custer, such as Montana and South Dakota. The statue in honor of the general at the United States Military Academy at West Point. Spinoff: The real Custer versus movie portrayals.

Favorite flowers of the presidents of the local garden clubs. The flower gardens of these women and the numerous varieties of flowers. The presidents as flower photographers.

Poisoned! Lifesaving in cases of poisoning locally. How first aid is administered following advice from the poison center at a hospital emergency room. Use of the poison safeguard kit with syrup of

ipecac and activated charcoal. The service of the National Poison
Control Network. Phone numbers to call for emergency assistance.
Poison-proof your home.

26

Hollywood comes to your state. Summer attractions that feature
movie and television stars. The boom in this type of summer entertainment that can be imported to places without scenic wonders.
How fans deluge the luminaries for autographs; beginning actors
who seek advice—and assistance. Mention fees, if available.

Bicycling families in your city. Men and women have turned to
bicycling with equal enthusiasm. Couples who take daily bicycle
trips. Bicycling with the children. Popular routes in the area. Taking along bikes on vacation. Fifteen million adults are regular bike
riders in the United States. Bicycling fitness programs; commuting
by bicycle.

The Ice Age in your area. Exactly what was happening and what it
was like in your area. A scientist of your state can discuss the
periods of the Ice Age and the boulders pushed ahead by the ice
sheets. The effect of melting ice upon the oceans. Question for the
scientist: Will glaciers return? The remarkable collection of Ice Age
fossils at the Los Angeles County Museum of History and Science in
California.

What are the odds on beating the gambling habit? Former gamblers
of your area who have licked the temptation through the organization called Gamblers Anonymous. The number of chapters in the
state and also in the nation. The fellowship of the members and the
encouragement they offer each other. The main steps in overcoming
gambling fever.

27

Lost, strayed, or stolen. The local supermarkets lose quite a number
of shopping carts in a year, an expensive loss. Its kinship with
shoplifting. Trying to keep track of the buggies; anti-rustling
devices. Damage by cars. Spinoff: The disappearance of trays at
eating drive-ins in your city. Practical jokes by customers.

The use of the walls of buildings for advertising. Slant: How this practice dates back a century, or longer. The chief advertisers on walls through the years, as tobacco and medicine companies. Putting up huge posters on the side of barns in the county. Comments by the manager of an outdoor advertising agency.

The earliest duels on record in your state. The weapons and the results; the site of the duel and the seconds. Duels over political issues; graves of persons killed in duels. The last duel in your state and the public reaction; how the state outlawed this form of combat.

Helen Keller's most successful books in her literary career. She has been translated into more than fifty languages. Slant: How this native of Tuscumbia, Alabama, born on June 27, 1880, found beauty accepted as commonplace by persons with sight and hearing. The reception of the inspiring *The Story of My Life,* published in 1903, and also *Optimism,* which appeared the same year. Later works and her methods in writing them. Copies of Miss Keller's books in the local library.

28

The clothing manufacturing center of your state. The weekly output of the largest factory, the kinds of fabrics, and the number of workers. Small plants with big results. Competition from abroad.

How high are the cities, rivers, and natural elevations in your section? The altitudes are determined by the work of the Coast and Geodetic Survey, a bureau of the United States Department of Commerce. Use of the data by surveyors and engineers, and also by highway planners.

Lightning as villain in your county. Death and damage caused by lightning the past year—a single stroke of lightning packs the punch of 15,000,000 volts. The worst and the safest places to be in a thunderstorm; swimmers and golfers beware. Farm animals as frequent targets.

Local sisters who are surgical nurses. Number of operations in which both have helped. Their work in assisting surgeons. The most operations in one day. How many emergencies have to be rushed into surgery at once.

29

Five ways to improve government—city, state, and national. The views of a political scientist of your state, and his most urgent suggestions. Public opinion polls that support his opinions. How he would cure voter apathy.

The Hall of Fame craze. How states have developed Halls of Fame to honor their leaders, including heroes of the distant past. Displays and ceremonies of induction. Halls of Fame in sports, as the National Baseball Hall of Fame and Museum at Cooperstown, New York. The National Cowboy Hall of Fame in Oklahoma City, and South Carolina's recognition of historical and modern heroes with its Hall of Fame at Myrtle Beach.

The consumers' watchdog. The work of the commission on consumer affairs in your state, and the operation of the consumer protection code. The chairman's description of the assistance provided consumers. Serving as consumer complaint mediator. Actions taken after charges of ripoffs. Do retailers feel the pendulum has swung too far in distrust of people in business?

Telling the world about Africa, the Dark Continent. The explorations of Sir Morton Stanley, born on June 29, 1841, and David Livingstone. Stanley's famous search for Livingstone and his words as he came upon him: "Dr. Livingstone, I presume." Stanley's autobiography, edited by his wife. Spinoff: Emerging Africa today, no longer the "heart of darkness."

30

Fairy tales know no boundaries! The universal appeal of these stories, whether in the United States, Ireland, England, France and India. Favorite fairy tales of members of nationality groups in your city. Spinoff: Views of a child psychologist on the necessity and usefullness of fairy tales.

Samples of local salesmen. The food salesman, who captures instant attention with his samples. The shoe salesman, with his samples of shoes for the same foot; how thieves feel frustrated when they find they have stolen such shoes. The pencil and pen salesman who gets himself on the "write" foot as he pushes his wares. The experiences of salespeople; resistance and reluctance to sampling samples.

Dancing therapeutic treatment. A dance teacher whose instructions have spelled recovery for injured persons and led to improvement in the mentally ill. His or her most amazing cases. Types of dances that are most effective. Slant: How dancing can be of medical benefit as well as social advantage.

Outdoor murals that have brightened the unsightly walls in a city. Artists who have been busy with such projects, as in downtown sections. How are the subjects selected? The wide attention attracted by the murals.

JULY

Patriotism's High Mark

Public demonstration of patriotism in the United States reaches its
zenith on July the fourth—the day the people of France presented
the Statue of Liberty to Americans in 1884. The Grand Old Lady
towers on Liberty Island in New York Harbor as a symbol of
freedom.

A number of other lands observe Independence Day in July:
Argentina, Belgium, the Netherlands, Tunisia, Venezuela, the
Philippines, Peru, Liberia, the Bahama Islands, and Burundi and
Rwanda in Africa. The citizens of France celebrate Bastille Day on
July 14, the Holiday of All Free Men.

Although born on July 3, song writer George M. Cohan adopted
July 4 as his birthday, an appropriate gesture for the author of
"You're a Grand Old Flag." Sharing his birth month are Presidents
John Quincy Adams, Calvin Coolidge, and Gerald R. Ford, as well
as his vice president, Nelson A. Rockefeller.

Other July "natives" have been Stephen Collins Foster,
Nathaniel Hawthorne, David George Farragut, P. T. Barnum, John
Paul Jones, Elias Howe, James A. McNeill Whistler, George East-
man, Oscar Hammerstein II, Rembrandt, Mary Baker Eddy, Roald
Amundsen, John Jacob Astor, William Makepeace Thackery, Er-
nest Hemingway, Haile Selassie I of Ethiopia, Simon Bolivar,
Amelia Earhart, George Bernard Shaw, Booth Tarkington, Benito
Mussolini, Louis Armstrong, Henry Ford, and Julius Caesar, who
named the month in his own honor.

In July Americans observe, in addition to Independence Day,
American Stamp Day, Gettysburg Day, Atomic Bomb Day, Moon

Day, Wyoming Statehood Day, Hawaii's Flag Day, Alaska's Flag Day, and Idaho Admission Day.

This is how history has been made in July: 1. Gideons, the Bible-giving organization, founded, 1899; 2. Charles J. Guiteau shot President James A. Garfield, 1881; 4. The Continental Congress gave birth to the Declaration of Independence, 1776; 5. The Salvation Army established in London, 1865; 6. The Harry S. Truman Library at Independence, Missouri, presented to the National Archives, 1957; 11. Aaron Burr fatally shot Alexander Hamilton in duel, 1804; 16. The District of Columbia created, 1790; 16. First atomic bomb detonated in New Mexico, 1945; 17. United States formally received Florida from Spain, 1821; 24. Salt Lake City settled by Mormons, 1847; 27. Korean War concluded, 1953; and 30. The WAVES formed as women's reserve unit of the United States Naval Reserves, 1942.

1

Research by a commercial seed company in your state. Slant: Furnishing the nation with seed is a year-round operation. The latest projects and the results; achieving greater crop yields and new varieties; importing seed. Researchers with the longest period of service. Seeds—vegetables and fruit—that are favorites.

Restoring old portraits and photographs. A local studio that specializes in restoration and the expert who performs the work. Methods of restoring old paintings and photographs to their original clarity. Valuable paintings that have been restored.

A mummy in a museum in your state. How the methods used by Egyptian embalmers have defied discovery by modern scientists. How the mummy was obtained for the museum. Reactions to the mummy. The financial value of the mummy.

The general delivery window at the local post office. Number of letters handled daily, on the average. Are many letters unclaimed? Growth in volume of this service. The use of United States postage stamps began on July 1, 1847, so there are a lot of story angles.

2

How much have gypsies of today departed from the customs and traditions of their ancestors? Pry info from some members of a band in your section or state. Modern means of livelihood; the traditional practice of fortune-telling. How far has the band travelled during the past twelve months? The skill of the gypsies as musicians and dancers—past and present. Disputed origins of the children of Romany.

Flying at the turn of the century—the first zeppelin flight was made on this day in 1900, but it was not until 1907 that Count Ferdinand von Zeppelin, the German pioneer in aerial navigation, was able to obtain a successful flight. The speed of the earliest zeppelin, in contrast with speed records today. The Germans' success in using zeppelins for bombing attacks in World War One. Slant: How Zeppelin was past sixty when he revolutionized a field dominated by young men.

Busmen's holidays. What do local bus drivers do on their days off—any distant trips? Slant: The safety consciousness of the busmen whether at work or pleasure. The drivers' worst scares and pet peeves; antics of children—and adults—on buses.

The broiler chicken industry in your state. The leading raisers, and details of their operations. The daily overhead of the king of the operators. The magnitude of the marketing process. Spinoff: The latest in henhouses. A day with the owner, and his busy schedule. Protection against human and animal marauders. Number of hens; egg production; breeds that are the best layers.

3

The user of an artificial kidney in your section. Details of the machine, and how it filters waste from the person's blood. The frequency of its use. Who operates the apparatus. The size of the machine, compared with the first artificial kidney; the operating cost. New portable units in use. Importance of donor kidneys.

The clerk of the Supreme Court of your state. His or her record of service in this capacity; the wide range of duties. Extraordinary cases that have come before the Supreme Court during his or her years as clerk. Spinoffs could be the experiences of the court's librarian and also the court reporter.

Hunts for buried treasure in your county. Reports that have stirred the imagination of citizens for decades. Highlights of searches and the frustrations. Have mysterious maps been involved? Are ghosts or apparitions associated with the stories? Spinoff: Treasure hunting with a metal detector.

Riding the waves. The sport Hawaiians gave the world centuries ago continues to add disciples annually. Surfers of your section, of any age, who journey to the seashore in quest of the perfect wave. The feat of mounting a surfboard and maintaining a standing balance. Favorite materials for surfboards; styles preferred by local fans.

4

The spirit of 1776! How patriotic organizations in your city, such as the Daughters of the American Revolution, honor the memory of the members' ancestors who participated in the Revolutionary War. Paying tribute to the patriots of more than two centuries ago; historians as speakers before the groups; erection of markers.

How the Fourth of July was observed in your city fifty or more years ago, as revealed by old-timers and newspaper files. All-day gatherings at parks; the speakers and the wide variety of fun-making; fireworks displays. Sporting events, including baseball games and horse racing; sack races and the like. Chasing greased pigs.

Sheriff's sales in your county. Auctioning off household furnishings to the highest bidder; the average number of persons attending such sales; antique searchers. A typical auction.

The horseshoe pitching champion of your section. This old, old sport still thrives not only in rural districts but at state parks and recreational centers. Elimination games and the big tournament; youngsters and oldsters in stiff competition. The champ's schedule of practice.

5

The storyteller for children at the local library. The number of years she has been performing this service. The listeners' favorite stories and authors. Do the old stories hold more fascination than new ones? Do girls outnumber boys in the reading sessions? Is the storyteller a writer of juvenile stories, either for pleasure or professionally?

The veteran owner of a local foundry. The busy task of repairing machinery for industries and farmers. PDQ calls, as for a newspaper's broken printing press. Designing equipment for farmers.

The Davis Cup, an international tennis trophy since 1900. It was established by Dwight Filley Davis, born on this day in 1879. How he developed an interest in the sport. Countries that have won the cup the most times. The service of the St. Louis, Missouri, native as secretary of war and also as governor general of the Philippines.

The legal aide of the governor of your state. Unexpected matters that require instant handling. Legal questions pressing at this time. Issues that finally wound up in the state supreme court. The subject's legal career.

6

Roadside zoos in your area, particularly for advertising and display purposes at service stations and stores. History of some of the wild animals in captivity. Feeding the creatures and protecting them from extremes of weather. Can any perform tricks? Nationwide efforts to prevent abuses and neglect at roadside zoos.

The longest and the shortest sessions of the legislature in your state. The legislation; the most controversial bills; leaders during the sessions; pay of the lawmakers. The criticism and the praise from government officials, including the governors.

Experiences of a Railway Express Agency carrier of your city. The variety of railway freight. Some of the most unusual cargoes. Shipment of animals and machinery.

Busy beavers in your county. Are they as industrious as tradition credits them? The story as related by top farmers or the county agent. Locations where the beavers have constructed dams. Opinions on whether the dam-making activities are basically beneficial or harmful to the environment. The protected status of the beavers today. Any market for the magnificent fur? Habits of the beavers.

7

An interview with a barber college operator in your state. Training students in the ever-changing methods of hair styling. What the drastic changes in men's and women's hair styles have meant to barber training and barbers. Has the school's enrollment increased during the past few years? Standards of the barbering profession.

A veteran elevator operator of your city, as in a department store or office building. How courtesy is the motto, and how the operator has the chance to form new friendships. The opportunity to study human nature.

A male collector of wild flowers in your county. Slant: How he makes use of a camera during his field trips to double the enjoyment and value of his hobby. Frequency of expeditions in which specimens are collected; rarest of the flowers; preservation of specimens.

Are training rules in the various sports too rigid or too loose? Discussion by coaches of both amateur and professional teams in your section. Slant: How some coaches insist on enforcing discipline even in the case of minor infractions. Penalties for violations of rules; the most common alibis and the coaches' reactions. Training problems with stars.

8

The information clerk at a local bus terminal. How many questions does he or she answer daily? Odd questions. Strange happenings at a bus station. Putting rout to undesirable characters, as winos, drunks, chiselers, and pickpockets.

A set of twins in your city who are mothers of a large number of children. Names for the boys and the girls. Do the twins still wear similar clothes, and do they make their own apparel? Would they like to be mothers of twins? Do twins run in families?

Parties with a sales pitch. Local examples of parties, as household products or cloth, for example. How the salespersons stage parties in different homes to demonstrate—and sell—commonly needed items to large groups. What the sponsor receives for his or her efforts; the number of parties he or she averages per week.

The demand for city and county maps. The secretary of the chamber of commerce can tell about the number of requests and how many of them are from school children. The most unusual reasons for seeking the maps. How often are new maps printed? The task of preparing a map; including data about the city and the county; the cost.

9

The dean of local gravediggers. The estimated number of graves he has dug; epidemics that kept him busy; grave digging in terrible weather. Is the subject superstitious, any ghost stories to tell? How mechanical grave digging has pushed human diggers to the point of becoming an endangered species.

Fireworks every day—the operation of a fireworks factory. Slant: How fireworks are produced a number of months ahead of their biggest seasons, Christmas and the Fourth of July. The most popular types of fireworks; largest displays produced. Any fireworks mishaps in the plant? The leading firework dealers in your sections.

Welcome to the Indian reservation! The great tourist invasion in the summer, and how the vacationists are given VIP treatment. The variety of entertainment, including an Indian outdoor theater, at a reservation in your state or neighboring state.

Survival of the weather vanes. How this feature of bygone days has become a hot item on the antique market. Vanes with interesting histories; various designs, as recalled by old-timers of the county. Slant: How early residents of the county had to serve as weathermen themselves with "signs" and the vanes.

10

The duties of the grand jury of your county. How the names are selected from the county's honor roll of eligible citizens. The jurors' authority; preparing reports for the various committees of the jury. Calling attention to the reports on bad conditions of roads, the jail, and county buildings.

Distribution of dead human bodies in your state. The state board for such purposes. Slant: How the bodies are used for advancement of medical science. How are the bodies obtained; do some people will their bodies to science?

Parking meters—boon or bust? Slant: How downtown merchants in some cities now look upon meters as an enemy instead of an ally in business. How shopping centers, with their free parking facilities, have lured customers from the downtown areas. Establishing free parking lots downtown. Meter "policing" and meter cheaters. Meter robbing is not uncommon. Spinoff: "Mr. Fix-It" for local parking meters. The number of meters he must keep in working order; keeping spare parts on hand. Cases of vandalism. The cost of a meter.

Disposal of sewage in your city. The up-to-date plant that is filled with intricate machinery and chemists who are surrounded by test tubes and charts. The scientific principles at work; latest methods of waste recycling.

⟩11

The Home Demonstration Council in your county. The current officials. The group's leading activities; the Home Demonstration club with the largest membership; achievement awards given by the council and the latest winners. Scholarship and loan fund. Families with the most members in the council.

Your state's first air hero of World War Two. His greatest exploits and the medals he earned. Anniversary angle: Colin Purdie Kelly, the first United States aviation hero of that war, was born on July 11, 1915. The posthumous awarding of the Distinguished Service Cross to him. Another anniversary: The United States Air Force Academy at Lowry Air Base in Colorado was dedicated on this day in 1955.

A major grain elevator in your section. How farmers store wheat and other grain there; the size of the storage bins. The capacity of the elevator in bushels; and metric units. Pest control and safety measures. As a spinoff, relate the latest improvements in harvesting machines. Use of the machine in your county; the reduction in harvest time and labor. Developers of the devices.

12

Street sweeper stories. Newest improvements in machines in your city; the number of gallons in the water sprayer. The best hours to clean the city's streets, especially uptown. Days of the most litter, as the weekend and after a parade; finding objects of value.

Reenactment of slayings in your county. Experiences of veteran law enforcement officers, including the sheriff, in reconstructing murders. How slayers often break down during the process and confess. Small things that trip up suspects in their stories. Do criminals show an inclination to return to the scene of the crime?

Reminiscences about the traveling photographer in your section. How itinerant cameramen of several decades ago made their rounds in every conceivable conveyance. The cameras in vogue; the price of the early photographs. Tintypes owned by the oldest residents of your county. The anniversary of the birth of George Eastman, camera pioneer, on this day suggests all sorts of articles.

Money that goes up in smoke. What happens when large sums of paper money are burned through accident and the owner nearly goes crazy? Cases in your section when cash is burned as trash or when a house burns down. Gathering up the ashes and sending them to the Mint Bureau in Washington, D. C., in the hope of redemption. Spinoff: Life span of a dollar bill; what happens to worn-out paper money?

13

The assigning of house numbers in your city. Does the city building inspector issue the numbers? The problems of working out numbers. Do some home builders just select numbers they like and use them, and have some residents called upon the post office to give them numbers? The largest and most unusual numbers locally.

An automobile accessories company of your state. How owners of cars, trucks, recreational vehicles, and motorcycles depend on the firm for specialty products designed to set their vehicles apart from the rest. The number of items in stock; performance-oriented, purely decorative, and strictly for entertainment.

A local architect who has built himself "the perfect house." Slant: How he has expressed his personality in the home and at the same time peered into the future. Rooms in which he takes the greatest delight; innovations. The landscaping of the grounds.

The largest shoes worn locally. Special orders by stores; frequency of the orders; highest prices. The biggest size required by a local woman; how some ladies are unabashed by wearing large numbers. Do many teenagers have surprisingly large feet? What about the saying that policemen have flat feet?

14

The appointment secretaries of important officials in your state. Slant: How they virtually amount to "human clocks" working behind the scenes. Their worst headaches; their greatest pleasures. Meeting the great and the near great. Fitting in unscheduled visitors.

A tree doctor of your city. What to do for wounded trees; giving them new life. Blights within recent years; diseases hardest to cure. The most disease-resistant trees; the trees most likely to develop ills and die.

Folklore as an inspiration to musical composers. How a musician of your state has based songs on folklore characters and made hits out of the compositions. Olden figures who have been given fame via music.

The favorites of the seven natural wonders of the world as selected by vacationists of your section who take world tours. Impressions after gazing upon the Grand Canyon, which extends 217 miles in length and one mile in depth. The startlingly varying color of the rock formations. Come up with a list of seven natural wonders of your state. Attempting to put such majesty on film. Tips for other photographers.

15

The state organization of nurses. The president and other officials; the foremost objectives of the club; the dean of the members and her recollections of the group's growth. Is there a nursing shortage in any hospitals in the state? The school of nurses in your city.

Imagine Clement Clarke Moore as Santa Claus, because he gave the world "A Visit From St. Nicholas." Anniversary angle: His birth on July 15, 1779. His reputation as a biblical scholar, and his professorship at General Theological Seminary in New York. How his life was affected by his poem about Santa Claus written in 1822.

This and that about fire hydrants in your city. The number of hydrants in the city, and the amount of water pressure. Testing the hydrants from time to time. Damage inflicted by cars in accidents. Do hydrant color schemes vary much, and have they ever been decorated for anything but the Bicentennial? Unauthorized use of hydrants; use by kids who want to cool off.

Artists of famous battlefield scenes. An art authority of your state can name the most popular and discuss the artists. Do not overlook the panoramic view of the Battle of Atlanta in the Cyclorama Building in Atlanta, Georgia. The masterpiece of George Washington crossing the Delaware, and *The Battle of Bunker Hill* by John Trumbell.

16

SOS calls to exterminators because of wasps, hornets, ants, fleas, and termites. Slant: How an exterminator can be the friend of a family who finds its home beset by such insects. Waging war against stinging creatures, with the proper respect. Spinoff: Wild animal pests.

An interview with the president of the state motor club. Various projects being staged or planned; safety measures, as on the Fourth of July or at Christmas. Advantages of club membership. Promotion of annual events.

A retired newspaper publisher in your state. Highlights of his Fourth Estate career; his greatest editorial battles and the results; threats by persons who wished stories suppressed; scoops that gave the subject his most satisfaction. His hobbies and special interests.

Atomic Bomb Day. The dawn of the Atomic Age on July 16, 1945, when the first atomic bomb was set off near Alamogordo, New Mexico, a few weeks before A-bombs were dropped on the Japanese cities of Hiroshima and Nagasaki and revolutionized warfare. The weapons research laboratory of the Manhattan Project. Spinoff: Nuclear armaments today. "Safe bombs."

17

Members of Allied Youth, Inc., as foes of the drinking of alcoholic beverages. How this organization of high school students has carried on activities in your state to encourage temperance. The size of the membership in the state. Spinoff: Local youth organizations combating drug abuse.

Methods of memory improvement. Slant: Mnemonics, the art of training the memory, is far from new, for the ancient Greeks employed mnemonic systems. Rules, rhythmic lines and other devices used by local citizens. Tricks used by businessmen and politicians in remembering names.

The older, the higher priced? A local antique dealer's list of the most expensive antiques. What makes these antiques so special? Protection against damage. Determining that antiques are genuine. Spinoff: A local expert on the antiques of the colonial days. The prices of such antiques and the availability of the historical treasures. The expert's collection. The popularity of primitive or Early American reproductions.

An amateur or professional impersonator of your state. How the subject imitates well-known persons in both voice and appearance. Demand for his impersonations at entertainments or on television. How he masters impersonations. Do celebrities object to impersonations of themselves?

18

What construction workers of your city uncover in their excavations. Exposing Indian, or early colonial settlements, relics, or perhaps graves. Dreams of buried treasure when metal boxes are found. Tearing down old structures and finding rare things.

A mule dealer in the Space Age. In what condition is the mule market? Modern-day applications; the current price. Where the dealer obtains his mules. How long has he been in this business?

Your state's foremost contributions to the United States Navy. Admirals, or captains and commanders, for instance, and their most exciting periods of service. Naval heroes and the medals accorded them. Their main interests in retirement. Brothers who are big shots in naval circles.

Closed-circuit television in your state as a means of instruction for industries and professions. New techniques in industry or science shown at meetings or conventions. How surgeons benefit from watching closed-circuit TV.

19

The Yiddish language as spoken and written by millions of Jews. Its use for approximately one thousand years. Famous Yiddish writers, and their books in the local library. Yiddish poems and plays that have passed the test of time. Origins of Yiddish.

The county in your state that is the champion in fruit production. The kinds of fruits and the leading varieties; record yields. Sudden disaster at times, as by storms. The foremost orchardists and their orchards; the number of trees and the care of them; harvesting the fruit. Fruit yields from bushes, brambles, or vines. Spinoff: The five most nutritious fruits in the state, named by a nutrition expert.

Boxmaking is his business. The owner of a plant in your state that manufactures cardboard boxes. The machines that cut the cardboard into the desired lengths; the workers who form the pieces into boxes by gluing or stapling the edges. Sizes of boxes in greatest demand; industries that send the most orders. Spinoff: The great strength of corrugated cardboard and its many applications.

An amateur wire-walker of your city. How he or she acquired mastery of the high wire and receives frequent invitations to entertain. Is he or she an acrobat as well? Any mishaps? Consideration of a professional career.

20

Moon Day. In a poll of your city how many citizens can remember the name of the first moon walker—Neil Alden Armstrong—and the name of the lunar module that landed on the moon July 20, 1969? What emotions the historic occasion inspired in them. Did some of the citizens almost regret the landing because that last refuge of poetic mystery would be no more? Armstrong's and Edwin Eugene Aldrin, Jr.'s fantastic rendezvous on the moon's surface, in their own descriptions. Local high schoolers who want to make a moon excursion.

Experiences in the layaway department of the largest department store locally. The average amount of layaway business monthly. The merchandise most commonly purchased by this method. Lagging in payment; hard-luck stories. Do some layaway customers never call for the goods?

Prenatal clinics in your state. Activities of the state board of health in this field, as with lectures and motion pictures helpful to mothers and expectant mothers. Slant: How such instructions relieve doctors from much of the time consumed in teaching mothers the practical side of child care.

A flower seller at a curb market in your county. Kinds of flowers sold; days that bring the best business. Do some people buy flowers every week or oftener? Tips from the vendor on how to choose and extend the life of cut flowers.

21

A giant of your state and his problems. The size of his clothes and shoes; the hugeness of his furniture; and his traveling troubles, as in finding hotel or motel accommodations to fit his needs. His size and weight when a teenager. Does the giant possess more than average strength? Has he been something of an athlete? The size of his wife, if he is married.

Is newspaper work harmful or helpful to future novelists? How Ernest Hemingway, a Nobel Prize author who was born on this day in 1899, held a job on the *Kansas City Star* and received valuable training for his career as a short story and novel writer. His service as a foreign correspondent for the *Toronto Star*. How at the age of twenty-six he established his reputation with *The Sun Also Rises*.

Dental plate mishaps. Odd stories from local dentists about their patients, as losing dentures while swimming or leaving them in hotels, hospitals, and such. Dental plates that were accidentally switched, perhaps flushed, or disposed of as garbage. Long searches that finally paid off. Any plates pawned or stolen?

Are love letters eternal? What percentage of people save their love letters? Make a local survey of couples of various ages, including those observing twenty-fifth and fiftieth wedding anniversaries. Is love letter writing a declining custom? Favorite love poems of the interviewed pairs.

22

A boy choir of your city. Its history, as told by the director. Appearances over the state and elsewhere; letters of praise from listeners; selections that draw the most acclaim. Members who hope to spend their lives as professional musicians.

The chaplain at the penitentiary in your state. Slant: How the chaplain conducts religious classes among the inmates and encourages the prisoners to discuss their problems. Are there some penitentiary problems with which he can't help? What alternatives does he suggest?

As easy as falling off a roof! Unpleasant recollections of veteran roofers of your city. Has a miracle saved a life among them? Longest falls and hospital stays. Safety precautions taken by members of this trade. Latest trends in roofing.

Diaries prized by the state historical society. How they were obtained; the most valuable; highlights of the diaries; the earliest entries. Slant: How the diaries throw light on the styles and the customs of early days. Is diary or journal keeping a dying art?

23

A hermit of your section. Reasons for his going into seclusion; his mode of living; preparation of meals, as fish, garden vegetables, and berries. Nature as a food provider. Love—or lack of love—in the recluse's life.

Original ways to apply for a job. The personnel directors of large stores and industrial plants in your area can tell about the most unusual stunts used by position-seekers. Odd methods that clicked. Slant: Firms that put emphasis on originality, as displayed by the stunts.

The job of the attorney general of your state. How his duties are to protect the rights and the properties of the state, appear in court for the state, and to defend county treasurers against law suits, among other things. What new laws, or revisions of laws, does the attorney general recommend?

Radio and television stations as people finders. Slant: How the stations amount to unofficial missing persons bureaus by locating lost persons via broadcasts. Average number of appeals per month; the most unusual cases; making certain the requests are authentic and not practical jokes. Is the number of runaways mounting? Newspapers perform the same service.

24

Your city's printing. The city's purchasing agent, and his handling of the printing needs. The annual cost of printing items, as forms, tax notices, books and manuals for municipal departments, and even parking tickets.

The growth of the Mormon church in your state. Anniversary angle: The Mormons led by Brigham Young settled Salt Lake City on this day in 1847 and saw it become the capital of Utah and the world capital of Mormonism. The reputation of Mormons as industrious and temperate individuals whose meeting houses figure as community centers. The size of Mormon membership in your state; the service of young people as missionaries.

How newcomers to your city are welcomed. The hospitality program of the local chamber of commerce. Do a number of merchants give newcomers presents? The Welcome Wagon service. Slant: How the newcomers enter more enthusiastically into the city's activities as a result of the hearty welcome. Go a step further and describe how local clergymen visit newcomers. Spinoff: Newcomers' reactions and comments on your city.

The boom in private airports in your section. More and more pilots are building their own airfields. Prominent businessmen and ranchers who have provided themselves with such services. Aircraft as a help in carrying out work on large ranches.

25

A day at a community cannery as a county-sponsored operation. The equipment; preparing vegetables for canning; final processing. The supervisor and his or her advice on how to achieve the best canning results. Record days at the cannery.

"The first movie I can remember." Recollections of top citizens, including city officials. Their fondness for Westerns and the Saturday serials of fifteen chapters that prevailed in yesteryear. Movies they have seen the most times. Their screen favorites down the years— and those of today.

Portraits of the founder of your state. Does one adorn the walls of the state house? Artists who painted the portraits and their reputation in art. Value of the paintings. Any knowledge of descendants of the founder?

The manager of the city auditorium. Slant: How he or she is the key cog in the wheel of the numerous kinds of entertainment that brighten your city. Organization and preparation as his two main secrets of success. The full range of activities, as music shows, conventions, religious crusades, wrestling and other sports, holiday programs, and civic meetings. Types of entertainment that bring SRO crowds.

26

The younger generation of your city's bowlers. Best scores by the youthful keglers; the king and queen of the lanes. Coaching by parents and coaches of the teams; supervision of bowling among youths by the American Junior Bowling Congress.

The housekeeper of the largest hotel in your city. How she has no idle moments with her various duties. The amount of linen, towels, and other items needed to make daily changes. Her supervision of the maids who clean rooms after departures. Sticky-fingered travelers. Articles patrons forget and write back for.

George Bernard Shaw Day, in observance of his birth on July 26, 1856. How Shaw societies in your state will mark the anniversary and offer tribute to the British dramatist, novelist, and critic who won the Nobel Prize for literature in 1925. His views on social problems.

The official song of your state. The composer and the conditions under which he or she wrote the number. Is the composer an unknown hero? Local vocalists' comments about the state song; occasions on which they have rendered it. Spinoff: Official songs of nearby states, and the oldest of them.

27

The champion life saver in your section. The lifeguard at a lake, as at a state park, who has saved the most lives. How to rescue a person from drowning despite the swimmer's panic; administering artificial respiration. Recognition for the lifeguard's feats; the gratitude of the families. The swimming ability of the lifeguard and his longest swims.

A chemical engineer of your section who has a national reputation. His most significant contributions; honors given him. His activities in scientific societies, as the American Chemical Society.

A local researcher on any subject. How he or she will research anything; the range of information at the disposal of the specialist. The most difficult subjects to research. How fees are determined.

Cyrus W. Field's realization of his dream to link Europe and America by telegraph. Anniversary angle: The first permanent Atlantic cable was completed on July 27, 1866, fulfilling Samuel F. B. Morse's prediction that the two continents would be connected by telegraph one day. How Field encountered repeated failures in his enterprise, but always raised fresh capital. The miles of ocean cable a ship can lay today. Are communications satellites making cables obsolete?

28

Medical superstitions, as told by the president of the local medical society. Folklore cures for various ills, as the practice of stepping back across a creek for chills. "Charms" that are believed effective, including the use of fried onions around the neck to prevent respiratory trouble. Wearing objects to ward off rheumatism.

The operator of a riding academy in your section. Do more young people than adults patronize the stables? The horse and the trails; matching the temperament of horse and rider. The operator as a participant in horse shows.

The minister or the priest of your county who holds the record for baptisms. The most persons he has baptized on a single occasion; baptizing in rivers as well as in church pools. Oldest persons who have received baptism.

A ham expert of your section who has a reputation far beyond the bounds of his own state. Does he have a hog farm of his own? The demand for his hams, cured and smoked; sale to the general public and stores. Any mail order business? Receiving orders months in advance. The specialist's secret or unique process of preparing hams.

29

A gag-writer of your state. Slant: How he depends upon his wit— and wits—for his income. How he develops gags; using old ones over and over, with variations. The various categories of jokes; his collection of humor. Publications that have printed the gag-writer's work.

Scarecrows of the Seventies. Farmers or gardeners of your county who still use scarecrows. What the "best-dressed scarecrow" wears today. Will scarecrows really repel crows? Latest devices to prevent bird invasion of fruit trees or gardens.

The furrier keeps busy in the summer, too. How one of your city designs fur garments and also engages in fitting and alterations. The most expensive kinds of furs and their sources. Keeping furs in storage for the public during the summer. Repairing fur apparel.

A local woman who has a successful mail order business. Her small beginning and determination to succeed in spite of discouragement. Her business mottoes and secrets of success. Seasonal products; the types of products that sell best by mail.

30

Anything to help a drive! What athletes and other individuals do to benefit an organization that is raising money for a worthy cause. Sponsoring a long-distance runner or a bicyclist for so much a mile. Arousing interest in the campaign at every stop.

When trash isn't trash but treasure. Surprises for the trash collectors of your city who keep an eye open for valuables while making their rounds. Items thrown out by mistake. Pursue this spinoff: People who search through the city's dump for usable objects.

A commercial grower of walnuts in your section. His care and cultivation of the trees; the annual yield. Shelling machines. Sorting and sacking the nuts in the packing house for shipment. Leading walnut growing counties in the state. Furniture makers prize lumber from black and English walnut trees. Spinoff: Other kinds of nut trees that are behind a commercial enterprise, as pecan and chestnut.

Weapons of various wars in the possession of a local gun collector. Revolutionary and Civil War firearms, and how they were obtained; their value today. Guns that saw service in the Spanish-American War and World War One, and their power. Weapons brought home from World War Two. Slant: The collector's assortment of firearms forms a fascinating history of armament.

31

A school for mentally retarded persons in your area. How the teacher instructs the adults in performing simple tasks and enables some of them to do limited work in shops and factories. The emergence of unusual abilities.

The magic of seeing entertainment stars in person. How Hollywood, California, and the entire Los Angeles area serve as a magnet for hero worshippers throughout the nation. A family of your city who made a dream come true by vacationing in the motion-picture capital this summer. Making tours of the studios and watching movies in production. Seeing stars and acquiring autographs.

Lucky discoveries by inventors of your state and elsewhere. Anniversary angle: The first patent in the United States was granted to Samuel Hopkins of Vermont on July 31, 1790, for his process of "making pot and pearl ashes." Examples of how inventions have been born, step by step.

The real estate board of your state. How it deals with the regulation of the real estate business and the licensing of real estate brokers, salespersons, and appraisers, in addition to others. The wide powers of the board.

AUGUST

Month of Fun and Dog Days

With August comes the height of summer's heat and the vacation season. Resorts compete with each other for crowds, and at the approach of fall, cities and counties stage festivals and other community events.

History has made August unforgettable, both in war and in peacetime. The United States unleashed the first atomic bomb used in warfare, Union forces won the Battle of Mobile Bay, Japan gave up to the Allies, and Washington, D.C., fell victim to British troops in the War of 1812.

Writers of anniversary articles have a fertile field in August: 1. The United States completed its first census, 1790; 2. First Lincoln penny put into circulation, 1909; 3. Christopher Columbus departed from Palos, Spain, on his initial voyage across the Atlantic Ocean, 1492; 10. Smithsonian Institution established, 1846; 12. Thomas A. Edison amazed world with his invention of the phonograph, 1877; 12. Hawaii annexed by the United States, 1898; 14. Social Security approved, 1935; 16. British lost to Patriots at Bennington, Vermont, 1777; 22. Successful demonstration of a sidepaddle steamboat made by John Fitch, 1787; 26. The 19th Amendment, granting women the right to vote, proclaimed, 1920; 26. Patent granted Ottmar Mergenthaler for his Linotype machine, 1884; 29. Second Battle of Bull Run began, 1862.

Topping the list of birth anniversaries are those of three presidents—Lyndon B. Johnson, Herbert Hoover, and Benjamin Harrison—and Vice President Charles G. Dawes. Authors are well represented by birth dates: William Saroyan, Conrad Aiken, Bret

Harte, Charles Anderson Dana, Percy Bysshe Shelley, Guy de
Maupassant, Herman Melville, Ernie Pyle, Alfred, Lord Tennyson,
Sir Walter Scott, Marjorie Kinnan Rawlings, Edgar Lee Masters,
and John Galsworthy.

Other notables with August birth dates have been Orville Wright,
the explorers William Clark and Meriwether Lewis, Napoleon
Bonaparte, Davy Crockett, Julius Rosenwald, Francis Scott Key,
Oliver Hazard Perry, Lee D. Forest, Jonathan M. Wainwright, Bernard Baruch, and Ethel Barrymore.

August presents an array of special days, Hiroshima Day, V.J.
Day, Atlantic Charter Day, Coast Guard Day, Klondike Gold Discovery Day, and National Aviation Day. Additional observances
are Women's Equality Day, Isaac Walton Day, Indian Day in Massachusetts, Herbert Hoover Day, Huey P. Long Day, Hawaii Admission Day, and now Resignation Day, the anniversary of the end of
President Richard M. Nixon's White House reign.

1

How reliable are rain makers? The latest in rain making, as reported by a leading meteorologist or a professor of meteorology in a
college in your state. Methods used by the rain makers, as seeding
the clouds with silver iodide or dropping crystals or dry ice into
them. Experiments with other methods. How aviators "doctor" the
clouds, in contrast with primitive rain makers. Scientific snow making.

Off-duty jobs of law enforcement officers of your city. The question
of moonlighting, and the views of city officials, such as the mayor or
city manager, on the matter. Serving stores, schools, industrial
plants, and security firms in extra-duty capacity. Any restrictions?

Beginning the day's work. When does the postman report to work?
When does the dairyman start his duties? What about the cafe cook,
the newspaper reporter, the bank president, the zookeeper, the
television engineer, the school custodian, the lawyer, and the construction worker? Is there any scientific truth to the old saying,
"Early to bed, early to rise makes a man healthy, wealthy, and
wise"?

The hobby of verse writing paid off for Francis Scott Key, a lawyer born on August 1, 1779. How the sight of the American flag flying over besieged Fort McHenry in the War of 1812 inspired the native of Maryland to write "The Star-Spangled Banner." How the song was adopted as the national anthem 117 years later. Fort McHenry as a national shrine. Spinoff: The latest efforts to have "The Star-Spangled Banner" replaced as the national song.

2

The business of moving houses. A local operator's description of the time and preparations required for removals. The reasons the dwellings have to be moved, as highway construction, the sale of the location for a commercial enterprise, or the building of a large lake. The largest structures that have been moved. Those moved the longest distances; the most difficult operations; mishaps enroute to the new site. The cost of moving a house.

An ice sculptor of your section. Slant: The varied demand for this unusual service, such as providing sculptured figures at weddings, parties, and other occasions. The instrument he or she uses for carving. The largest pieces of ice sculpture; the time required for the average product.

Celebrated figures of the Early West who died with their boots on. For example, James Butler ("Wild Bill") Hickok was killed by Jack McCall in Deadwood, South Dakota, on August 2, 1876. The assassination of Jesse James by Bob Ford on April 3, 1882, as the outlaw was dusting a picture. Tombstones, like the one for James' grave with the inscription "Murdered by a traitor and a coward whose name is not worthy to appear here." How some legends about Early West figures do not correspond with reality.

Local hotels' service of baby-sitting for patrons with babies as well as older children. How the hotels keep a list of sitters with a reputation for reliability. Who seem to make the most dependable sitters, young people or middle-aged and elderly women, as grandmothers? Spinoff: Finding a neighborhood baby-sitter, current charges.

3

The model farm of a chapter of the Future Farmers of America in your section. The operation by and for the members; the various crops and the most remunerative of them. The adult advisory committee and the sponsors who give funds and farming tools. Use of the profits.

The nicknames of professional baseball clubs in your state down the years. The origins of these nicknames and mascots. Managers of the teams and their recollections; interview old-time umpires, if available. Nicknames of the stars themselves.

How many kinds of birds can be bought in your city? Check with pet shops and variety stores. The most expensive birds, and also the cheapest. The sources of the birds; local raisers who supply a large number. The best-selling bird.

The conjugal rights program for prisoners in your state. Providing for conjugal visits by the wives of inmates as during the weekend. The officials' opinion of the practice and comparison of results achieved across the nation.

4

A camera repairman of your city who has repaired thousands of cameras. The most frequent repairs. The most common kinds of camera carelessness, and accidents. The latest word in cameras and equipment; imported cameras. Are parts hard to obtain? The paraphernalia of the repairman. Does he collect cameras?

City versus farm poets. The opinions of city and rural verse makers about the best places of inspiration. City poets who find the muse more cooperative in the country. Favorite subjects of poets in your county, no matter what their locations. Poems with city locales. Slant: The kindred spirit and purpose of all poets regardless of their surroundings.

The old, old fight for the freedom of the press. The acquittal of John Peter Zenger, a German immigrant who established the *New York Weekly Journal*, on charge of libel for criticizing the governor of New York. Anniversary angle: He was acquitted on this day in 1735. Slant: How the acquittal marked a major milestone in the freedom of the press in America, since Zenger had opposed the colonial government.

A local interior decorator who specializes in designing interiors for hotels and clubs. Selecting the furniture and arranging it; color schemes that have created the most attention. Also the most eye-catching wall decorations. Any decorative accents or artwork by local artists?

5

The Marco Polo of your city — a tour director. Slant: How he or she gratifies the desire to travel by this service and makes the tours abroad more interesting by his or her enthusiasm. The close friend-ships he or she has made with fellow travelers. The joys of interna-tional friendships; favorite foods of tourists overseas. Trips to ma-jor cities and chief attractions. Illnesses that produce problems.

Dreams of fame and fortune in cartooning. Observations by an in-structor in cartooning in an art school in your state. Steps in developing talent; the ability to interpret situations with humor in gag cartooning. Opportunities in commercial cartooning.

The business side of the arcade at an amusement place in your sec-tion. The coin games that are highest in popularity; new devices that claim heavy attention. Making change for customers. Do the machines require frequent repair? How patrons try to cheat with slugs. How long do the devices last, and are some examples of Americana?

The champion watermelon grower of your county. The acreage given to cultivation, and the favorite varieties of customers. Methods of disposal, as selling to stores and operating roadside markets. Size and weight of the grower's largest watermelons. Spinoff: The Number One producer and shipper of cantaloupes or vegetables, as potatoes, tomatoes, cabbage, and peppers.

6

An interview with a radio or television script writer of your state. Fundamentals of such work, and the opportunities in the field. The differences in radio and television writing. The most popular types of programs at present, according to stations' surveys.

Weight of the first atomic bombs. Anniversary angle: Uncle Sam in-troduced warfare on August 6, 1945, by dropping the Little Boy, weighing four and a half tons, on Hiroshima, while on August 9,

Fat Man, with a weight of five tons, was dropped on Nagasaki. Formation of the Atomic Energy Commission.

Information, please. An employee of an insurance company who conducts confidential checks of applicants in your city. Interviewing the person's neighbors, friends, and business associates about his or her habits and living style. Spinoff: How stores and credit bureaus seek information about the reliability and assets of a person. Consumer's right of access to the material; what to do about a bad report.

A young pantomimist of your city. Slant: How in this type of show biz the expression "Silence is golden" sums up a successful career. Largest groups the actor has entertained. Training in the art of facial expression, gestures, and body movements.

7

Which "paints" the prettier scene, the sunrise or the sunset? Artists and photographers of your area can wage their own "battle of beauty" with their choices. Those who make it a point to rise early enough to view the rising of the sun. How the sun provides sky spectaculars twice a day in clear weather—to begin the day and to begin the night.

Life of a computer salesman in your state. What he or she finds the most fascinating aspects of this position. Providing computer service to companies that use it for such purposes as accounting, inventory control, billing, order processing, and production scheduling. How many bits of information will the company's most elaborate machine store? Installing computers and training the operators. The highest priced models. Computer technology of the future.

A well-known crop duster of your section. How the operation is carried out from an airplane, taking into consideration the wind, the dusting solution, and the danger of low altitude flying. Various crops for which dusting is needed. Other phases of the pilot's aviation career.

The successful marriage of a local woman who is confined to a wheelchair. Slant: Her remarkable record as both a wife and a mother despite her handicap. Performing the housework and also the cooking; special equipment in the home. How she entertains on special occasions. How she brightens the lives of her relatives and friends.

8

An engraver for a jewelry store in your city. His or her artistic skill in personalizing items. Watches, bracelets, and necklaces as among the items most frequently engraved. Occasional mistakes or slip-ups by the engraver. The heavy amount of work on gifts on February 14. Unusual uses of his or her talents.

The work of a pressroom superintendent. Slant: Combining the skills of the pressroom workers in your city into a human machine that gives subscribers their paper on time. Operating the press and its speed; the color process. Latest technological advances. "Making over" pages when big stories break. Amount of ink and newsprint used each week. Pressroom humor—including pranks.

The drama behind a symphony orchestra of your section. Slant: How the players, of various occupations, are so dedicated that they find the time for constant practice. The headaches—and joys—of the conductor. The excitement of the opening concert; the most successful numbers during the season. Ticket campaigns.

Preparing monthly statements for customers. The largest machines of your city, including the water and light, gas, and telephone firms. The supervisors of the offices and the machine operators; days on which the mailings are made. The total amount of postage per month.

9

A historian of the National Park Service who is identified with your state. Slant: The Service's conservation of historic structures and objects as well as scenic areas and wildlife. The maintenance of museums and the chief exhibits. Current research by the historian and his assistants; debunking history.

The chain letter craze. Outbreaks of the letters in your city from time to time despite their illegality. The most enticing letters, and the benefits of getting in on the ground floor. The postmaster's comments on such an operation. Spinoff: Pyramiding and other financial swindles.

The souvenir business in your city. Slant: Oddly enough, a great percentage of the souvenirs originate in distant places. What kind of souvenirs lead in abundance? Postcard views, pennants, T-shirts, plates, jewelry, and risque items in demand by tourists. Good and bad taste in souvenirs, today versus twenty years ago; changing—or unchanging—tastes in travel memorabilia over the years. A merchant's opinion as to what constitutes an honest versus a dishonest (aesthetically, that is) souvenir.

Quarrels over boundaries and their solutions. An example is the Webster-Ashburton Treaty, which established the eastern border between the United States and Canada and was signed on August 9, 1842. How the treaty ended a long dispute known as the Aroostook War over the northern boundary of Maine and made an almost equal division of the territory in question.

10

What's the best location? How chain stores select sites for new stores. Interview the head of a real estate division of a large chain. The chief factors involved in choosing a location. How the necessary parking is estimated. Market surveys and long-range planning. Gambles that paid off.

The accomplishments of the city gardener or landscape artist. Slant: Carrying out his ambition to transform the city into a metropolis of beauty. The latest acts in his beautification program; number of flowers and shrubs he has planted within the past year. Adding to the beauty of the city parks. The cooperation of the garden clubs; vandalism and flower-nappers.

Abandoned babies in your county. The most dramatic instances as related by caseworker of the county's social services department. Official routines when a baby has been found; seeking clues as to parents. Finding foster homes for babies. The emotional problems that beset abandoned boys and girls.

The old custom of husking bees among farmers in your county. Slant: How it combined work with the social enjoyment of dancing and singing, plus refreshments. The competition between the two sides at the event. How the finding of a red ear of corn gave a young man the privilege of bestowing a kiss on the girl of his choice.

Leaders of farm groups in your county who can relate whether "bees" of any kind persist in today's rural America. Barn raising and other rural cooperative efforts. Spinoff: Block associations in urban areas.

11

A commercial hunting preserve in your section. The operator and how he or she has transformed it into a sportsman's paradise. Hunters from the longest distances; children's hunting ability. Placing game in the preserve and maintaining the animals and the birds. Bagging limits. Greatest problems of the operator. Spinoff: A fisherman's heaven in your county—a pay-pond. The species of fish and the biggest catches. Spinoff: Wildlife refuges, public and private.

Your state's largest club of Toastmasters International, a nonprofit organization devoted to making better public speakers. The variety of the members' occupations, all the way from insurance agents and store managers to engineers and real-estate agents. Steps in speaking improvement; the mastering of fear through practice. A survey has found that fear of public speaking outstrips fear of death two to one. The selection and arrangement of material, and the arts of presentation.

How about a pass? Disturbing words to the manager of a theater, auditorium, or a sports event. Impressions of local managers and their techniques in meeting the situation. How almost perfect strangers attempt to impose upon their hospitality.

Stories from the operator of a local storage company. Unusual reasons for storing things. The most commonly stored articles; the oddest. Items that remain unclaimed, and their disposal. The trend toward the mini or individual warehouse.

12

A government veterinary inspector of your state. Passing on the health of animals; number of animals he inspects annually. Finding animals unfit and condemning them. A typical day with inspector.

A local collector of early phonograph records. Anniversary angle: Thomas A. Edison invented the phonograph on August 12, 1877, and his original records were cylinders. The earliest phonograph dealers in your city. Early Victrolas owned by the collector. Record stars in the early years.

A literary agent in your state. How he or she markets the literary products and receives a commission for services. Notable writers who were discovered by the agent. The writing career of the subject. Making stories and articles salable. The quickest sale ever made by the agent.

A day center for elderly persons in your city. Is it a civic, church, or government operation? The head of the center and the assistants. The activities of the Senior Citizens. Birthday celebrations and other special events. Gabfests among the old-timers. A turnaround in subject would be local nurseries for children.

13

The "bargain basement" at a local bakery or a store outlet. How outdated loaves, rolls, and cakes are sought-after merchandise at reduced prices. How bakery bargain stores sell a wide range of day-old products. The largest number of customers every day; buying for animal, as well as human, consumption. Removing bread and cakes from the shelves of grocery stores after the freshness deadline. Tips on preserving or revitalizing day-old products.

The cleanest career in your city—window washing. A veteran window washer who regularly cleans display windows of stores. How often are they washed? Cleaning the windows of high-rise apartments and skyscrapers. The window washer's greatest frustrations; his oddest experiences. How the subject became accustomed to heights. Accidents just short of fatal.

State tourist bureau. Promoting tourist travel; distributing road maps and literature about the state. Main attractions for visitors. Telephone calls; strange requests from tourists. Slant: How the organization, in increasing tourist travel, is a stimulant to a number of businesses in the state.

The first woman physician in your county. Where she received her medical education; prejudices against a woman doctor when she opened her practice. Did she encounter any opposition to her entry into the profession? Winning acceptance into the community. If she was an obstetrician, or GP, how many babies did she deliver during her career?

14

A typist for hire in your city. What trades give him or her the most business? Small companies that need a typist only part-time. Typing manuscripts for writers. How he or she makes vital checks for accuracy. The typist's speed, especially with rush assignments. Editorial services.

Projects of fire stations in your county. Events, such as fish fries, dances, chicken suppers, that have been big money-makers for the volunteer fire-fighters. The assistance of the members of the auxiliary in the undertakings. The most successful occasions and the use of the funds. Turkey and ham shoots.

V-J Day, or Victory Day, and how local citizens demonstrated their emotions over the surrender of Japan to the Allies in World War Two. Number of your county's servicemen who lost their lives in the conflict with Japan. How they are remembered in memorial services today.

The art of giving titles. How the best known artists of your state have bestowed such and such titles on their work. Changing titles at the last moments. Titles suggested by friends. How novelists of the state hit upon ideas for titles of books.

15

Napoleon's Day, which commemorates the birth of the Little Corporal on the island of Corsica on August 15, 1769. His reputation as one of the world's greatest generals. Would a local historian include Napoleon among the top five military generals in world annals? The height of Napoleon's power.

The head of the Employment Security Commission in your state. How he is the state's leading expert on the rise and the fall of employment. The state's total work force, and the percent of it that is jobless at present. The most unemployed professions currently or in the past year. Seasonal declines in construction and trades; months with the largest unemployment. Statistics about the rate of employment in various industries.

Opening of the Panama Canal to world commerce on this day in 1914. The first complete voyage through the Big Ditch was made by the S.S. *Ancon,* a passenger-cargo ship owned by the Panama Railroad Company. Local newspaper files of 1914 can reveal citizens' reactions to the opening of the canal. Victory over disease in the construction. The pros and cons of the furor that raged over recent canal treaties.

The first newspaper of your state and neighboring states. For instance, the first newspaper in California, the *Californian,* was issued at Monterey on August 15, 1846. The first daily newspaper in that state was the *Alta Californian,* launched in 1850. Editors of the first newspapers of your state; the circulation and the subscription rates. The oldest newspaper still appearing in your state and its slogan.

16

A commercial grower of sunflowers in your section. Slant: How the sunflower is hailed by botanists as one of the most highly developed plants in existence. The wide, wide market for sunflower seeds. The seeds are made into poultry feed because of their richness in fat and protein. How edible and industrial oils are obtained through crushing. Roasting of seeds as tasty nourishment. Food for birds.

"What my father wanted me to be." Reminiscences of business, professional, and religious leaders of your city. Did most dads hope their sons would follow in their footsteps? Mothers who openly opposed such plans. The ambition of fathers for sons to carry on their businesses. Partnerships of fathers and sons, as in medicine, law, or engineering.

Centennial costumes. The experiences of the leaders of a centennial celebration in a city of your state. Designing authentic costumes. Research into the attire of a century ago; enlisting the aid of professional seamstresses. Producing the hats; the hair styles and the use of wigs; accessories with the clothing. Beard contest winners.

What's in a number in your city? How about racing car numbers? Also boat numerals. The unusual numbers chosen by private citizens in states where you can pay an extra fee and have anything you want on your license plate. The number of the badge worn by the chief of police; numbers of baseball and football stars.

Telephone numbers every citizen should know—those of the police and fire departments and the hospital. And who can ignore the numbers applied to highways?

17

Sales day at a cattle barn in your county. Slant: How the event can pack as much fun as the antics and sideshows of a county fair. Scenes on the floor, and the sales spiel. Present prices.

Mixing business and flowers. How business places in your city make a habit of saying it with flowers. Brightening up lobbies, dining rooms, desks, and dentists' and doctors' offices. Flowers for special occasions. The favorite flowers of business houses.

The inventions of Robert Fulton besides his steamboat, the *Clermont,* which revolutionized sailing. Anniversary angle: His famous vessel started its initial trip from New York City to Albany, New York, on this day in 1807. Other inventions: Flax-spinning and ropemaking devices, a substitute for canal locks, and dredging machines.

The art of food packaging. Slant: Combining attractiveness and sound sanitation in putting products in containers for store shelves. Preserving freshness. Use of glass and cellophane to show the contents. Applying labels to canned goods; listing the ingredients. Spinoff time: The trend in no-name or generic brands at lower prices.

18

A woman embalmer of your state. Her reasons for selecting this career. Are other members of her family in this profession? Her training. Her most interesting experiences. The number of women embalmers statewide.

What happened to Virginia Dare, the first English child born in America? She was born on this day in 1587, and is considered to have had the first English christening in America. Facts about her mother and father. Theories of local or state historians about the fate of Virginia and other members of the Lost Colony.

Airplanes versus ships in model building locally. Which leads in total number of hobbyists? The making of the most elaborate models; assembly kits that are available in your city. The radically different types of model kits made in recent years. Radio-controlled airplanes and winners in contests. Girls who are fervent model builders. Model car building.

States that are twins with yours. Similar characteristics, such as the average temperatures, the population makeup, the size, and physical characteristics. Comparison of rainfall and days of sunshine. States that came into existence about the same time. Similar industries.

19

The vacation capital of your state. Notables who have summered there; the wide-awake work of the Chamber of Commerce. The climate and attractions of the city. Recreational facilities and special events.

Bottles bottles, bottles! Keeping the bottle situation at the local plants of soft drink manufacturers well in hand. How many new bottles must be purchased monthly? What percentage of used bottles are returned? How both youngsters and adults gather castaway bottles over the city and the county. Nonreturnable bottles and recycling.

National Aviation Day, honoring Orville and Wilbur Wright and other pioneer aviators. The marvels of the jetport in your section of the state. The largest and swiftest jets that serve the place, and the number of passengers handled there in an average week. Latest improvements at the jetport. Stress on safety.

The oldest city park in your state. Is it in the oldest city? The marker describing its historic role. Any statues? The trees and flowers that are drawing cards; paths for walking; the benches for resting and observing. Is there a pond or a fountain? History and use of the early parks known as commons.

20

A psychiatric village facility in your state. Slant: How the facility represents a step toward decentralization of the mental hospital complex. How the state's mental health commission operates the facility and provides a level of intensive treatment between outpatient and inpatient services so that patients may return home earlier.

Cleaning rural cemeteries. The long-time practice of families gathering on a designated day for a mass attack upon weeds and grass. Slant: The pride and the reverence of the families for the cemeteries. Cemetery improvements; the erection of fences.

The record gourd-grower of your area. The acreage that he devotes to gourd cultivation, and the varieties. His pride in his gourd dipper supply. How he likes to give gourds to his friends; his sale of dippers. The range of practical and decorative uses for gourds; how flower designers feature gourds in winter arrangements.

Patent laws in various countries, as explained by an inventor of your state or a patent lawyer. Anniversary angle: The United States signed the International Patent Convention on this day. Patent legislation abroad past and present. Largest lawsuits over patents.

21

Courting industry over the nation. The efforts of the city government to bring new industries to your region. Fierce competition with other cities and states. The sales talk offered by the local Chamber of Commerce. Number of plants erected within the past few years, and their expansions.

In the midst of August heat waves wood stove dealers are preparing for winter. The kinds of wood stoves and fireplaces local dealers will feature. The renaissance of wood stoves, wood furnaces and fireplaces as a result of energy problems. The customers' concern for both warmth and economy. Wood best suited for stove use.

The political opponents of presidents of the United States. Stephen Douglas began his debates with Abraham Lincoln on this day in 1858. How the Little Giant donated his services to Lincoln after the beginning of the Civil War. How the Vermont native disdained ownership of slaves, but did not take a stand against slavery.

A professional woman wrestler of your state or one performing in your city. Her expertise as a grappler on the mat; her favorite holds. How she gained her great strength and learned this sport. Any serious injuries during her wrestling career? Has she married a professional wrestler?

22

Mysteries that arouse the greatest curiosity among local residents. Speculation about the Abominable Snowman, who reputedly makes his home in the high Himalayas; the Loch Ness monster of Scotland and the annual fanfare about it; and the Bigfoot, sighted in numerous places in the United States. A mystery creature legend in your area.

The tax collector of your county who has heard everything, excuses as well as gripes. The old saw about only two things being certain—death and taxes. Special efforts to collect delinquent taxes.

Grass "mowers" extraordinary—goats and other animals. Places in your section where goats are put to use to reduce the cost of grass and weed cutting. Shoot down the myth that goats are trash eaters. Spinoff: Ten leading myths about animals that can be exploded.

Winning ways of a pedodontist of your city. Slant: How the specialist in the care of children's teeth displays skillful diplomacy in ridding boys and girls of their fear of dentists. Making tooth care lessons fun and memorable for the young patients.

23

The manufacturers' association of your state. Slant: Exchange of technical knowledge among the members and joining hands for the benefit of industries and the community. Present objectives. Latest developments in manufacturing processes. Plants that have increased their production the most. Spinoff: Activities of manufacturer's lobbies.

The latest traffic surveys by the state highway department. Highways with the heaviest travel and the fatality rate on them; the increased use of danger signs as well as more traffic lights. Roads in your county that will be widened due to survey findings. The highways with the largest truck traffic. Moves to limit truck usage during certain hours on some highways.

The worship of Rudolph Valentino, motion picture idol, still goes on. Pilgrimages to his place of rest; the mysterious woman visitor down the years. The death of the screen star on August 23, 1926, and how local newspapers handled the story. Romantic figures of the silent movies headed by Valentino. Reactions to the deaths of other stars; Elvis Presley.

The mailing list might get you! How such lists are used in direct-mail advertising by local stores as well as mail-order companies. Sources of the mailing lists, slanted toward occupations, interests, income levels, and age. How to stay on—and get off—a mailing list. Mailing listings become multiplied through the manifold sale of lists, which means somebody is making dollars for your name. Companies that sell lists, how much per name.

24

The barbecue master of your area. His estimate of the number of barbecues he has prepared; the most persons he has served at one time. His most sought-after recipe, and the amount of ingredients he uses on an average occasion; the cooks under his supervision. Does he travel out of state to concoct this gourmet's delight?

The day the White House burned. The damage to the structure on this day in 1814 during the War of 1812; the loss of priceless or ir-replaceable items; the smoke-stained stone walls. Reconstruction by James Hoban, the White House architect, and President James Monroe and his family as the first occupants of the reconstructed mansion.

The long-time operator of a fruit store in your city. His reputation for freshness and variety. The most popular fruits—and the most exotic—that he carries. His close friendship with patrons young and old. Sources of his fruit supplies.

Annexation battles that have aroused cities in your region. Leaders pro and con in the efforts; their touting of advantages and disadvantages. Cities with the largest population gains during the past few years because of annexation.

25

The county of your state with the most post offices. The largest and the smallest of them; the newest post offices and their self-service features. The dean of postmasters in the county and his reminis-cences of his early years in the postal service. Salaries now and then. Number of postmistresses; husbands and wives who are postal workers.

The work of the parole board of your state. Who serves on the board. Seeking to maintain good morale at the penitentiary. Main points when paroles are under consideration by the board. Frequency of paroles being revoked. The most compelling problems at present; prison improvements; reducing terms for good behavior.

Advances in the nuclear power industry in your state and elsewhere despite crusades against it. The protestors' main claims about the danger from nuclear stations. Developing new uses for nuclear energy and predictions for ten years from now.

Farming as a part of the Amish religious beliefs. How the members engage in tilling the soil in about two dozen states and Ontario. Their existence without telephones and electricity, and their reliance upon horses. The wearing of old-timey clothes, including bonnets. Amish craft and food-selling enterprises.

26

The task of maintaining a large public aquarium in your state. How the fish are kept in good health by such devices as filters and pumps. Where and how specimens are acquired, and how about the compatibility of the species? How often are the fish fed? Questions that visitors ask the attendant. Comparison of keeping a large aquarium to maintaining one in the average home.

The most unusual experiences of a crane operator in your section. The numerous uses to which a crane is put; uses of cranes in emergencies. Largest cranes manufactured. Spinoff: Other types of heavy equipment and the operators.

Furniture of the future. How the designer at a furniture factory in your state sees chairs, tables, sofas, beds, etc., as time marches on. A feature can be unfolded about home architecture of a decade hence, with a local architect as the crystal ball gazer.

The largest private art collection in your state. How the most valuable of the paintings and sculpture were obtained, and the original owners. The value of the entire collection, and the protection provided for the art treasures. Lending the collection to museums for display.

27

Air traffic controllers at the local airport. Slant: How they fill the role of hero in carrying out their duties. The equipment that enables personnel of the control tower to direct the planes. Latest fail-safe devices. Busiest hours; traffic rushes.

The dawn of the oil production age in the United States. The big moment came on August 27, 1859, when Laurentine Drake discovered oil. The beginning of commercial production; statistics a century later. States that lead in oil output at present. New technology for getting the most out of wells.

The trials and tribulations of a men's suit salesman in your city. Trying to please both the prospective customer and his wife. The color consciousness of men versus women. Times when Mr. and Mrs. do not mince words about their differences of opinion.

Maintenance of an ice skating rink in your area. Slant: How the rink requires constant upkeep to keep the ice in perfect condition. Supplying skates for customers. Instructions for beginners; the worst faults of tyros.

28

Equestrian statues in your state, including any on the State House grounds. Such statues on courthouse grounds or in large parks. The persons so honored and their heroics that earned the recognition. Descendants of these heroes and their pride in the statues. The sculptors. Horses the military owned, and their favorites. The symbolic conventions of equine statuary. Latest examples of horse statuary in widely-known public gardens in your state. Spinoff: Any recently installed pieces of modern sculpture; reactions to it.

Henry Hudson's discoveries in America. How he discovered Delaware Bay and the Delaware River on this day in 1609. His greatest adventures in commanding the *Half Moon* for the Dutch East India Company. Meeting his doom at the hands of mutineers in 1611 when Hudson, his son John, and seven sick men were set adrift in a small boat.

The textbook depository of the county. The person in charge of the mountains of textbooks that will be distributed to the students of the county with the opening of school. How many textbooks are on hand? Are many replaced because of wear and tear? How often are textbooks changed by the board of education? The main publishers of textbooks.

Turning back the clock to 1565 when Spanish explorers landed at St. Augustine, Florida, on this day. How Pedro Menendez de Aviles founded a settlement there forty-two years before the English settled in Jamestown. The old Spanish dwellings in the city today.

29

The highest dam in your state. Details of the construction; the engineers; the area served by the electricity generated by the plant. The use of the lake for recreational purposes. Slant: The dam's impact on the industrial life of the section and on fish and wildlife.

The dean of solicitors in your state. Steps in his legal career. His terms as solicitor, and the most celebrated cases prosecuted by him. The most baffling cases he has won. Any threats against his life?

Once a stock broker, always a stock broker? A leading broker of your section, and his fascination with this business. Details about his work. Attributes that contribute to success in this occupation. Financially speaking, what does the broker expect by the first of next year?

Results of research by an astronomer who works at a planetarium in your state or nearby state. The most elaborate equipment with which he performs his star-gazing. The most startling information in his lectures to the public at the planetarium.

30

How a county in your part of the state has solved the problem of garbage disposal. The results of landfills and the number of people served by them. Amount of garbage dumped into the landfills weekly. Visits by federal environmental officials. The "green box" system, in which garbage is stored and picked up by special trucks. Trash disposal at the city dump; incinerators. Predictions about garbage disposal in the future.

A baseball fan of your city who has not missed a World Series in two decades or more. Slant: How his devotion to the sport has overcome weather, health, job, and distance problems. The most thrilling Series games he has witnessed, and the greatest heroes, and scapegoats, during the long period. Hobnobbing with the stars; the fan's autograph collection.

Merchandise that sells best door-to-door in your city. Are inexpensive items quick sellers? The inevitable magazines and encyclopedias. Demonstrations of money- and time-saving devices. A van, or a clothing store on wheels, with routes for selling the merchandise. Salesladies who take orders for cosmetics.

The emotional problems encountered by both husband and wife after the woman undergoes a mastectomy. Views of the head of a university's department of psychiatry in your state about such an operation's effects upon the pair. Counseling and the latest advances in cosmetic restoration.

31

The youngest member of Congress from your state. Slant: How the public demonstrated faith in the saying youth must be served, by sending the subject to Congress. The lawmaker's accomplishments as a congressman. His business or professional activities since his school days.

The ambitions of hotel bellboys in your city. The ones with the greatest aspirations and their preparation for the big opportunity. Top thrills for the bellboys, as rubbing elbows with celebrities. Handling of drunks and strange characters.

Landslides that have spelled tragedy in your state. Those that have resulted in the most property destruction and loss of life. The causes of the disasters, as too much rainfall, snow accumulation, and earthquake vibrations. The ever present danger in mountain areas. Tree and grass planting as a preventive measure.

Monkeys as pets in your area. Reasons for their popularity. The price of monkeys at pet shops; types of monkeys that make the best pets. Monkey quarters and menus. Spinoff: The survival of the organ grinder and his monkey—once a familiar sight in large cities. An organ grinder of today who is a unique figure at events in your section. The devotion between the grinder and the agile monkey. History of the portable organ; tunes associated with the instrument.

SEPTEMBER

Month of Fairs and Sports Classics

September means the start of a new school year and the harvest season with its distinctive feature, the county and the state fair. The harvest moon makes its appearance about September 23. Its name comes from the illumination it provided that enabled harvesters to toil in the fields later than usual.

In September the football season erupts in all its frenzy, and the college and the professional teams claim their following of millions in the stands and in front of the television. Meanwhile, baseball rushes down the final stretch for the October classic, the World Series.

Labor Day is marked by a legal holiday on the first Monday of September, followed by such special days as National Anthem Day, Citizenship Day, Gold Star Mother's Day, American Indian Day, American Legion Charter Day, Defenders' Day in Maryland, Pacific Ocean Day, California Admission Day, and (hear grandmothers cheer) Grandma Moses Day.

September boasts the birth dates of one president, William Howard Taft, and two monarchs, Queen Elizabeth I of England and Queen Liliuokalani of Hawaii. September birthdays also belonged to Richard J. Gatling, General John J. Pershing, J. P. Morgan, Francis Parkman, William Faulkner, Elmer Rice, James Addams, Frances E. Willard, H. G. Wells, George C. Gershwin, Henry L. Stimson, Samuel Adams, Margaret Sanger, T. S. Eliot, James Fenimore Cooper, William Sydney Porter, Walter Reed, James J. Corbett, Carl Van Doren, Sherwood Anderson, Elizabeth Kenny, Upton Sinclair, Sarah Bernhardt, and John Chapman, of

Johnny Appleseed fame.

The anniversary parade: 1. German invasion of Poland ignited World War Two, 1939; 5. First Continental Congress convened, 1774; 7. Germany launched London blitz, 1940; 10. Battle of Lake Erie won by Oliver Hazard Perry, 1813; 16. Voyage of Pilgrims from England began, 1620; 23. John Paul Jones led the *Bonhomme Richard* to victory over the British vessel *Serapis,* 1779; 25. The first newspaper in the American colonies, *Publick Occurrences,* was published in Boston, 1690; and 27. Mutual military aid pact signed by Germany, Italy, and Japan, 1940.

1

One of fall's highlights centers on the farmer and his family: the gates of your county fair swing open for recognition and fun, and agriculturalists put their best wares forward to vie for prizes. The youngest and the oldest winners. Blue-ribbon exhibits by farm women. The interest created by the animal shows. How judges grade animals. The newest features of county fairs.

An old-time mineral prospector of your county. His most exciting— and most rewarding—experiences in mining; the richest mine he has worked; the number of states in which he has prospected. Has he tried his mining hand abroad?

The demand for your state's crops abroad. The county agent or state commissioner of agriculture can supply data. The crops of your state most in demand abroad. Countries that are the greatest buyers; predictions about the next decade.

A prominent writer-in-residence at a college in your state. Persistence despite rejection slips in the early part of his or her career. Books to the writer's credit, and the ones with the largest sales. Teaching methods; the number of students; those who have broken into print.

2

It's official. The formal surrender of Japan aboard the U.S.S. *Missouri* on this day in 1945. Servicemen of your county who brought home Japanese brides. Revelations about the marriage today; the pair's joys and problems. The greatest delights of the family circle.

A day with the ringmaster of a circus appearing in your city. Slant: How a circus program, with its multitude of acts, always teems with excitement. Soothing performers' (and animals') temperament; the circus band. Unexpected thrills—and injuries.

Handicapped workers in your county who have not missed a day of work in years. How these employees demonstrate their reliability and workmanship. Mastering new techniques; praise from co-workers and managers. The value of the rehabilitation office in industry. (For Labor Day, the first Monday in September.)

All eyes on the thermometer! The amazing range of thermometer types in your city. Don't forget the one at the weather bureau and the one at the airport. The most unique thermometers locally. Temperature and time signs in front of business buildings and their change every minute. Spinoff: The sale of barometers and rain gauges. "Weather bureaus" for the home.

3

Foreign investments in your state. How companies abroad have purchased tracts of land and constructed industrial plants to take advantage of the state's assets. The officials and workers from overseas, making new homes and new friends. How the industries and the foreign families have adapted themselves to American customs. The extent of local help. Why the concerns preferred your state for their operations.

Local doctors always on call. Making the deadline at various occasions. Slant: How physicians, especially baby-deliverers and heart-patient tenders, attend religious services and meetings with sickness and maternity cases liable to "strike" at any minute. Paged at meetings and at theaters?

The daily whirl of a personal shopper at a large store in your city. Slant: How she enables people to shop at home with perfect confidence by telephoning their wants to her. Choosing what the callers would like for special occasions, as birthdays, anniversaries, and holidays. Are men easier to please than women?

Checking utility meters. How the local utility companies check water, light, and gas meters; replacing meters. Customers dissatisfied with their bills. Slant: Take it from the utility industry, the customer is not always right. How some people cook up schemes or devices to cheat the meters.

4

Irrigation practiced by a leading orchard owner of your county. The size of the area served by the system; frequency of watering the trees. The source of the water, as a pond or creek. Improvement in the yields of fruit since the installation. How many orchardists in the county have adopted irrigation?

Student safety in your city. The number of patrol boys who help with the traffic at street intersections near local schools. Slant: How a patrol boy imparts invaluable lessons in safety with his directions to students in crossing the streets. Dealing with violators. What motivates a young person to be a crossing guard? The kind of training he receives and what he learns from being a patrol person.

A veteran judge at water ski tournaments in your section. The states he or she has visited serving as a judge; the largest tournaments and the most thrilling of them. A discussion of champions. Tourney events, as slalom runs, tricks, and jumping. Families with several outstanding skiers. The judge's own achievements in skiing.

Founder's Day in Los Angeles, California, movie and television center. How Felipe de Neva, as the Spanish governor of Upper California, established Los Angeles on this day in 1781 and named it, in English translation, The Town of Our Lady, Queen of the Angels of Porciuncula. Descendants of early residents, including Mexicans, Portuguese, Chinese, and Japanese; the sections they inhabit; and their types of employment. Activities along the city's oldest street, Olvera Street.

5

The latest in city hall architecture. The design of the newest city hall in your state; the architects and their most interesting innovations. Slant: The vision of the architects in designing a building that will meet the needs and taste of future decades.

Ballads about infamous outlaws. A ballad collector of your state and his or her observations about the ballads with the highest popularity. Songs that stress romance—and tragedy.

Happy days of an organ salesman or teacher of your city. The perennial popularity of organs, especially among the I-always-wanted-to-play-an-instrument types. The fancy special-effects technology available on organs. The prices of reed and also electronic organs. Spinoff: An organ builder of your section. The main kinds of troubles; obtaining new parts; the demand for secondhand organs.

A college placement bureau in your state. How the bureau offers college counseling and matches a student with the right kind of college. Subjects in which colleges are concentrating more attention; rapidly expanding vocations. The role of junior colleges. In view of the controversy about overenrollment and scarcity of jobs in some areas, a counselor could offer his or her opinion on who really should attend college today and why. The increasing interest in alternatives to college.

6

A commercial diver of your state who carries out dangerous missions for industry. How he or she risks life by performing difficult tasks underwater. The diver's part in building or repairing bridges, piers, docks and pipelines. The expert's equipment, and how it is checked for safety. His experiences in a recovery or search operation. The worst scares of the underwater specialists. Jobs with the highest pay. Diving for sport.

A hero's name lives on. How the Indiana city of Lafayette received its name in honor of Marquis de Lafayette, born on this day in 1757. Forms of tribute to the French statesman and soldier who gave aid to the colonies in the American Revolution. Slant: How Lafayette lost his fortune, social position, and his freedom because of his beliefs, but earned American and French admiration.

Park rangers to the rescue! How they help when accidents occur in a park. Giving emergency aid; instances of heart attack and overheating. Troubles that develop in a park's wilderness area, as hikers who become lost. A ranger's safety tips.

The McKinley tragedy. President William McKinley was shot at a public reception in Buffalo, New York, on this day in 1901. How his wife remained in ignorance of the shooting for several hours and refused to attend the funeral. In her shock she would not set foot in the White House again. Improved, but still not perfect, security measures for chief executives.

7

The return of the king of fall sports. Football as big business for the colleges of your state. How a large hunk of the revenue from the games goes for the salaries of coaches, trainers, and other staff members. Specifics about the expenses of the varsity and lesser teams, including uniforms and equipment. The upkeep of the stadium and the costs of transportation.

Key troubles in your city. Loss of keys among the occupants of apartment buildings; finders of lost keys in the building or nearby. Shoppers who lose their car keys in stores. How the post office reissues keys to the boxes after losses. The embarrassment of store owners who misplace or lose keys to their establishments. Special types of keys and locks.

Local women's clubs of political parties. The oldest club and the size of its membership. Charter members of the clubs and the leadership they have provided. Political races by members; members as campaign speakers. Circulation of political literature.

What past candidates in the Miss America pageant are doing today. Those who follow careers, as airline hostesses, interior decorators, singers, and actresses; examples from your state. Talents that the candidates displayed in the contest staged in Atlantic City every September. The lure of modeling. The professions of the husbands.

8

Blood transfusions for dogs, administered by local veterinarians. Number of canine blood-types; the most transfusions given one day; the champion blood donor among the canine population. Canine conditions that call for blood transfusions.

The oddest names of cafes, diners, or nightspots. Names local operators of eating places have seen in various states. The most offbeat, and the most elegant appellations. Memorable motto signs, such as those for discouraging requests for credit.

The dean of bridge players in your city. How often do the most devoted players meet to play, and do they rank among the leading players? Trips to other cities for competition; championships they

have held. The number of bridge clubs locally; the total membership. Favorite bridge menus.

The popularity of the snuffbox long ago. How people even before
the Civil War prided themselves upon their snuffboxes. It was a
point of etiquette to offer a friend "a pinch of snuff." Famous personalities who indulged. The elaborate or ingenious decorations of
snuffboxes. The snuff market today; kinds of brands available. The
present medical viewpoint on snuff, as, for example, compared to
smoking.

9

"Selling" religion on the airwaves. An interview with the manager
of a Christian radio station in your state. The various ways it
concentrates on spreading the Gospel. How the station offers live
programs as well as taped, such as dramas with Christian morals.
Programs that bring in the most fan mail. How listeners phone in
their prayer requests. Shows slanted for children. Telethons to raise
funds.

A senior citizen of your county well known for making bedspreads.
What she considers her most beautiful designs; the average time
consumed in fashioning a bedspread. Bedspreads she has given to
her children and grandchildren; commercial demand for her output.

A local collector of first-day covers in the stamp world. How he or
she takes more pride in these covers than in other parts of his or her
stamp collection. The newest and the most striking covers. Keeping
up with the latest developments through stamp publications and
philatelic clubs.

Searching family trees. A local genealogist who aids persons preparing family histories. The local demand for such services and the
rate of payment. The principal sources for research, as private
family records, including letters and wills, and government and
legal documents. Use of church records. Local descendants of notables of a century ago.

10

Indifference to inventions when they were introduced. Take the example of Elias Howe, who patented his sewing machine on Septem-

ber 10, 1846. He failed to arouse any interest in his product in the United States and let his brother, Amasa, sell it to a corset manufacturer in England. The inventor's struggle to eke out an existence, until he hit the royalty jackpot with as much as $4,000 a week.

Woes of program chairpersons of local organizations. The task of booking speakers; prevailing upon notables to appear; celebrities who traveled the longest distances to address the groups. Program changes at the last minute. Slant: How the duties of a program chairperson requires him or her to be nothing less than a lecture bureau.

Popping the cork for a toast. Is champagne consumption in your city on the increase, according to distributors? Occasions on which the drinking of the sparkling wine is traditional. Which leads in consumption, dry or sweet? Details of champagne production; the authentic French process and the domestic.

Portraying famous personalities on stage. Such experiences by a professional actor or actress from your state or one visiting in your section. Slant: How he or she has studied lives of national or world leaders so as to sharpen portrayals. The most demanding roles. Meeting relatives of the notables and winning praise from them.

11

The anti-litter officer of your county. Has the institution of antilitter laws meant a distinct improvement in the county's appearance. The difficulties and technicalities of proving litter violations. Worst seasons of the year for litter. The most frequent offenders. Maximum fines and penalties. What further remedies does the officer propose?

Headaches of local dentists. Emergency appointments; squeezing extra patients into busy schedules. Breaking appointments without notice. Scheduling students for non-school hours; dentists who have been bitten, as by kids. The question of unpaid bills. Are dentists and members of other professions in accord with their hours?

The newspaper days of William Sydney Porter. Anniversary angle: This author, noted for short stories with surprise endings, was born on September 11, 1862, in Greensboro, North Carolina, where he gave up public school at the age of fifteen. Writing for the *Detroit Free Press*, operating his own paper, the *Rolling Stone*, and working for a newspaper in Houston, Texas. How he adopted the pen name of O. Henry.

An interview with a landscape architect. Slant: How landscape architecture fills two purposes, beauty and usefulness. The subject's largest and most difficult assignments. How cities employ such architects to design or improve grounds and gardens; these gardens as assets to the cities.

12

Chewing gum, the present popularity of this peculiarly American habit. New and exotic flavors as well as the traditional ones. Bubblegum and bubble-blowing contests, formal or impromptu. A psychologist's explanation of how chewing gum reduces tension.

A well-known scientist's predictions about space exploration during the next decade or so. The Russian's launching of the first rocket to the moon came on this day in 1959. Visions of space travel in the twenty-first century, and the projected costs.

Clergymen of your county who engage in farming or in other occupations, as sales and music, part-time. Members of congregations who raise produce on a large plot of land jointly as part of their creed—God's acre. Sharing crops with the needy.

Pulling power of classified. Anything goes, from advertising for a wife to garage sale notices. The old and familiar "lost" and "found" ads; those by persons who wish to buy or sell something. The human interest in help-wanted, job-wanted, and "personal" ads. "Freebie" ads, such as those concerning pets to be given away.

13

A veteran operator of a grass seed or sod company in your area. The varieties of grass in greatest demand; those best suited for certain types of soil and shade. Promising new varieties. Kinds of grass best suited for winter survival.

What's in a wastebasket? The manufacture of them in your state. The latest styles in "file 13." Designs in keeping with the times; the largest sizes; the world of colors, and materials. The so-called woman's touch.

Reaction to name changes in your state. How the changing of geographical names has aroused people's resistance. The feelings when roads, highways, and bridges are renamed. How churches have changed names amid opposition by some members. Renaming of manufacturing companies after a change in ownership. How a person can change his or her name; the legal procedure.

Barry Day. Contributions of John Barry, the country's first commodore, to the nation. The native of Ireland drew plaudits as the first American naval officer to seize a British warship in battle. Rising to the highest position in the Navy. How Barry Day commemorates the hero's death on September 13, 1803.

14

First graders' sense of humor. Revelations by a veteran teacher; the most amusing incidents. Are boys really more prankish than girls? Small-fry comedians; their wit and wisdom even at a tender age. Has the teacher recorded any of her classroom experiences?

The activities of the broadcasters association of your state. The most pressing problems confronting the organization; improved technology in the radio industry. Officials of the association and their plans for the future. Providing scholarships for high school graduates. What characteristics and talents speak to a career in broadcasting?

Food examination by home economists of the government. How they test foods—such as pork, cornstarch, and peanut butter—to learn things that may help consumers. Determining how cooking methods affect the various aspects of food, as the flavors, nutrition, bulk, and consistency. Other research carried on by the home economists.

The demand for safe deposit boxes at local banks. How customers keep their valuables, including important documents and jewelry, in the boxes. How more and more citizens prefer bank security because of fear of break-ins at their homes. The limitations—and advantages—of safe deposit boxes. The oddest things ever kept in them.

15

A garment manufacturing plant in your area that specializes in sportswear and swimsuits. Months in which the most of these products are manufactured; scenes in the cutting, sewing, and shipping departments. The designers and the pattern makers; materials from which the items are made; use of fashion models at times.

When illness strikes students. An insight into the infirmary or hospital of a local or nearby college. Experiences and observations of the college physician. The most common diseases among students, as flu, measles, mumps, and mononucleosis, the so-called "kissing disease." Students who require emergency operations. Quarantining some patients; the worst epidemics.

Introduction of military tanks. Anniversary angle: The British Army became the first to make use of military tanks on this day in 1916. How this invention altered the mode of warfare. Other innovations in World War One, on the ground and in the air; aviation heroes of the war, as Eddie Rickenbacker.

A children's museum in your state. Founders of the museum; the number of exhibits; leading features, as art, ceramics, and nature field trips. Details about the museum's operation.

16

The superintendent of the county farm in your county. Slant: How the county operates the farm for the purpose of supplying county needs, as food and meat for prisoners. Number of county employees who work on the farm. Amount of grain harvested annually; the largest vegetable crops; the size of the cattle herd. Is irrigation used on part of the farm land?

The origin of your state's nickname. Who first suggested it? Spreading the use of the nickname, through advertising as well as by manufacturers. Does the state live up to its nickname today?

Cherokee Strip Day, an Oklahoma holiday commemorating the fabulous land rush on this day in 1893. The frantic dash of more than 50,000 individuals for the giveaway of 6,500,000 acres on this day in north-central Oklahoma.

A well-known evangelistic musician of your city. The most successful revivals in which he or she has participated; ones with the largest attendance and the most conversions. The most effective songs at revivals; songs that the musician has composed and their popularity. The number of miles the musician travels annually.

17

Model railroading as a fad among girls of your city. Girls who possess the most extensive sets. Daughters of railroad employees who indulge in this love and share the thrills of their fathers.

Citizenship Day, which commemorates the signing of the United States Constitution on September 17, 1787. What do the signatures of the best known signers mean to a local graphologist? His or her comments on traits revealed by the handwriting. Spinoff: Other intriguing uses of graphology, as in demonstrations or tests at universities. How graphologists contend they can deduce the personality, character, and health of a person from handwriting. What slanted lines, closed a's and o's, and heavy lines mean to a graphologist.

The use of dry ice in your city. Industrial uses, as in refrigeration of food, fire fighting, and bottling of carbonated drinks. Local firms that make the greatest use of dry ice. How it is made and where it comes from.

The spoon-licker's best friend—a jam and jelly maker of your state. Growing and/or buying the fruits and other ingredients. Preparations for the jam and jelly making; the number of assistants; a day's production. The marketing strategies. Jams and jellies that lead in sales; exotic types. Spinoff: The pride of local residents and farm families in the county in the making and canning of jams, jellies, and marmalades. Recipes that have passed from one generation to another.

18

A showman in the sport of archery. His most amazing feats with the bow and arrow; championships he has won in tournaments. The use of human targets and the boldest tricks. What the archer considers his most difficult performances. Does he make his own bows and arrows?

Blessed events at the local zoo. Slant: How the zookeeper responds to his role as the midwife of the zoo population. What animals at the zoo are the most prolific? The youngest mothers. What baby animals are the most valuable? Pointers on bringing up animals.

A long-time roof repairer in your city. How his good work keeps his services in constant demand. Most common types of repairs; outpouring of calls after a severe windstorm. Hardest kinds of roofs to stay on; safety measures. Unusual perils; discoveries of wasp and bird nests.

American Gold Star Mothers in your state. The founding of the national organization in 1928, and how membership is open to mothers of servicemen who were killed in World War One and subsequent wars. Number of members in the state's chapter and their correspondence with others. How the last Sunday in September is observed as Gold Star Mother's Day. Spinoff: Local members of Gold Star Wives of America, Inc., their activities, and programs at national conventions.

19

Official state flowers—and your state. Interview the president of a local or state garden club about how many state flowers grow in your state. What the president considers the most exotic of the flowers; tips about the cultivation.

A haven for homeless people and vagrants. An organization of your section that provides shelter and meals for such persons. The founders of the home and its present operator; the sources of funds, as donations by businessmen and churches. The average number of patrons each month; finding jobs for the men and the women. Religious services.

The commissioner of labor in your state. The variety of his duties. Enforcing the state's labor laws; investigating industrial disputes. Inspecting factories, mercantile establishments, workshops, and commercial institutions. The commissioner's report.

Hayriding is not dead. How beaus and belles in rural areas of your county still indulge in this practice. Use of trucks to transport the hayriders; favorite destinations and the entertainment.

20

The head of the voters registration board in your county. The qualifications a person must meet in order to obtain a voting certificate. Age and length of residence in the state required. How many county residents are qualified to take part in elections? Are many voting registrations not renewed? How the names of voters are selected for jury duty.

Are bandleaders good or bad matrimonial merchandise? Confront a top maestro in your state for his observations. Conflict of careers that put a marriage to test. Marital disasters of the past; idyllic marriages among the musical great. Cases of love at first sight.

The oldest spinning wheel in the possession of antique collectors in your section. Slant: How the spinning wheel was once a standard household fixture. How this instrument of colonial times served Europeans as early as the 1200s. The value of the spinning wheel on the antique market. The use of the wheel by alternate-lifestyle folks and in special handcraft applications today.

For children only! Boutiques in your city that carry kids' clothing exclusively and meet the criteria of the ultra fashion-minded. How the buyers keep their pulse on the latest styles. The children's motif in the stores, and appropriate names for the businesses. Local shoe stores devoted to boys and girls.

21

The world of male modeling. Facts and figures on this profession as furnished by the operator of a model agency in your state. Their demand for newspaper and magazine illustrations and television commercials. Are the opportunities for a male model as great as for a woman? Actors who pick up extra remuneration by modeling.

The largest and most luxurious houseboats in your section. How the houseboat provides the water lover with a convenient, portable modern home and recreation at his doorstep. The number of rooms and their furnishings; sunning on the decks. The rivers and lakes where houseboats are used in your area; houseboats for rent.

The career of a veteran paperhanger of your city. His remarks about wallpaper styles past and present; the current demand for hangers. Funny episodes in paper-hanging. Hard-to-please customers. Plans for retirement.

College athletes of your state who are leaders in the Fellowship of Christian Athletes. Number of chapters in the state; how the athletes speak to youth and church groups. Do any of them hope to become ministers? Experiences of prayers being answered.

22

The food and drink of longevity. Octogenarians and older residents of your county who credit their long life to the drinking of buttermilk or plain milk. Favorite foods of centenarians, as cornbread, cabbage, spinach, turnip greens, and honey.

How spies in various wars fell into the enemies' hands. Nathan Hale was captured after spying on British forces and was hanged by the British on September 22, 1776. His declaration on the gallows: "I only regret that I have but one life to lose for my country." Slant: How he was only twenty-one years of age when he paid with his life for a deed that transformed him into one of America's heroes. The seizure and execution of Mata Hari, the one-time dancer, by the French on charges of being a German spy in World War One.

The farm news department of a local radio or television station. Slant: How the station promotes agricultural progress with regular educational programs designed for the county's farmers. The county agent and the home demonstration agent as speakers; preparing the information and making it down-to-earth.

Recruiting for the branches of the military service. The activities of the recruiting officers in your city, and the branch that pulls the most volunteers. Are there quotas? Number of young women who have volunteered since the first of the year; their reasons for enlistment. Statistics about the all-volunteer army.

23

The busy role of a local allergist. Slant: How the hay fever season accounts for only a small part of allergic troubles, for foods form a major group of allergens. How the allergist diagnoses a disorder; keeping of food diaries by patients. Conducting skin tests. The allergist's estimate of what percentage of the population is afflicted by allergies of one kind or another. The latest allergy treatments.

Who can dump the clown? The carnival attraction of the taunting clown who challenges one and all to hit the target and plunge him into the pool of water below. The showmanship of the clown and a day's and night's pay for the "abuse."

Citizen's arrests on the increase in your city? Figures given by the chief of police about persons using their authority as citizens. Outcomes of trials under such circumstances.

Frontier Days. Salutes to the adventurous past. Features of the celebrations, as rodeo shows, and portrayals of the pioneers. The citizens of Cheyenne, Wyoming, staged their first Frontier Day on this day in 1897. The stores, saloons, gambling joints, and shacks that made up a frontier town. Actual life on the frontier versus movie portrayals.

24

A butler in your city who may be carrying on a family tradition. The duties in which he takes the greatest pride and enjoyment. Is one of them his handling of personal services? Directing other employees of the household, and the chief problems. The butler's off-duty interests. Comparison to fictional butlers.

Favorite salads of chefs in your city and their delight in serving them. The grand, and now nearly ubiquitous American institution of the salad bar. The peculiarities of human nature as observed at a salad bar. Salads of various nationalities; Caesar salad, named for Caesar's, a restaurant in Tijuana, Mexico; shrimp salad Louisiana, Waldorf salad, Hollywood salad, and Saratoga salad. How salad lovers perform hallowed rituals of preparing the greens.

The fashion expertise of a leading chanteuse in a nightclub of your section. How the singer is widely acclaimed for both her singing and her stylish attire. Does she have a designer? Her thoughts on dressing for the spotlight; her off-duty or street fashions; sportswear.

The "king" or "queen" of paperbacks in your state. The author who leads in the paperback field, and the total number of sales. Are most of the paperbacks reprints? Characters who are featured in more than one book. The most novels written by the author in one year. Awards won by the writer. The amount and nature of fan mail; readers who plead for writing advice.

25

Questions a fortune teller of your city is asked the most. Do romance and marriage figure as the leading topics? Concern over sickness and marital problems. Questions about whether to change jobs, invest money in a business, or move to another city.

Pacific Ocean Day, with focus on Vasco Nunez de Balboa. The explorer hailed the ocean as the Southern Sea when he beheld it from a mountain peak for the first time on September 25, 1513. Staking the claim for the Spanish monarch. Balboa's ironic fate: He lost his head on a false charge.

The drama of selecting photograph proofs. A veteran photographer of your city has a storehouse of experiences. How most parents beam with pride as they choose from the proofs of their children, but there are some moms and dads who can't be pleased. Persons who want the wrinkles removed, eyebrows touched up, and the bald spots covered.

26

Ancient newspapers can be news. A resident of your state with the hobby of collecting such newspapers. Has the flavor, or manner, of newspaper reporting changed over the years? Stories with the most interest; newspapers published during wars; accounts of famous battles. The advertisements as a history of the lifestyles of the various generations. Take another angle: Where are the files of local newspapers of a half a century or older preserved?

The textbook market. A textbook salesman of your state; the extent of his travels, and the average number of appointments he makes in a month. Slant: How styles in school books, like clothes, change. The problem of keeping textbooks up to date; educators in your state who are textbook authors. The salesman's views on educational methods. Latest theories on what makes a textbook effective.

The kitchen of a local fire station. Preparation of meals and midnight snacks; do firemen ever burn food? The fire fighter who reigns as favorite cook. Favorite recipes from the firehouse.

The "song plugger" for a music publisher at age sixteen who made good as a composer—George Gershwin. A native of Brooklyn, New York, he was born on this day in 1898 and hit the musical jackpot at twenty-one with "Swanee," which Al Jolson popularized. His composition of *Porgy and Bess*, set in Charleston, South Carolina, ranks as his final major work. Catfish Row in Charleston as a tourist attraction.

27

Handicapped persons in your state who have won progress in their fight for freedom from architectural barriers. Leaders of the campaign and their efforts to amend building codes. How local handicapped men and women raise objections to buildings, as churches, clubhouses, lodge halls, auditoriums, stores, and even medical offices, without accommodations for them.

An old dream book owned by a local citizen who puts strong faith in dreams. The popularity of dream interpretation since earliest times; how Joseph was given his freedom because he interpreted a dream of the Pharaoh. The meaning of different dreams. Dreams that have solved crimes, as robberies and murders.

Musical scales and sales at the vanishing pawnshop. How operators of pawnshops in your city find ready markets for instruments that have been sold to them. Any hard-luck stories by original owners? Young music lovers eager to buy the instruments; the most common instruments, some of them almost new, that have been pawned. The number of used instruments of a particular type on the market might be an index of its faddishness. How is a used instrument judged?

A jockey of your state who has won large purses in horse racing. His love of horses—and competition around the track. The first major race he won; his victories with the most prize money; winning by the proverbial nose. The jockey's best time. How to keep fit in jockeying; handling the horse to achieve the best results.

28

Do Indian legends never die? How Indians of your state still relate legends to their children and grandchildren, just as the stories were told to them by their parents. How much Indian folklore resembles that of slaves who were brought to the American colonies from Africa. The importance of this oral tradition in maintaining a people's identity.

What a test driver of your state looks for in his assignments. Putting an automobile or a motorcycle through the works to make his assessments. His frame of mind in expecting the worst. Kinds of courses the driver uses.

Confucius' claim to fame—a lifetime of wise sayings. The populace of Taiwan honors the Chinese philosopher today with a national holiday called Teacher's Day. Examples of his famous observations. Erection of temples throughout China as tribute. His thirteen years of wandering and voluntary exile.

Trees that contribute to naval stores, as described by a forest authority in your state. How resinous conifers and particularly pines furnish such products as rosin, turpentine, and pitch. How much of the world's supply of naval stores originate in the forests of Georgia.

29

The point of this story is the needle, all kinds of needles. The largest and the smallest you can find in your city. The wide range of uses besides the sewing machine: The surgeon's needle, the shoe repairman's needle, the record player's needle, and crocheting or knitting needle. The price tags.

The wrath of Neptune, god of the sea. Vivid memories of retired sailors of your city about the worst storms they encountered during their careers on the high seas. Highest winds and the damage. The hurricane season.

War on noise pollution. What your state is doing to reduce the menace, especially at jetports. Medical authorities' warnings about the effects of noise upon people, including workers in industrial plants. Enforcement of noise ordinances.

Get the message on car license plates? Display of state nicknames on regular plates; lettering that spells names; and titles, as governor or senator. How a fee enables a person to have almost anything on the plate. Purely decorative front tags and clever statements, as "Let Me Tell You About My Grandchildren." The range of oddities, humorous, and cryptic plates. Spinoff: The variety of bumper stickers.

30

A specialist in pictography in your state. How he or she has made a thriving career out of pictographs in which statistical data is presented in the form of illustrated charts, graphs, or diagrams. The art of presenting statistics to provide fast and easy understanding.

The premier of football games on television. The reaction of the showing of the first game on this day in 1939, the year the National Broadcasting Company introduced television as a regular service with Franklin D. Roosevelt as the first president seen on TV. Early football broadcasters on television, and the equipment. First owners of TV sets in your city and their recollections.

Passing judgment on new products. How members of a buyers panel in your section test articles, including grocery goods, and list their likes and dislikes. Items the panelists call a rip-off.

The mysterious rites for casting a spell against warts. A local resident who claims the power to remove warts through a secretive process. Legends relating to warts and other folklore cures for them. Current medical opinion.

OCTOBER

Fall Beauty and Observances

The days of October are a panorama of flaming beauty as autumn foliage bursts into brilliant colors. This period is popularly known as Indian summer and receives it special character from the hazy sunshine and the tang in the atmosphere. It is the time of final harvesting of crops as well as the gathering of apples; long-heralded king of the orchard paid homage with countless festivals.

October sparkles with favorite occasions, notably Columbus Day, the birthday of the United States Navy, United Nations Day, and Halloween, with its witches and goblins and cries of "Trick or treat"?

Other days of significance are Child Health Day, Leif Erikson Day, Alaska Day, Yorktown Day, National Magic Day, Missouri Day, Fire Prevention Day, Ether Day, International Red Cross Day, Frances E. Willard Day, Statue of Liberty Dedication Day, and Nevada Admission Day. October also brings the observance of National Newspaper Week, National Employ the Handicapped Week, Fire Prevention Week, and National 4-H Week.

The birth anniversaries of six American presidents come in October: John Adams, Rutherford B. Hayes, Chester Alan Arthur, Theodore Roosevelt, Dwight D. Eisenhower, and Jimmy Carter. Other noted personalities born in the month have been James Lawrence, Cordell Hull, Thomas Wolfe, George Westinghouse, James Whitcomb Riley, Juliette Low, Martha McChesney Berry, Eddie Rickenbacker, George Bancroft, William E. Boeing, Helen Hayes, Eleanor Roosevelt, William Penn, Noah Webster, Eugene O'Neill, Richard Evelyn Byrd, Sir George Hubert Wilkins, Alfred Nobel, Pablo Picasso, John Keats, and John Dewey.

Anniversary angles in October are good for article excursions into such fields as the automotive industry, war, the Space Age, the arts, discovery, and government: 1. Model T Ford made its appearance, 1908; 2. British Major John Andre hanged, 1780; 4. Russia's first artificial satellite launched, 1957; 6. American Library Association established, 1876; 12. Columbus discovered America, 1492; 13. Cornerstone of White House laid, 1792; 16. John Brown led seizure of the United States arsenal at Harper's Ferry, Virginia, 1859; 19. Lord Cornwallis' troops surrendered to General George Washington at Yorktown, 1871; 22. Sam Houston became first president of the Republic of Texas, 1836; 23. Metropolitan Opera House opened, 1883; 24. United Nations charter ratified, 1945; and 28. United States experienced worst stock market crash in history, 1929.

1

Hot air ballooning in your state. An enthusiast who has set a record in this sport, and the greatest height and distance he has achieved. How long has he remained aloft at one time? Controlling direction and altitude. The cost and size of the average hot air balloon.

A therapist of your section who teaches amputees how to wear artificial legs, arms, and hands. Slant: How, in addition to giving the instructions for use of the "new parts" he or she instills confidence in the wearers. The time needed to teach users of artificial legs to walk and climb stairs. The materials out of which prostheses are made.

A local restorer of antique clocks. Is this a hobby that combines pleasure and profit? His workshop and the number of clocks he has restored; the nature of the repairs; fashioning parts. The growing interest in clock restoration. How many antique clocks are highly decorative. Spinoff: Antique pocket watches in a watch collection in your section and their worth. Old timepieces upon which railroad men relied.

The number one cattle brander in your section. How the custom of branding, dating back to the arrival of the Spaniards in the New World, assumed new importance as a result of cattle rustling. The brands used by the top brander. Can brands be doctored or forged? The number of cattle that can be branded in a day. Trapping modern-day cattle thieves.

TOBER 189

2

What can you rent in your city? Slant: The vital service rendered by
concerns that specialize in renting equipment by the day or week, a
boon to persons who have only limited use for an item. Popular
items: floor sanders, carpet shampooers, and chain saws. Renting
typewriters, TV sets, garden tillers, apartment furniture, party
equipment, wheelchairs, hospital beds, trucks, and moving vans.
Businesses that lease equipment; the advantages.

The municipal golf courses. Slant: The courses provide year-round
recreation for men and women without country club membership.
How the courses have somewhat different personalities, with their
physical features and degrees of difficulty. The average number of
players per week; champions and their trophies; holes-in-one; green
fees. The golf pros of the courses.

Master politician—or saint? Mahatma Gandhi was born at Port-
bandar, India, on this day in 1869. The leader's devout life and his
campaign for India's independence, as detailed by a well-known
professor of history in your area.

Calculators of all descriptions. The various models sold by local
stores, their size and features. Special units for special needs; business, banking, engineering. Calculators programmed like a computer, by means of card and key. Top manufacturers of calculators.

3

Helicopter pilots as heroes in the war against forest insects. Slant:
How countless trees are saved by these aviators, who spray forests
in order to destroy destructive insects. A veteran pilot of your state
who performs this service; the kinds of chemicals used, and the cost
of the operation. Forest pests that cause the most damage.

Patenting of flowers and vegetables. The fascinating details from a
leader of local garden clubs. Introduction of new varieties within
recent years; the advantages; how names are chosen. The leader's
preferences in varieties. Keeping up with developments in the
flower and vegetable world.

The car-wash of your choice. The washes run from the do-it-your-
self kind to the automatic system in which wax can be applied. The

attendants who clean and vacuum the automobile's interior. The time required for an automatic wash. The rush business on Saturdays. Young people who wash cars to raise money for a project.

First novels that made authors famous. Anniversary angle: Thomas Wolfe, who wrote *Look Homeward, Angel,* was born on October 3, 1900. First novels that have been autobiographical, like Wolfe's masterpiece. The most successful first novels, as Margaret Mitchell's *Gone With the Wind,* in the opinion of the local librarian. These novels' present popularity among library patrons. The statistical probability of a first novel's success, or, for that matter, the statistical probability of its being accepted for publication.

4

Blood donor clubs among organizations in your city. Men and women who have made the most contributions; "gallon donors." Donors with rare types of blood. Record number of transfusions for a person in your city. Building up blood supplies. Spinoff: A commercial blood bank; the usual pay to a donor, and the shipment of blood to distant states.

Carnival time—and cotton candy and candy apples. Slant: The perennial appeal of these treats, especially among children, has made them a trademark of the fair. The dean of the makers at the county fair. How cotton candy machines spin sugar, coloring, and flavoring through heat bands to make the airy concoction. The dipping process in producing candy apples; the ingredients of cinnamon, red coloring, and a blend of cane sugar and corn syrup. How candy apples can be made at home.

Gardens of your section that contain a gazebo, a souvenir of bygone years. Builders of the small structures and recollections of their use by the family during the summer. Social leaders who joined the gazebo trend; flowers and shrubbery that increased the charm of this vanishing institution. Spinoff: Any topiary gardens?

What makes a champion cat? The experiences of cat owners whose pets have won prizes in cat shows in your state. The standards used in passing judgment upon the felines. Keeping a cat in good physical condition and grooming its coat; number of breeds generally presented in a show. Prices offered for champions.

5

Commercial polls. Slant: Not all public opinion polls are political; some are conducted by corporations and industries to learn how the public feels about products and services. How the results enable the companies to make improvements in products and sales. Employing polling organizations to make the surveys. How individuals are chosen for polling; the difficulties or perils in poll-taking.

Wild plants that make a landscape complete. Types that a local landscaper recommends; their cultivation and care during summer and winter. Tropical plants that are favorites; strangest plants grown in your city, and how they were obtained.

Scheduling weddings at local churches. How the large number of weddings makes it necessary to obtain reservations far in advance. Unexpected cancellations and postponements. Leading seasons and favorite dates. How people try to read the weather far in advance for this purpose.

The world of the snail as revealed by a local student of nature. Slant: The expert's admiration for this mollusk, especially its amazing homing instinct and its persistence at a "snail's pace." The kinds of snails in your area and their characteristics; their remarkable sense of smell. Flower and crop damage by certain types of snails. The beauty of some snail shells. European snails as the gourmet's delight.

6

Performance barometer for athletes? The interest of athletic coaches of your state in biorhythm, a theory which holds that three internal cycles in the body—physical, emotional, and intellectual—influence each person from their date of birth. Preparing charts that predict the best and the worst days in a month. Football players who put their faith in biorhythm to find out their most favorable days in competition. Experiences of athletes in other sports.

The youngest orchestra leader in your state. Touring with his aggregation, traveling by bus and meeting deadlines; the booking agent. Recruiting musicians and topnotch vocalists; practicing; longest engagements. Is the orchestra leader also a composer?

The champion check signer in your county. Is the person the cashier of the largest company? The amount of time each day spent signing checks; distributing the checks. The total amount of checks in a year. Characteristics of the cashier's signature. Spinoff: Anti-forgery features of check design, or check papers. Any decrease in forgeries or bad checks?

Out of the ordinary insurance policies. Rain insurance carried by fairs; unusual policies taken out by entertainers. Insurance issued to farmers. Little-known kinds of policies offered by local companies.

7

Repossession of cars locally. How owners lose their automobiles when they are unable to keep up the payments to banks, finance companies, and credit companies. Preparing the automobile for resale. The techniques of the snatchback.

Annulment. Enumeration of reasons by a local attorney such as either person being underage or of unsound mind; claims that fraud or force was employed. Is alimony involved in cases of annulment?

The education of mountain children today. Compare it with the schooling hardships when Martha McChesney Berry founded the Berry schools for girls in the mountain sections around Georgia in 1907. Anniversary angle: The educator was born on a plantation near Rome, Georgia, on this day in 1866. Her highest honors, including her selection as one of the twelve greatest American women in a national poll.

The manure boom. How compost from barnyards and pastures is sold at stores in your section. The best manures for specific purposes; the necessary processing or aging. The months with the most sales, as in the spring. Other natural products for soil enrichment.

8

Is the boarding house still alive in your city? The operator of the largest one, and his or her views on the situation; the plague of constantly rising costs. The problem of preparing and serving three meals a day to a roomful of patrons. The typical run of boarder types, including construction workers and men and women without families. Famous boarding house figures or operators in literature. Spinoff: Residential hotels.

An importing firm of your state. The most common items imported for dealers. Radio and television sets, clocks, novelties, jewelry, and art shipped from abroad. Hard-to-find merchandise. Countries from which the importer receives his goods; comments on the workmanship. Changing import patterns. Problems with fluctuating values.

Fire Prevention Week in your city. Anniversary angle: How the great fire of Chicago, Illinois, started in a barn on De Koven Street on October 8, 1871, and in twenty-seven hours claimed about 250 lives. The inspection of homes and buildings by local firemen as part of the fire prevention program. Fire drills in the schools; fire safety regulations for business structures. Spinoff: The largest volunteer fire department in your county, in regard to the number of firemen and the amount of equipment.

The sauna bath is here to stay. The pleasure and benefits of the steaming experience, described by patrons of a local sauna. The temperature and length of the session. The traditional Scandinavian rituals of the sauna; home saunas, which are growing in popularity; hot tubs.

9

Timber! Lumberjacks of your county who must remain alert for falling trees. Mishaps despite precautions taken by the workers. Largest trees cut down in the county; the equipment. The most valuable species of trees; various uses of the timber.

The sources of play plots. Experiences of the best known playwright of your state. Has he or she based many plays upon real-life incidents? Reaching back into history for plots; engaging in research for such productions. Milking new styles and tastes for stage material; delving into socio-political subjects.

A resident of your city who specializes in Indiancraft. How he or she took up this activity and has attained a high proficiency. The products, such as moccasins, beadwork, war bonnets, traditional costumes, and jewelry. The sales outlet for the items.

The shortest city names in your state. How they received their names. Other cities in the nation that bear the same names. The longest names and their origin. How names have been transplanted from place to place, from abroad to the United States and from one spot in the United States to another.

10

Keeping the hearses and limousines of local undertaking establishments spic and span. The daily care, rain or shine. Frequency of washes; maintaining the vehicles in tip-top shape mechanically. What is the fate of old hearses? Does a local mortuary have a collection of historic hearses, even a horse-drawn one?

A clergyman who serves retirement homes in your city. Providing the patients with spiritual comfort; Bible reading and prayer; religious services. Has the clergyman performed a wedding ceremony for patients?

A kennel in your state noted for its hunting dogs. Slant: How the operator finds it profitable to be "in the dog house" every day. Dogs most in demand; raising and training the different breeds, as coon, fox, rabbit, squirrel, and deer hounds. The kinds easiest to train; boarding dogs; shipping dogs over the nation. The most expensive breeds.

"And so to bed." The varied types of beds that can be bought locally. Changing styles. Care for a brass bed or a canopy one—a trundle bed or a Hollywood twin bed? Convenience of roll away beds. The water bed and also the inflatable bed into which air is pumped. Beds with orthopedic value. Japanese futons and hammock beds.

11

The "chain gang" at college football games. The work—and the emotions—of the chain toters up and down the side of the gridiron to measure and mark first downs. Staying on the alert with every play, despite the game's excitement. Any injuries due to pileups? The best players of all time, in the opinion of the chain carriers.

The old-time iron washpot still has its uses. Local citizens who use them as ornaments and also as containers for growing flowers.

Memories of boiling clothes in the pot and using the scrub board. Price of washpots in antique market. Spinoff: Another picturesque item of the past is the anvil, on which metal is hammered into shape. Its presence and the uses to which it has been put in your county today.

The service of Eleanor Roosevelt in the United Nations. How the First Lady, born on this day in 1884, held a delegate's seat in the United Nations General Assembly from 1945 to 1951 and in 1956 became chairwoman of the UN's Human Rights Commission. Her part in drafting the Universal Declaration of Human Rights; her championship of equal rights for minority groups.

The tribute of a prominent historian to General Casimir Pulaski, a native of Poland and a hero of the American Revolution who died on this day in 1779. How he received fatal wounds in an attack on Savannah, Georgia. Pulaski Memorial Day is observed in a number of states on October 11 to commemorate the death of the nobleman whom Benjamin Franklin persuaded to aid the colonies in their struggle for independence. Spinoff: Poland in World War Two, when the Nazis shipped two million Poles to Germany as compulsory laborers. The activities of the Polish Underground. Local citizens with Polish blood.

12

The star of fast foods rises. The growth of restaurants in your city offering quick service in hamburgers, hot dogs, pizzas, fried chicken, roast beef, french fries, and milk shakes. How the ready-in-a-jiffy fare meets the challenge of America on the run. Newspaper coupons as business boosters or competition gimmicks. Building up the number of breakfast and dinner customers. Spinoff: Nutritional analysis of popular fast food items.

Traditional Columbus Day. Cities that bear the name of the discoverer of America, as Columbus, Georgia; Columbus, Indiana; Columbus, Mississippi, and Columbus, Ohio. The Ohio capital received its name in honor of the explorer because "to him we are primarily indebted in being able to offer the refugees a resting place."

A handwriting expert of your state who testifies in court cases.

Slant: How handwriting is as much a revelation to him as fingerprints are to investigators. Testifying about handwriting specimens, as from documents; enlarging handwriting by photography. How persons slip up in trying to disguise their writing.

Church bells or chimes? How many churches in your city still ring the bell on Sunday morning? The most elaborate chimes and the cost; donation of chimes as memorials. Pastors who still prefer church bells. Churches that have ventured into even more varied and unusual sound effects, including recordings.

13

A day with paving crew of the state highway department. Preparation of the road base and experimental new materials, if any. Use of a mechanical spreader in producing blacktop or concrete pavements; compressing several layers. Making the surface strong enough to support the heaviest trucks. How often do heavily-traveled highways need repaving? How roads are tested for strength.

Laying of the cornerstone of the White House in Washington D.C., on this day in 1792. Debunking the legend that George Washington laid the stone, since he was in Philadelphia at the time. How a native of Ireland, James Hoban, won first prize in a contest for the best design for the White House. The selection of the site by the founder of the city, Major P. C. L'Enfant. Spinoffs: L'Enfant's careful design of the city. Planned communities today.

A woman who sells motorcycles in your city. Slant: How she draws both men and women who are in the market for a motorcycle. The saleslady as an inveterate rider, practicing what she preaches; longest trips and/or most adventuresome. The latest motorcycle styles; the most deluxe.

Scenes in your city and county that are favorites with artists. Are facades, church steeples, lakes, waterfalls, and bridges among them? Landscape preferences. Out-of-state artists who have been attracted to the places. Prizes won by the artists.

14

Current research on arthritis and rheumatism. Local specialists in these fields can reveal progress against the two diseases. The activities of the chapters of the Arthritis Foundation and the Pan American League Against Rheumatism. How arthritis sufferers comprise ten percent of the world's population. The sharp decline in the mortality rate of rheumatic heart disease; the big battle to conquer rheumatoid arthritis. Treatments now in use. Spinoff: Gout—no longer the disease of kings.

Kiddie lands as business boosters. Slant: How stores in your city have activities for customers' children. Riding contraptions that claim the most attention; animal antics. Staging of small circuses; presenting movies.

Term paper research by local students. How the city librarian helps in locating material. The most popular subjects, as in biography. Do headlines influence subject selection? Worst headaches of the librarian, as theft of pages from books. The practice of college students buying ghost-written theses that aroused the nation a few years ago. Spinoff: Book synopses for sale. How professors feel about these "notes."

National Friendship Day, marking the birthday of President Dwight D. Eisenhower. Ike's knack of easy friendship, his grin and friendly nature. His leadership in civil rights legislation during his administration. His actions in school segregation crises, as at Little Rock, Arkansas, and his efforts for unity during his White House years.

15

Where do all the flowers go? The life of the deliveryman of a local florist. The usual destinations—hospitals, mortuaries, churches for weddings, and homes for special occasions, as anniversaries and birthdays. Unusual destinations: The airport, and sporting events for presentation of bouquets to queens. The most expensive flowers. What were the most flowers the deliveryman has ever seen sent at one time? Mix-ups in the delivery of flowers. New streets that are problem makers; asking directions. The language of flowers is alive and more eloquent than ever.

When a county prisoner becomes ill. Experiences of the county physician. The most common kinds of sickness; emergency operations; guarding prisoners as patients in hospitals. Do many prisoners try to fake sickness in hope of escaping work? Do some criminals fear shots—of medicine, that is? Spinoff: Prisoners as guinea pigs in testing new drugs.

White Cane Safety Day, by presidential proclamation. The white cane as an indispensable aid to the visually handicapped of your city, especially on downtown streets. How sightless residents like the feeling of independence; security with seeing-eye dogs. Your area might contain a nature trail for blind persons with Braille signs along the routes. Vacation activities, as at state parks.

The life of a bugler—in local Boy Scoutdom. Reasons a Scout chooses to become a bugler; the time required to master the art. The youngest buglers; brothers who are bugling experts.

16

The operator of a card shop in your city. His or her helpful nature that has made the store a must-stop. The perennial best-sellers in this field; the newest types and styles of cards to catch the public's fancy; the wider than ever range of novelty and special effects cards. Do humorous cards outsell straights? Modern sentiment cards; trends toward poetic/personal/inspirational cards.

Full speed ahead! The owner and driver of a racing boat that has won more than its share of races in your state. Setting records; number of trophies. Mishaps during the racer's career. Kinds of boats he owns, and his knowledge of motors.

The dictionary as best-seller. The word master—Noah Webster— was born in Hartford, Connecticut, on this day in 1758. Consult book store owners in your city: The lowest and the highest priced editions; newest and/or most popular types, and features; months of the greatest sales, including September when schools reopen. Compare dictionary sales with Bible purchases.

First aid to animals. The steps to be taken when an animal—such as a horse, cow, dog, cat, or bird—has an accident and is awaiting the arrival of a vet. Advice from vets, Humane Society workers, and operators of animal shelters and hospitals.

17

Does every woman—and man—love a mirror? Revelations by

salespeople in local stores. How people try on garments and admire themselves in front of the store's full-length, multi-sided mirrors. Special mirrors for shoe and hat selection; make-up mirrors. Slant: How the customer has faith in the saying "Seeing is believing."

Black Poetry Day. This commemorates the birth of Jupiter Hammon in 1711. How he became the first Negro in the nation to put his poetry into print. Black poets in your section and state today, and their dominant themes.

Branches of your state museum. The persons in charge of these places and the importance of the museums to the communities. The diversity of the exhibits and collections that have been featured during the past year. Acquiring items, as historical photographs and even tintypes.

A poultry raiser of your county who specializes in bantams. His or her special fondness for the small domestic fowl, and the market for these chickens as a novelty. The demand for bantam eggs. Spinoff: An area resident who raises Oriental breeds of chickens.

18

The highest paid professional athlete in your state. The salary in his or her first professional contract; largest moneymaking moments. Which sport offers the greatest financial rewards to the professional? Slant: The attraction of being a professional, including the opportunities of travel and meeting people. Keeping in training. Preparing for retirement.

Motion pictures in surgery. An insight given by the president of the state medical association. Special cameras and lighting; other technological aspects of this type of photography. The skill of the photographers, and uses of the movies.

The ramp serviceman at the local airport. His speed and ability in handling cargo and baggage. Refueling of planes. Meeting celebrities and obtaining autographs. Other jobs he may have held at the airport.

New inventions for farmers. The most useful of them, in the opinion of the county agent. The inventors; their other inventions. Spinoff: A poll of the area's farmers on the question: What kind of invention would benefit you most of all?

19

City codes and their consistency with state codes. Revision of city codes to bring them up to date and remove conflicts. Attorneys who pressed for the changes to make ordinances uniform. Do county codes need attention, according to some legislators?

Yorktown Day. Anniversary angle: Lord Cornwallis surrendered to General George Washington at Yorktown, Virginia, near Chesapeake Bay, on this day in 1781. Features of the Colonial Historical Park at Yorktown, including the Moore House where the Articles of Capitulation were drafted.

The most unusual experiences of a drivers' agency in your section. Providing drivers for distant trips, including emergencies. The longest drives; worst kinds of weather; travels in the name of romance, as honeymoons. Biggest tippers; handling would-be deadbeats.

What will people buy? How local department stores select merchandise. The judgment of the managers and their buyers in purchasing seasonal and holiday goods. Do customers differ in their various suburban branch stores: any variance from region to region in their taste and buying habits?

20

The best-known heart surgeon in your state. His most difficult operations; "miracles" on the operating table. Latest advances in heart surgery; reduction of death rate among heart disease patients. The surgeon as a speaker before medical groups. Spinoff: Diets and exercise programs that can reduce heart disease.

A forester of your state as wildlife's best friend. Slant: How the forester—for the United States Forest Service or the state forest services—safeguards the wildlife as well as the water and soil of the forest lands. A typical day, in both summer and winter. Knottiest problems.

Franchises. Examples of franchises operated in your section, such as ice cream, doughnuts, fast food chains, printing and copying service, dry cleaning, motels and hotels, and employment agencies. Experiences of your section's franchises. The advantages of obtaining a franchise. How the franchise companies furnish the know-how, or expertise, for the franchise license and a continuing royalty.

The geographic center of your county. A geodetic official can pinpoint this interesting location. What city is it nearest? The family who resides in the center of the county, probably without realizing the distinction. Owner of the property and how he or she has capitalized upon the location. Travel advantages offered by the county's center.

21

Honorary citizens of your city. The most famous persons who have been accorded this honor; their visits, as recalled by city officials. Red carpet treatment for government leaders and entertainment stars. Foreign dignitaries who rated the honor. Who makes the "keys" to the city?

An expert on oceanography in your state. What latest research has revealed about ocean geography. The ocean bottom's topography; the deepest points of oceans. Methods of exploring the oceans and the mysteries. "Mining" the ocean.

The fastest growing city in your state. Reasons for the rapid growth, and the leading industries. The large increase in building permits for construction of manufacturing plants. Housing developments. Annexations that have made the population figures zoom.

Visiting at the state mental hospital. The days on which visitors are allowed, and the hours. The visiting quarters and regulations. Are visits by relatives and friends encouraged in most cases? A supervisor's recommendations on how to conduct a visit with a mental patient. Passes for outside recreation.

22

The chef at the country club in your city. His busiest days; the largest banquets he has prepared. The size of his weekly grocery bill; the wide variety of meals served the members; favorite courses and desserts. Number of assistants in cooking and serving.

Protection for the local police and county officers. Where they buy weapons and other equipment, as bulletproof vests. The full range of items carried by the business. Most expensive pieces.

A local collector of pocket knives. The wide variety of knives, with a multitude of purposes. The most exotic knives; highly decorated or engraved pocket knives. The accessory tools of some pocket knives. Knives prized the highest by the collector. Spinoff: Local maker of custom knives.

More hair—for a price. Americans have been wig addicts since colonial days, and today hairpieces are worn more than ever for a variety of reasons, professional and business, romantic, and plain vanity. What a hairpiece specialist of your city offers in styles. The price of top-quality wigs. New strides in "looking natural." Leading country in hairpiece production. Spinoff: Latest developments in transplanting hair. The growth time and the charge.

<h1 style="text-align:center">23</h1>

Assistants to officials in your city and county. Range from the assistant fire chief and the assistant police chief to the assistant postmaster and the assistant county officials, such as the assistant superintendent of education. Assistant pastors. Little-known tasks of the assistants.

Counting sheep? What physicians of your city recommend for insomnia sufferers. Methods used by local citizens and the results. A psychologist's explanation of insomnia, as overexcitement and worry, and his or her suggestions.

The president of the fox hunting association of your county. Slant: How the hounds' barks are music to the ears of the fox hunter. The president's description of the sport and the thrill of participating in a fox hunt. Just how foxy is the fox in a hunt? Foxhunt customs and etiquette.

The touch of Scotland in the United States. How citizens of Scottish ancestry keep customs alive by holding annual gatherings, as in Charleston County, South Carolina, and at Grandfather Mountain in North Carolina. Bagpipe musicians and dancing. Athletic contests, as tests of strength; tossing the caber. The Parade of the Tartan. Spinoff: Nationality celebrations, as the Chinese New Year in San Francisco, New York City, and elsewhere. Observances by foreign-born groups as Irish, Italian, Puerto Ricans, Polish, German, Russian, Greek,, and Japanese.

24

Voices out of the past. The use of sound tape by historians and archivists. Slant: How they treasure the sound tapes as much as microfilmed documents. How historians interview elderly citizens for their recollections, preserving their interviews in the archives of your state. Keeping the records under proper conditions of temperature and humidity. Indexing and arrangement.

New uses for glass in home and in industry. Disclosures by the operator of a glass company in your city. Extensive research by the leading glass manufacturers to develop glass with remarkable new qualities and to further its usage.

United Nations Day. The official birth of the UN on October 24, 1945, after ratification of the Charter by the United States, United Kingdom, France, China, Soviet Union, and a majority of other signatories. Opinions of United States congressmen and senators about the greatest achievements of the UN. Evaluation of secretary-generals.

Has mining lost its romance? The impressions of a mining engineer in your state. Recently-found mineral deposits; analysis of ores. The worst problems that face a mining engineer. The most profitable mines in the subject's career.

25

Laminating as a business in your city. How the operator of such a business laminates various things, as Social Security cards and driver's licenses. Spinoff: A person of your section who laminates newspaper obituaries and also engagements and wedding announcements. The number of newspapers he or she uses.

Hitchhikers' laments. Thumbers of your section find the going tough most of the time because of the bad name given the hitchhiking fraternity by its violent members. Hitchhikers who still thumb rides and find motorists willing to take a chance. How hitchhikers size up and evaluate possible prospects. New hitchhiking techniques, such as the ones employed to get around no-hitchhiking postings and designations.

The zipper is an oldie. Back in 1892 Whitcomb L. Judson, a Chicagoan, introduced a slide fastener with hooks and eyes. Twenty-one years later Colonel Lewis Walker entered the field with a mesh-tooth type of zipper. Old-time merchants of your city with memories of the revolution in the clothing industry caused by the zipper. Foremost manufacturers today. Velcro; new fastening devices.

Admiral Richard E. Byrd, pioneer in polar aviation. Anniversary angle: The flying explorer was born in Winchester, Virginia, on this day in 1888. In 1926 he and Floyd Bennett made the first flight over the North Pole. Byrd's South Pole flights. The scientific research projects undertaken by the native Virginian.

26

The carpenter shop of the maintenance department of your city's schools. The number of carpenters and their work with the buildings, even in the summer. Repairs that keep them busy; construction to meet new needs; replacing broken windows. Safety features of the shop.

The perennial lure of puzzles, especially jigsaw and crossword. The most elaborate puzzles in local stores. Variations of word puzzles. Cryptograms, word fill-ins, and acrostics. Sections in newspapers and magazines devoted to puzzles; puzzle magazines on the news stands.

Counties in your state with the highest rate of venereal diseases. On the other hand, the lowest. The constant campaign of the state board of health against VD; progress cited by the epidemiologist assigned to your area. Age brackets with the most infections.

The frequency of bankruptcy in your state. How a United States District Court receives petitions in bankruptcy; hearings before judges; referees in bankruptcy who take testimony. The requirements for the action, and the results of bankruptcy.

27

Women receiving training at a technical college in your section. Types of skills that demand the highest salaries; learning jobs dominated by men, especially construction work, surveying, and mechanics. A noted psychologist's list of careers that give women the greatest sense of achievement today.

Traveling telephones. How automobiles, trucks, airplanes, and even trains are equipped for mobile telephone service. Use among business and professional people in your city. The monthly charge. Spinoff: Bleepers, or CB's and valuable services.

The thread market in your city. Best-selling kinds of thread—in fiber and in color. Thread made of Sea Island cotton as well as silk; production of man-made fibers. Variety of thread in textile plants. Spinoff: The popularity of the art of embroidery and other forms of decorative needlework in your city.

Navy Day. The observance was launched on this day in 1922, on the anniversary of the founding of the American Navy in 1775. How the Continental Army used fifty-three vessels during the American Revolution. The most dramatic sea battles in the war, and John Paul Jones' famous words, "I have not yet begun to fight." Observations by a local historian.

28

The leading toll bridges in your state. The total of tolls collected from motorists the past year. The longest toll spans and their cost. Streamlining toll collection. Resistance to toll hikes. Catching up with toll runners. Spinoff: Drawbridges in your state. Details of their operation and unique features of their construction. Mishaps resulting in loss of life or extensive damage.

Real-life Biblical locations, as discussed by local religious leaders. Do they agree with the beliefs of archaeologists that the Tigris-Euphrates valley was the site of the Garden of Eden? Claims that the remains of Noah's Ark have been discovered on Mount Ararat in Turkey. Visits of clergymen to Biblical lands; photographs they made.

The Christmas spirit comes early for the toy wholesalers of your city! Beginning the flow of merchandise from toy factories in your state or elsewhere to catch the full advantage of the season. Doll and train manufacturers. New toys expected to hit the jackpot.

Founder's Day at Harvard University, the oldest institution of higher education in the nation. Its founding on this day in 1636 followed the landing of the Pilgrims at Plymouth by only sixteen years; the first graduating class in 1642. The university bears the name of John Harvard, a minister who bequeathed half of his estate to the school in Cambridge, Massachusettts. Presidents of the United States and also leaders in your section or state who have been Harvard graduates.

29

How to "read" features of the human body. A phrenologist of your state who claims that he or she can judge the mental faculties and character of a person by the study of the skull's conformation. How he or she interprets the features. Do the contours of the skull indicate anything? Spinoff: An insight into body language and its purported meanings.

The trade associations in your city as a boosting business throughout the year. How each association carries out special promotions; other activities. Example: Dairy Month, featuring ice cream and other dairy products. Shows devoted to one kind of product, as boats. Local associations with the most members.

Rattlesnake meat. Is the old fad of eating rattlesnake steak still going strong in your section? Sources of the meat; a visit to a rattlesnake ranch. Number of ways in which the meat can be prepared. Spinoff: Wild foods, as grasshoppers, ants, turtles, squirrels, opossum, and raccoon, and recipes for them. Giggers in quest of frog legs.

Lure of cruises for local vacationists. Voyages in winter are gaining in popularity, as local travel bureaus can attest. Are bookings heavy for this winter? The lines that offer the cruises, and the rates. Menus and activities aboard ship. Spinoff: The popularity of freighter travel.

30

Stuttering can be cured. How a speech pathologist of your state treats the speech disorder suffered by two million Americans. How the technique involves giving confidence to the stutterers. Methods of treating the patients; the time needed for recovery. Research by a speech pathology unit.

Variety is the strong selling point in the handkerchief industry. The report of managers of local stores about the demand for various kinds of handkerchiefs—even the red bandanna. The favorite materials of customers, as linen and silk. The different styles, some purely decorative and others meant for serious use. Kinds of hankies identified with certain countries. We can thank the ancient Romans and Greeks for the introduction of handkerchiefs.

Fake or real? Remarkable mind power performances by a psychic in your state. Tests made of the psychic's abilities; observers' close check for any deception. Predictions that hit the mark—and those that flopped.

A long-time country correspondent for a weekly newspaper in your county. Slant: Her service to community and the newspaper in writing folksy letters of small happenings in the area. Rounding up the news; injecting cheer and bits of philosophy into her column. Her greatest pleasure in writing; her output; what interested her readers most? The columnist's most startling or embarrassing experience with the items she has written.

31

Halloween—and National Magic Day, which commemorates the death of Harry Houdini on this day in 1926 and also honors the skill of magicians. The five most popular tricks of a professional magician. Some of the oldest tricks that are still baffling audiences today.

The long-time association of the owl with ghost stories. How the weird cries of this bird at night undoubtedly started it. The superstition that the hoot of the owl in the night signifies an approaching death. Slant: Despite its association with wisdom, the owl is as entrenched in superstition as the black cat. What the owl is really like, as revealed by an owl raiser of your county. Spinoff: Other birds and animals prominent in myth, folklore, and superstition.

The owner of a costume rental agency in your state. Slant: How the customers include not only theatrical people but also partygoers, centennial observers, and pageant players. How some kinds of costumes seem to grow on the wearers and renters because they fail to return them, or come back and purchase them. The most common damages to rented costumes. Varying costs, to make or rent. The number of costumes for rental by the company; making costumes and enlarging the wardrobe from time to time; the chief seamstress. The average life of a rental costume. The most unusual costumes.

Pros and cons of a universal language. Do well-known linguists of your section believe the advantages would outweigh the disadvantages? The invention of over two hundred languages, including Esperanto, for international use. How does a language expert of your city rate English as a candidate for a global language?

NOVEMBER

Month of Milestones and Firsts

Plymouth Rock—under a granite canopy in Massachusetts —symbolizes November because here the Pilgrims embarked upon their new existence and in the autumn of 1621 began the custom of Thanksgiving in gratitude for an abundant harvest. In the tradition of the Pilgrims, the United States observed its first Thanksgiving on November 26, 1789, with a proclamation by President George Washington.

In November Americans devote one day—Veterans Day, formerly known as Armistice Day—to honor members of nation's military. On November 11, 1918, the Allied and Central Powers signed the World War One armistice. The tomb of the Unknown Soldier at Arlington, Virginia, serves as another symbol of this month.

November has a star-studded role in American history in both war and peace. Lewis and Clark caught sight of the Pacific Ocean on November 7, 1805; the first United States telescope was patented on November 11, 1851; the cash register was invented on November 4, 1879; the first radio broadcasts were inaugurated by station KDKA in Pittsburgh on November 2, 1920; Richard E. Byrd made the first flight over the South Pole on November 29, 1929; and the United States exploded the first hydrogen bomb at Eniwetok in the Pacific Ocean on November 1, 1952.

Other highlights of November are: 2. San Francisco Bay discovered by Gaspar de Portola, 1769; 8. Wilhelm Roentgen discovered X rays, 1895; 9. Kaiser Wilhelm II fled from Germany into exile in The Netherlands, 1918; 15. League of Nations Assembly first met at Geneva, 1920; 18. Panama Canal Treaty signed by the United States and Panama, 1903; 19. Gettysburg Address given by President Abraham Lincoln, 1863; 22. President John F. Kennedy slain, 1963; and 28. Fire at Cocoanut Grove Nightclub in Boston claimed nearly five hundred lives, 1942.

Leading the birthday anniversaries in November are Presidents James K. Polk, Zachary Taylor, Franklin Pierce, James A. Garfield, and Warren G. Harding; King Edward VII of England, Charles de Gaulle, and Winston Churchill. Humorists Will Rogers and Mark Twain were born in the month, along with a number of other literary figures—Robert Louis Stevenson, Stephen Crane, William Cullen Bryant, Voltaire, Louisa May Alcott, and Jonathan Swift.

Other November birthdates: Robert Fulton, Louis Daguerre, Marie Curie, Martin Luther, Maude Adams, George S. Patton, Andrew Carnegie, John Harvard, Cyrus West Field, and Crawford W. Long.

Beginning with Author's Day on the first of the month, November has a full range of special days: John F. Kennedy Day, Churchill Day, Father of Texas Day, Will Rogers Day in Oklahoma, John Harvard Day, Sadie Hawkins Day, Marine Corps birthday, and Admission Days in North and South Dakota, Oklahoma, Montana, and Washington.

Add to the list of observances American Education Week, National Farm-City Week, National Bible Week, National Children's Book Week, National Diabetes Month, and National Retarded Citizens Month.

1

A resident of your city who designs and makes jewelry. Slant: The originality and skillful craftsmanship displayed by the subject in fashioning such objects as earrings, bracelets, necklaces, buckles, rings, and cuff links. The studio and the variety of tools; the products most difficult to make. The various materials, and their relative cost. Custom orders, personalized designs.

A veteran molasses maker in your county. How he devotes a large number of acres to the cultivation of cane and then produces molasses through the grinding and cooking processes. Utilizing old-time "horsepower" for turning the grinders. The annual output of molasses; sales outlets. Modern-day uses of molasses.

An old cannon on display in a park of your section. Wars in which the relic was used; the weight, size, and material of the cannon. Was a veterans' organization responsible for mounting the cannon in the park? Any other war relics on local display?

Shoplifters will be prosecuted! The kinds of stores in your city most victimized by shoplifters. Types of merchandise preferred by the thieves; methods of concealing the goods. Hiring of security guards to combat the menace, and the variety of increasingly sophisticated detection devices in use. The disease of kleptomania.

2

The weather forecasting equipment of a local television station. How weather reporting ranks as one of the most important public services of television, especially in flood and tornado crises. Activities of the weatherman or the weatherwoman—gathering and presenting the weather data. The most expensive equipment.

Foreign language newspapers in the United States. Hundreds of them are published in the nation. Those received by local residents who once lived abroad. The most popular features; the dailies with the largest circulation.

Beyond ribbons and bows. The wide variety in gift wrapping today. New and unusual materials and methods. Spinoff: Free and "fee" gift wrapping at local stores. Tips for achieving professional results in home gift wrapping.

The dean of substitute teachers in the local school system. Number of generations she has taught; one-time pupils who have become national figures. How a substitute teacher wins the confidence of the students. Changes in classroom atmosphere. Comparison of textbooks old and new; varying of teaching methods.

3

The production manager of the printing house of a religious denomination in your state. How the establishment prints all sorts of religious material for state and national distribution. Publications that are tied in with the activities of churches. Filling rush orders. Progress in the printing industry.

Father of Texas Day. How today honors Stephen F. Austin, born on November 3, 1793; he combined his wisdom and diplomatic skill to bring harmony between Mexicans and American settlers in Texas. How he prevailed upon more than five thousand persons to make settlement in Texas.

Upswing in the popularity of down, the soft feathers obtained from ducks, geese, and other waterfowl. The advantages of down, and the products in which it is used. Kinds of feathers best suited for pillows and upholstery. Care of down products.

Year-round gardeners in your city. How the greenhouse makes it possible for the "green thumb" people to pursue their love throughout the year. Heating, cooling, and watering facilities for the greenhouses. Rare or exotic plants that thrive; kinds of flowers and vegetables grown. Use of plant food. Spinoff: The largest greenhouses of local florists and their equipment.

4

The problems caused by color blindness. Testing for such a condition; the nature of the tests. How color blindness is more prevalent among men than women. How the defect may prevent a person from taking certain jobs or entering military service. Problems with traffic lights. Recent use of a single tinted contact lense to correct this disorder.

Wedding bells for Abraham Lincoln and Mary Todd, the long and the short of a future First Family. It happened on this day in 1842; the Kentucky belle's declaration to friends during the courtship: "His heart is as big as his arms are long." The minister who married Abe and Mary after a number of temperamental clashes between them. Pastors who "tied the knot" for other presidents.

A hockey goalkeeper who has a sensational record defending the goal cage. His most enthusiastic supporter; perhaps a friend or an athlete who has followed his career closely. The design and weight of his equipment. Injuries—a matter of course.

Formal opening of the Erie Canal, on this day in 1825. Slant: Its importance as the first major national waterway in the nation, connecting the Great Lakes with the Atlantic Ocean. The foresight of the canal's planner, De Witt Clinton, who was governor of New York State when the project was completed. Spinoff: The building of canals in your state for ship or barge navigation, avoidance of rough parts of a river as waterfalls, and adapting the water flow for generating hydroelectric power.

5

A veteran animal trapper. Slant: How trapping not only reduces his meat bill but increases his revenue. Animals that command the highest prices; the value of the furs. The slyest animals. Spinoff: Attacks upon trapping by conservationists and humane society workers.

The biggest problems of the delivery personnel of the United Parcel Service. Are deliverers plagued by dogs, like postmen? Mix-ups in street names. Are there many COD's? Difficulties in making change. Trying to catch customers at home. Have they noted an increase in business in the face of soaring parcel post costs?

A restaurant supply house in your city. Its principal products, including microwave ovens, food warmers, deep fat fryers, charbroilers, and heat lamps. Is owner a former restaurateur? Equipment innovations; sales of used items. Servicing the products. Spinoff: Increased use of commercial items by value conscious consumers.

Making a good living from junk. The revelations of a junk dealer who prides himself on the variety of his "goods." Does the enterprise cover acres? Kinds of junk worth the most. Customers attracted from other states. Competition from freelance collectors, theft problems.

6

A well-known marathon runner in your area and his or her plans for the future. Is the runner a record holder? The longest distances and fastest times for the runs. The dedication and training demanded by this sport. The reactions and emotions in a long race. The time the runner devotes to practice.

Cities that have served as the capital of your state. The most noteworthy events during that period. The governors and their records as chief executives; the state houses and their preservations; markers erected by historical societies.

Animals with the best memory. Opinions of leading farmers and pet owners of your county and incidents to back up their contention. Dogs that do a remarkable job in rounding up cattle. Do farmers think the hog is dumb or smart? Horse sense! A zoo keeper of your section can select the five animals that lead in memory.

Downtown malls in your section of state. Closing streets to automobile traffic and building malls as downtown attractions to compete with suburban shopping centers. Designers of the malls and their comments about the trend. Features and special events there.

7

What price entertainment? A nightclub owner can tell about the expense of keeping the customers entertained—and coming back. The highest paid acts and the best paid entertainers. Breaking in new acts that wow the audiences. Comedians who have been overnight successes. Taking a chance with unknown talent.

Counties in your state that were named in honor of war heroes. The first county to be so named; the wars represented by such names. Monuments that some cities have erected in tribute to generals; the greatest feats of the battlefield heroes. Relics of these leaders in museums. Capitals of counties that have been given names of military notables. Spinoff: Cities, streets, and parks of your area that bear the names of war heroes.

Population findings. Cities in your state that have gained the most in population, and those that have experienced the largest losses. Statistics about minority groups; number of American Indians in the state, if any. Density of population in the state. Growth in large metropolitan areas.

A plastic surgeon of your city. Restoring or repairing parts of patient's body after car and airplane accidents, burns, and injuries. Facial operations and the transplanting of skin from other parts of the body. Cosmetic remodeling, as the nose and the ears. Covering up scars. His greatest challenges.

8

The most prolific inventor of your state. The number of patents to his or her credit, and the best known of the inventions. His first as well as his latest invention. Has he reaped considerable money from his devices? His laboratory and its equipment. His favorite or most productive hours for working. How and when his best ideas are likely to come to him.

The Civil War as a passport to fame for Georgia novelist Margaret Mitchell. Anniversary angle: The author of *Gone With the Wind,* which appeared in twenty languages, was born in Atlanta on November 8, 1900. How she used her native city as the locale of a large part of the action in her novel that won the Pulitzer Prize. Her life after the great success.

The electrical inspector of your city. Slant: How inadequate wiring presents fire hazards in the business and residential districts. Points of safety checks. Does the inspector suggest the adoption of a new electrical code? His most urgent advice.

The timetable of the local railroad station. Slant: How timetable has been a symbol of the accuracy and dependability of trains over the years. The number of arrivals and departures each day and night; how engineers adhere to schedules to the minute, if possible.

9

Experiences of an insurance adjuster. The average number of adjustments made a month; ironing out disputes. False claims; legal actions; strange accidents. Storms that have wrought the heaviest damage in the past decade.

The most unusual staircases in your city. Features about the stairways of local mansions; historic homes with unusual staircases. Public buildings, such as city halls and courthouses, and college structures with unique stairways.

Daredevils on skateboards. Youngsters of your city who have won acclaim with their amazing feats. How they mastered their most sensational performances. Girls who "steal the show." Skateboards as a cause of injuries; wearing helmets, knee and elbow pads.

Musicians' other jobs. Do most local bandleaders have other jobs?

Is teaching a second occupation for members of the local symphony orchestra? Wives who are accomplished musicians and vocalists.

10

What everybody wants to know about photography and is not afraid to ask. Interview a well-known college photography teacher about how friends and strangers constantly seek advice. How the students learn from actual experience. Careers open to graduates of the course. What the professor sees as the most fascinating branch of photography.

Founder's Day of the United States Marine Corps. The creation of the Corps on November 10, 1775, by the Continental Congress for participation in the American Revolution. The adoption of the motto *Semper Fidelis* ("Always Faithful") in 1868, and examples of the expression about the Corps, "The Marines have landed, and the situation is well in hand."

The workers of the Salvation Army as the firemen's friend. The long-time custom of the Salvation Army aiding firemen while they are fighting major fires. Providing canteen service; giving dry socks and gloves in addition to coffee and food.

The sundial in the Space Age. A local or county resident who has an undying fascination for the use of this instrument of time-telling, whose history dates back to about 1300 B.C. in Egypt. How he prides himself in a sundial handed down for generations. Does he make sundials? Is he interested in clock and hourglass collecting?

11

Veterans Day. Continuation of friendships a local veteran of World War One made while in military service abroad; reunions with his one-time comrades since that time. Recollections of the signing of the armistice that ended the war on this day in 1918. The worst battles in which the subject participated. Miraculous escapes from almost certain death.

Activities of the auxiliaries of veterans' organizations. Slant: How they sponsor projects that train girls in citizenship, as Girl's State and Girl's Nation conducted by the American Legion Auxiliary. Goals for the coming year. Spinoff: The role of women in various wars, including World War One. Close calls as a nurse; also experiences of WAC's.

Records of local painters in painting a house. The time spent on the jobs and the number of painters. The sizes of the dwellings; the methods of painting, as by rollers. Unusual problems or obstacles encountered.

Projects by a science club in a local school. Slant: The club as a stimulus to the scientific-minded students of the Space Age, providing an outlet for their abilities. Planning entries for the next science fair. Achievements of the members; the officers and their ambitions.

12

Bald-headed barbers of your city! The great amount of kidding that they have to take. All kinds of cures suggested to the barbers. The extent of baldness among women. Spinoff: Barbers, bald-headed or not, who like to carry harmony, in barbershop tradition. Any quartet aspirations?

Object: Matrimony. A matrimonial agency of your state and its service of linking interested parties. How the operator gathers lists of men and women who seek mates because of loneliness and other factors. How Dan Cupid operates through the mails; unusual correspondence. Spinoff: Computerized courtships.

A local citizen who is well known for bird feeding. The kinds of birds that flock to the feeders in summer and winter. Types of feeders, including ones easily made at home. The ever-pressing problem of keeping unwanted eaters, of various kinds, away. The types of food and the price. Bird traits the subject has noticed.

Let's go to a ladder factory in your state. The range in the height; highest ladders for use by construction companies; the smallest and the extent of their sale. The lumber or metal most popular for ladder manufacture; states that are the chief sources. A construction supervisor can explain ladder safety.

13

Undertakers and tents. Keeping an ample supply; tent woes in rough weather; average life of a tent. Slant: How funeral directors are weather watchers as well as clock watchers. Are many funerals postponed on account of unruly elements, including heavy snows? The Holland Tunnel as the first vehicular tunnel. Anniversary angle: The tunnel was opened in New York City on this day in 1927, when it ranked as the largest in the world. The greatest engineering problems; the danger from poisonous exhaust gases, and devising ventilation systems. Spinoff: The greatest engineering marvels in creating mountain tunnels, either for vehicular or train traffic.

A minister of your county who is a prominent raiser and rider of horses. Slant: The love of early preachers, or circuit riders, for the horse, on which they travelled from place to place, delivering the gospel. The clergyman's longest trips on horseback.

Leading high school and college wrestlers of your state. Their coaches. The most effective holds. Are many girls wrestling minded? Slant: The advantages of wrestling as a body builder, as recognized by schools. Do any of the athletes contemplate a professional career in wrestling? Differences between professional and college wrestling.

14

The highest railroad trestle in your state. The date of construction and the cost; the height and the length. Have floods ever threatened its destruction? Accidents or near accidents of trains while crossing the span. Other high trestles in the state.

Nellie Bly, traveler extraordinary. Anniversary angle: How the reporter set out on November 24, 1889, to circle the globe in less than eighty days. Her modes of transportation; chief difficulties; what she enjoyed about her travels most of all. How she cashed in on her fame.

Soil that spells doom for the criminal. How the arm of the law in your section analyzes soil from shoes and trouser cuffs for vital evidence; examining dust from clothing. The equipment of the soil detective. Spinoff: An ink detective is another type of sleuth who can identify inks linked to suspects.

The longest strikes in the history of your state. The issues at stake in the union-management conflicts; picket lines and outbreaks of violence. Terms of the settlements. Industries in which most strikes have occurred. Arbitration as a method of settling disputes. The unions with the largest membership in the state.

15

Teachers' pets—the animal kind. The most extraordinary pets kept for companionship and protection; names on the strange side. Range of oddities, as animals, birds, reptiles, and fish. Any pets particularly suited to the teaching life?

How automobile license plates of your state are made. Are they manufactured at the state prison? The amount of metal used in the tags this year; the total number of plates. Who decides on the design? The price of tags since inception of the automobile.

The champion couple of your city. The longest-married pair and their activities at present. The part they take in the program of a Senior Citizen club and their travels. Does husband or wife play a musical instrument? Number of children and descendants.

Pike's Peak—or bust! Anniversary angle: Zebulon Montgomery Pike, general and explorer, first sighted Pike's Peak in the Rocky Mountains near Colorado Springs, Colorado, on this day in 1806. Pike scaled part of the peak in November, 1806, but turned back because of lack of supplies. Major Stephen Harriman Long led an exploring party that made the ascent fourteen years later. How motorists of today can attain the top by a highway from Colorado Springs. Annual footrace up the mountain.

16

Neighborhood clubs of your city. The objects of the groups; a typical meeting. The largest club and its officials. How the clubs participate in city-wide campaigns or projects. Taking outings or tours.

Unique aprons in your city. Aprons with interesting stories, as those made out of material brought from foreign countries. Very old aprons and bonnets worn by elderly farm women. A local apron maker who finds the market good. Aprons for industrial use.

Statehood Day in Oklahoma. Oklahoma gained admittance to the Union on this day in 1907, when Guthrie was the state capital. The prominence of Guthrie as an agricultural and oil region today; the annual '89'er Celebration there that commemorates the opening of the Oklahoma Territory in 1889.

The fate of the old-time country store in your county. Slant: How some rural emporiums have survived by converting to tourist or recreational needs, especially in resort areas. The sale of bait and fishing supplies; picnickers, campers, and hikers who turn to the country store. How this institution of the past has stayed essentially the same; how it is different in some ways today.

17

An interview with a prominent entomologist of your state. The cataloguing of the different species of insects in the state. The task of collecting insects. How do you count insects? The techniques of the workers. The state's most harmful insects; newest insects to make their appearance.

The amusements of the first settlers of your section. Did they include running footraces, jumping, fiddling, dancing, shooting, and swimming? Dig into the records of a historical society. The pride of the pioneers in their guns and marksmanship, a characteristic of their descendants today who express this love in hunting.

Ways of being self-employed. Examples by residents of your city— raising fishworms, saw and scissors sharpening, piano tuning, genealogical research, typing, nurseries for children, sewing and alterations, freelance writing, door-to-door selling, and raising animals for sale. Home businesses that require little capital; semi-retired merchants who like to stay busy with a mini-business.

A legal aid society in your section. How persons financially unable to obtain a lawyer may receive free legal aid from the group. Do many of the problems concern domestic squabbles? The officers of the society and the staff attorneys. Number of cases handled since the group's founding. Spinoff: The position of the public defender in your county, and the amount of work it requires each month.

18

Buffalo meat. What gourmets of your section think of it. Its qualities, and how it compares with other meats; price. A buffalo ranch as mecca for animal lovers and curiosity seekers. Buffalo ranches in your state. Experiments in breeding bison with ordinary domestic cattle.

Famous firsts in your state. How people accomplished them in various fields, as agriculture, industry, medicine, education, inventions, and literature. Were some of the first-makers unsung heroes? Did any of the first-makers become wealthy. Proving claims about inventions; taking the matter to court.

Troubles of a theater usher. He has to be an escort, a diplomat, a night nurse, a bouncer, and also an encyclopedia, all in one. Trying to be equal to any occasion. Summoning physicians and other persons from the audience; helping patrons find objects and money they have dropped; assisting in cases of sickness.

Scissors cut to fit. Kinds of scissors that are used in your city, including household scissors, barber's scissors, medical scissors, and industrial scissors. Electric scissors, miniature scissors, extra-large scissors.

19

School records that make an absorbing history. Slant: Tracing the progress of the city's school system since its inception via the mementoes. Preservation of photographs, as of trustees, early classes, and first schools. The file of high school yearbooks through the years. Reminiscences by the oldest school teachers.

Art from natural materials. A craftsperson of your section who creates art using wood, pods, cones, seeds, and the like. Steps in fashioning a work. The most delicate masterpieces. Market for such creations; objects most in demand.

How to prepare for disaster. Stark facts from the director of Civil Defense in your city. What he or she expects if and when disaster strikes. Civil Defense equipment and supplies.

Residents of your state who have been portrayed in literature. How did they feel about being put between the covers of a book? Novelists who have depicted members of their family in fiction. Cities and towns that are recognizable.

20

An interview with the president of your state's chapter of the National Wild Turkey Federation. The growth of the group as proof of the high interest of sportsmen in the welfare of the American wild turkey. Accomplishments of the state members in carrying out the goals of the national federation. Periodic attempts to make the wild turkey the official United States bird. Tie-in with Thanksgiving Day.

The program research department of local radio or television station. Slant: The extensive efforts of the station to ensure accuracy. Types of programs that require the most research; errors that almost slipped by. The vast amount of data at the fingertips of the department.

Two drinking giants in competition—coffee and tea. How does the sale of coffee compare with that of tea in grocery stores in your city? The ratio of coffee to tea served in local restaurants. What percentage of coffee is decaffeinated? The institution of the coffee break in local places of business or professions. Doctors' remarks about coffee and tea drinking. Exotic coffees and teas available in your city.

Excuses, excuses, excuses! Those that a debt collector hears day after day. The most familiar excuses and hard-luck stories. Who can tell the most convincing lies, men or women debtors? The largest delinquent accounts. Bringing suits to collect bills.

21

An interview with the business manager of the state penitentiary. Slant: How even a place of punishment and rehabilitation must be operated on a business basis. Daily and monthly cost of operating the pen; the major items of expense. Revenue from the manufacture of products; the prison factory.

Driving a car despite handicaps. Slant: How such drivers in your city have overcome their handicaps by "intestinal fortitude" and the special equipment in their automobiles. The devices that enable handicapped or paraplegic persons to drive; the problems of getting in and out of cars.

The state's chief food sanitation inspector in your area. Number of eating establishments that he and his assistants have to inspect; those that have opened in the past six months. Inspection of school lunchrooms. The checklist of the inspector and what is needed for the best grade sticker.

The wide, wide range of games in your city. Put at the head of the list the games with the video computer system in which a unit allows as many as fifty game variations from a single game cartridge. The kinds of games and sports available in such cartridges. Other favorites in games, as judged by managers of local stores handling games and recreational sports. The sales charts of billiards, table tennis, and shuffleboard. Board games; dart boards.

22

The custom of singing conventions, particularly in rural communities in your section. Churches where the sessions are held. The officers and other leaders. Dean of the singers and the musicians; persons who travel the farthest distances. How the conventions have been of benefit to the music of rural churches for decades.

Silence and the chase are golden—for clowns. Observations of a circus clown playing in your county. Do most clowns remain silent during their acts? The art of pantomime; memories of the Keystone Kops of silent movie days. The traditional chase and mishaps that never fail to produce laughter. Good-luck pieces of clothing the clown likes to wear for performances.

A couple of your city engaged in medical practice. How long have the physicians served the medical needs of the community? Did they study at the same medical college and fall in love there? The task of being a wife, a doctor, and possibly a mother.

The woodpile on farms in your county. Old-time farmers—and younger ones, too—who still depend upon wood for heating and cooking purposes. Kinds of wood the farmers prefer; utilizing the chips. Farmers who still champion the wood stove and hail its cooking powers. Spinoff: Many farmers provide wood for urban and suburban fireplace users today.

23

For Thanksgiving Day, observed on the fourth Thursday in November: Favorite Thanksgiving paintings, as chosen by the head of the local art society. Is one of them Doris Lee's *Thanksgiving*, which depicts the kitchen where women are preparing the Thanksgiving dinner? Thanksgiving scenes a local artist would like to depict.

The king of river cities in your state. Slant: How the city owes its origin to the advantages of the river location when the various forms of transportation were slow and difficult. The founders and pioneer citizens who capitalized upon river cargoes; how fortunes were made; mayors through the years. The main industries today and their leaders; combatting river pollution.

Gambling laws in your state. Are some forms of gambling permitted? Nevada as a gambling center; how New Jersey initiated a legal lottery to help finance education in 1963. Gambling taxes imposed by states. Horse race betting; the numbers game in sports events as a form of lottery. Questions about bingo and slot machines.

The luck and pluck of Horatio Alger, Jr., who in his long stretch of books preached the philosophy of strive and succeed. How the native of Revere, Massachusetts, was a Harvard University graduate and a Unitarian minister who turned out such novels as the *Ragged Dick* series. Today members of the Horatio Alger Society observe the anniversary of the founding of the group in 1961. How the members put Alger's principles and goals to good use today.

24

Hobbies of former mayors of your city. Prescriptions for enjoying life. Their choice of authors as well as movie and television stars. The extent of their travels. Collections of any kind, or any art hobbies? Do the ex-mayors and their wives share the same hobbies?

A veteran service engineer of an equipment company in your section. Slant: His dependability that is behind the slogan of making a customer satisfied. His travels in supervising the installation of equipment; insuring the proper operation. How he rushes to the rescue and saves the day when a breakdown stops production.

The registrar of a local or nearby college. The years with the largest enrollment. Recent expansion in the institution's buildings, especially dormitories. States represented at present. Statistics about the student body; the average student of today, as compared with yesterday's. Are student loans from government increasing?

Months and years of the largest land deals in your county. Skyrocketing prices in building booms; sites selected for industrial plants. Largest sums involved in transactions during the past year. Land sales as an index to business conditions.

25

A rape prevention program in your state. The leaders' discussion of psychological approaches to dealing with a rapist instead of using weapons or physical violence. The most effective self-defense. Top authorities as speakers at seminars.

Indian chiefs who signed peace treaties with the settlers in your state. The most bitter engagements; how sites of such battles are marked today; Indian mounds in the area and the discovery of relics. Are the graves of the chiefs known?

Local masters of checkers and chess. Their expertise in these games and their championships, perhaps the state title. Playing checkers blindfolded. Longest games; playing by mail.

The family Bible as a record keeper, both past and present. The custom of recording births, marriages, and deaths, as well as other family history, in the Bible, and its importance in preserving a significant record. The family Bible of a centenarian of your county. How family Bibles are used as aids in securing birth certificates in your county.

26

An old-time "herb doctor" of your section. How long has he or she followed the practice of making medicine from herbs? The various herbs used. Has his practice picked up in the wake of the organic living tide? Slant: Modern medicine's rediscovery of herbs' therapeutic value.

The drawing power of garage and rummage sales locally. Slant: The twofold purpose of raising money and disposing of unwanted items. Advertising the sales by various methods, as newspaper classified ads, street signs, and circulars. How church organizations and clubs sponsor such sales as money-makers. The easiest items to move, and the hardest. Are any real finds made at garage and rummage sales?

The most unique and picturesque stone fences in your county. Did any of them come into existence because of an overabundance of stones in the fields? Endowing gardens with a rustic note by means of stone fences; marking land boundaries with this type of fence. Spinoff: The most interesting rock gardens in your city, and their designs. Flowers that thrive best in shade.

Electric railways in your state. Introduction of electric locomotives in 1895; development of electrified suburban service. How the railroads were revolutionized by the diesel electric locomotive, extensively adopted after World War Two. Spinoff: The advent of the electric trolley system in your city. The company that operated the trollies; the excitement the streetcars produced.

27

The luckiest breaks of the wealthiest men or women in the county. How do they define luck? Beginnings in the business world; making the first dollar. Does he or she believe in taking chances? Worst investments and the lessons learned from them.

Groups that share with others. Organizations in your section that give a hand; checking out family needs. Kinds of assistance. The activities of the National Jewish Welfare Board and the National Catholic Welfare Conference over the years. How CARE has been sending food and clothing to needy persons abroad since 1945.

Conducting the rehearsal of a local orchestra. The main points in a rehearsal, as the bandleader or conductor explains. The meaning of the numerous signals given by a conductor. Devoted musicians who report for rehearsal—or even performances—despite sickness or other problems.

Telegram and telegraph services today. Telegrams for special occasions, as weddings, birthdays, and anniversaries. Observations of the manager of the local telegraph office. How messages are selected from a large group of greetings. Holidays and controversies are inspirations for a flood of telegrams; heydey of the singing telegram.

28

A flying club of your city. The family with the most members, and their combined number of flying hours. A husband-and-wife team with the plane as the second home of their children. Newest members of the club; the dean of pilots; war veterans who have continued their flying.

A slingshot wizard of your city. An adult who "draws a mean bead" and draws admiration from the younger generation. The shooter's incredible feats of marksmanship. Does he make his own slingshots?

Belts—or suspenders? How extensive is the use of suspenders in your city today, in comparison with the wearing of them a few decades ago? The volume handled by local stores and the styles. The once common red galluses. Are elastic sleeve holders still in demand?

Common-law marriage. An estimate of the prevalence of the practice today from county and state officials. What percentage of couples of this type eventually undergo a wedding? Experiences of probate judges and ministers.

29

Working dogs at a military base in your state. How dogs are trained to be "detectives"; some can smell out bombs. The kinds of dogs best suited for military duty. The guard duties of canines, and also spying performances. Dogs used by the police and customs authorities.

Recognition via postage stamps. Natives of your state, including any presidents, who have been honored by stamps. What value does foremost philatelist of your area place upon such a collection?

The most severe earthquakes in the history of your state. Records of the tremors and the loss of property and lives; cities and counties that suffered the most damage. Believe-it-or-not stories about escapes from death. Light earthquakes felt in the past decade.

Automobile makes that bit the dust. Recollections of a veteran car dealer of your city. Cars with the shortest life span; manufacturers who could not make the grade. Prices of automobiles a few decades ago. The "oldest" cars on the market today.

30

The Mennonites in your section as good neighbors. How they give a helping hand to neighbors and others who need assistance, as rebuilding fire-destroyed homes or in times of other disasters. The Mennonites' simple way of living and dressing; their reputation as expert cooks.

The oldest house in the historical district of your city. Its builder, and the number of rooms. Preserving the building; the present owner. Antique furnishings and other objects. Each room as a revealing glimpse into the past. The advantages and disadvantages of residing in a "living museum."

Mark Twain's beginnings as an author. Anniversary angle: Twain, as Samuel Clemens, was born at Florida, Missouri, on November 30, 1835. He first tried his hand at writing on the *Enterprise* at Virginia City, Nevada, and introduced his pen name there; his later work in San Francisco.

How manufacturers of your state test their products, ranging all the way from sporting goods to musical instruments. How tests are conducted. Final inspection of products before shipment. The meaning of those mysterious little inspection number slips you find. Spinoff: Local stores that specialize in "seconds" in clothing and other goods at discount prices.

DECEMBER

Month of Good Will and Winter Holidays

December makes its appearance as the grand climax of the year, the eagerly awaited season of festivities teeming with joy and good will. It represents a bonanza for article writers amid Christmas parades, the rush of buying or making gifts for family and friends, the delight of putting up a Christmas tree and spreading cheer with decorations, and the singing of carols.

Writers can distill into timely features the customs, religious and otherwise, that surround the season highlighted by Santa Claus' visits on Christmas Eve and the celebration of Christmas Day.

December introduces the winter season, along with the wide variety of winter/snow sports, and snowfalls and ice storms can transform cities and farms into the fabled winter wonderland—a continual wave of activities that fairly beg for feature treatment. Then on New Year's Eve families assemble for a fond farewell to the old year and a toast of anticipation to the new. As for writers, you and I, we make open resolutions to write—and sell—more stories.

While Christmas dominates December, special days begin with Pan American Health Day, set by presidential proclamation, and proceed through the month with such observances as Heart Transplant Day, Pearl Harbor Day, Human Rights Day, Boston Tea Party Day, Wright Brothers Day, Forefather's Day, International Arbor Day, and Louisiana Purchase Day. A number of states—including Illinois, Indiana, Pennsylvania, New Jersey, Iowa, Texas, Delaware, and Mississippi—observe Admission Day, in recognition of gaining statehood.

December brings the birth anniversaries of Presidents Martin Van Buren, Andrew Johnson, and Woodrow Wilson. In the literary world Noel Coward, Maxwell Anderson, Joseph Conrad, Willa Cather, Joyce Kilmer, Jane Austen, John Greenleaf Whittier, John Milton, and Rudyard Kipling were born in December.

Other notables with December birthdays have been Admiral George Dewey, George Armstrong Custer, George C. Marshall, Kit Carson, and Billy Mitchell of fighting fame; Louis Pasteur, Eli Whitney, Charles Goodyear, and Harvey S. Firestone, contributors of scientific progress; and also James Oglethorpe, Joseph Smith, Edwin W. Staunton, Ludwig van Beethoven, Gilbert Stuart, and Clara Barton, the "angel of the battlefield."

From the arrival of the Pilgrims on the New Continent to the birth of powered flight on the sand dunes of North Carolina and the utilization of atomic energy for electricity, the December chart of historical events abounds in a wide variety of article subjects: 2. President James Monroe gave the world the Monroe Doctrine, 1823; 5. Twenty-first Amendment, which repealed prohibition, added to Constitution, 1933; 7. Japanese aircraft attacked Pearl Harbor on day that will "live in infamy," 1941; 9. Jerusalem fell to British, 1917; 10. Nobel Prize awarded President Theodore Roosevelt, 1906; 12. Wooden golf tee invented in Boston, Massachusetts, 1899; 14. George Washington died at Mount Vernon at the age of sixty-seven, 1799; 16. Colonists staged Boston Tea Party, 1773; 17. Wright Brothers opened Age of Aviation with first heavier-than-air flight at Kitty Hawk, 1903; 20. United States produced electricity from atomic energy for first time, at Reactor Testing Station in Idaho, 1951; 20. France sold the Louisiana Territory to the United States, 1803; 21. Pilgrims stepped ashore at Plymouth Rock, 1620; 24. War of 1812 ended with signing of the Treaty of Ghent, 1814; 26. George Washington's troops won Battle of Trenton, 1776; and 30. Fire at Iroquois Theater in Chicago took 639 lives, 1933.

1

"Mr. Toastmaster" of your city. The Number One after-dinner speaker and his fund of sense and nonsense. Kinds of jokes that get the greatest response; favorite jokes. Putting over serious points. Filling the chairmanship of fund-raising campaigns.

The president of your city's largest fan club of an entertainer. The enthusiasm and amount of work he or she puts into the club's operation; methods of recruiting members; activities at the meetings. Visits of the entertainer to the city or the state, and the outpouring of his or her fans. How a certain number of fan clubs are for "dear departed" entertainers.

Weddings of blind persons. The superintendent of the state school for the sightless is a top contact. Slant: How the blind put the lie to the old saw that love is blind. Stranger-than-fiction romances. Means of livelihood. Are there many divorces among the blind?

Tightrope walkers of the construction industry. They are the ironworkers on tall buildings who risk their life daily. The knack of walking the narrow beams with seeming nonchalance. Dean of workers in your section and his injuries, if any. Rules of safety that have kept him alive. Chief worries of the daredevils of high iron.

2

A chemist of a paint manufacturing company in your state. Slant: His constant search for a better tomorrow in paint. New ingredients that give better finishes and longer life in paint. Current research projects of the chemist. His company's annual production.

The use of personalized holiday greeting cards in your city. A store or photographic studio that features cards with family photographs, especially children. Original or unique poses. What is the Christmas season without photographs?

Taxicab passengers as humorists. Slant: Local cabdrivers are a captive audience for men and women who imagine themselves great joke-tellers. Do some of the cabmen swap jokes? The best-loved jokes of the drivers.

Coldest spots in your state. Record low temperatures and the deepest snowfalls in the state's annals. Is December generally the month of the first snow? Old-timers can describe winters more than half a century ago and the worst inconveniences. The never-flagging interest in snowmen and snow ice cream.

3

Daily flag raising in your city. At how many buildings do the American flag and other flags, as that of the state, fly? The persons who hoist the flags at the largest places; flag raising at schools. Tallest flagpoles; obtaining new flags; flag etiquette today.

The role of school marching bands in the local Christmas parade. How their appearance, along with the arrival of Santa Claus, ranks as a highlight of the event. Preparation of the musicians for the parade.

Heart Transplant Day, as tribute to Dr. Christian Barnaard, who performed the first successful heart transplant on December 3, 1967. The death of the patient, Louis Washkansky, eighteen days after the surgery in Cape Town, South Africa. New research findings about heart operations and transplants discussed by the president of the state heart association.

Do most bosses in your city come to work early? Do the owners or the managers of businesses or manufacturing plants believe in being early birds? First duties every morning. Earliest risers among the local bosses. At what time do they retire?

4

The zoning board of appeals in your city. How the body considers cases in which enforcement of the zoning regulations might be contrary to the public's best interest. Restrictions and exceptions that have aroused controversies. Latest residential sections that have been converted into business areas; types of commercial activities to which citizens of neighborhoods object most vehemently.

The operator of a large pigeon farm in your state. Slant: The heavy demand for pigeons—for table use, research work, and foundation stocks of pigeon breeders. When was the plant established? The original and present investment; the number of employees. How much food is consumed by the pigeons each day? Types of pigeons; prices of the birds; largest orders. Spinoff: A farm that specializes in ducks, geese, or perhaps quail.

A bowling instructor of your area. The most common faults of beginners. Furthering the interest of boys and girls in the sport. Conducting bowling clinics. The highest scorers among local men and women keglers. Do women have their own bowling association? Travels of the instructor; giving exhibitions; trick shots.

Christmas clubs at banks of your city. How the banks employ
special tellers to handle the clubs' accounts; the years the clubs
have been in existence. The inducements and recruiting campaigns.
What percentage of people actually finish up the payment schedule?
Do many Christmas clubs end up getting spent on something else?

5

A singer of your section who also sings in foreign languages. Slant:
Music is the universal language, as shown by the success of American vocalists in recording in foreign languages in the past. How
many languages does the singer know? Most difficult songs to
deliver in other languages. Current hit tunes in other lands. Spinoff:
English songs most difficult to deliver in various languages; the
easiest.

An extensive grower of holly trees in your state. Slant: How the
cultivator finds a market for the leaves and the berries as well as
the timber, which is in wide demand for making such products as
piano keys, cabinet inlays, and rulers. Largest holly trees in the
county; varieties; the holly as the state tree of Delaware. Spinoff:
Examples of Christmas decorations provided by members of local
garden clubs.

The top hobbies of millionaires in your section. Wealthy persons
who engage in rather expensive hobbies; in contrast, the most expensive pastimes among the richest residents. Millionaires who
cling to their boyhood or girlhood hobbies. Preferences of
millionaires' spouses in hobbies.

The amusement park and theme park craze since Walt Disney—
born in Chicago on this day in 1901—opened Disneyland Park for
children near Los Angeles. The success story of Disneyworld in
Florida and places like Six Flags in Georgia and Texas. New rides
and shows; skylifts; train and showboat rides; haunted houses or
castles. Porpoise and animal shows.

6

A theological school in your state. The founder and its heads since
the inception. Growth of the institution and erection of new buildings. The best-known teachers, and the oldest of them. Noted
religious leaders who have received their preparation there. Total

number of graduates; alumni activities. Courses and studies, such as psychology of human sexuality, that were not in the curriculum many years ago.

Who arranges your movie fare? The work of a motion picture booking agent in your state. How a booking agent is one of the unheralded figures in the cinema industry. How films are booked for regular theaters and drive-ins. Crusades by parent-teacher associations and other groups to lower the boom on sex-oriented and excessively violent pictures.

Garbage that finds its way to livestock. How owners of cattle, hogs, etc., call upon food establishments daily for scraps. Is there much demand for such refuse? Slant: How garbage and castaway food has a market like scrap metal. Spinoff: Rescue of garbage at landfills by persons who sell the material or items for recycling or other purposes.

Construction barriers—and human nature. Comments by the head of the highway department in your county. Are detour signs frequently ignored? Motorists who ride on freshly treated roads in defiance of signs; disasters that have occurred as a result.

7

Pearl Harbor Day. How a professor of history at a local college compares the Japanese attack on Pearl Harbor with other military acts that started wars. The teacher's evaluation of General Douglas MacArthur's direction of the occupation of Japan. The present-day interdependence between the United States and Japan; top Japanese exports to the American market and vice versa.

A professional home economist in the field of clothing in your section. How she serves the government by helping families plan their clothing. Preferences in fibers because of durability and other advantages; giving instructions in the making of clothes and the care of them.

The smallest county seat in your state. Slant: The achievements of the city in spite of its small size. The county's history; the founders; and the present officials. Reminiscences of oldest citizens; most historical buildings.

The story of a float in the local Christmas parade. Deciding upon a theme and designing the float to carry it out. The amount of cloth, paper, and other materials; special decorations and lighting effects. Unusual characters for floats. Features of prize-winning floats in the past.

8

A well-known animal sculptor of your state. Slant: How he or she has captured the personality of animals in sculpture. Best pieces of sculpture and honors they have won state-wide and nationally. Animals he or she has sculptured the most. The sculptor's knowledge of animal characteristics. Spinoff: An illustrator of your state who has a wide reputation for animal drawings; publication of the art in magazines and possibly books.

Insurance in the sports world. A discussion of the cost by professional athletes of your state, as well as team physicians and insurance experts. Their views on the subject. High-hazard athletes, including racing drivers, high divers, boxers, and wrestlers. "Parts" insurance in sports, as a pitcher's arm and a skater's legs. Are fatalities in sports increasing?

Safety is the watchword at a gasoline storage plant that serves service stations in your area. Precautions on the part of every individual. Number of gallons generally stored at the place; keeping watch at all hours. Precautions for consumer use of gasoline.

Progress in the conservation of energy. An interview with the operator of an insulation business in your city about how homeowners of the area are reducing fuel costs. The most common types of insulation, as mineral wool, urea formaldehyde, polystyrene, cellulose, perlite, and polyurethane. Methods of installation in floors, walls, and ceilings. Insulation recommendations by the local utility company. Tax credits for insulating.

9

Flower problems at funerals. Talk with local funeral directors. The art of arranging flowers at the church or the mortuary. Transporting the flowers to the cemetery after the service so that they will be there before the arrival of the procession. Rain and wind as headache-makers. People who want to see their wreaths, in order to determine whether florists filled their orders. Spinoff: The trend to flower alternatives, such as memorial funds to churches, institutions, medical research, and the like.

Secrets of a glamour photographer of your state. How to shoot for glamour; variety in posing, as striving for a different angle. Clients who are in the news. Magazine assignments; covering beauty contests. How the reader can put some of the tricks of the glamour photographer to use.

The creator of the Uncle Remus stories, Joel Chandler Harris, an Atlanta, Georgia, journalist born on December 9, 1848. How he based the tales on black folklore associated with animals and presented them in the book, *Uncle Remus: His Songs and His Sayings* in 1880. His latter volumes and their sources. Confrontations between Br'er Rabbit and Br'er Fox; Uncle Remus characters in the movies. Harris' home in Georgia as a shrine.

A square dance club in your section. How this form of American folk dancing has the enduring enthusiasm of young and old. Founders of the group and present teachers. A veteran square dance caller and the basic calls. Dance patterns. Eye-catching square dance costumes, and ones made by the dancers themselves.

10

The charity work of organizations in your city. Playing Santa. Finding the neediest and most deserving families. Emphasis on food and clothing. Raising funds for the Christmas project.

War is hell. How General William T. Sherman's witnessing of destruction in the Civil War led him to coin the celebrated phrase. Anniversary angle: The native of Lancaster, Ohio, completed his March to the Sea from Atlanta to Savannah in Georgia with a force of 60,000 on this day in 1863. How he launched his march to destroy supplies instead of lives and thus earned the title of the first modern general. Burning of the cities of Atlanta and Columbia, South Carolina.

The record-holding cake baker of your city. The person who makes cakes at the largest bakery locally, the deluge of orders as a tribute to his or her talents. The largest number of cakes baked in a single day. Spinoff: Baking birthday cakes as a home business. A local woman known far and wide for this skill. Most popular kinds of birthday cakes; the largest she has baked; the most unusual; decorations. Her own favorite recipes and suggestions for better cake baking. Slant: Cake as the birthday symbol, be it the seventh or the seventieth.

Human Rights Day. The adoption of the Universal Declaration of Human Rights on December 10, 1948, and the official observance of the day by the United Nations. International crises over human rights issues; involvement of famous writers. Recent human rights campaigns and the results. Countries named by United States senators and congressmen from your state as most flagrant violators.

11

The variety of cosmetics offered in local drug stores. The face as a focal point for the cosmetic industry, with cleansing and softening cream, lotions, powder, lipstick, rouges, mascaras and myriad other products. The latest on the market. A cosmetic authority's advice about effective use of facial aids.

The role of radioactive substances in cancer treatment. The average number of local patients who are irradiated in a week. The cancer experts who administer the treatments and their discussion of the effectiveness. Spinoff: The industrial uses of radioactive substances.

Activities of the Better Business Bureau. Any increase in calls about consumer problems in your city at this time of year? Investigating claims of false advertising, deceptive selling methods, inferior merchandise. Traps shoppers should avoid.

Magnets that can move "mountains" of material or save a life in your area. The use of electromagnets in industry in handling heavy objects. How salvage companies capitalize upon these devices to move metal—a far cry from the horseshoe magnets of childhood. Physicians' and surgeons' use of magnets in removing objects that have been swallowed. Special magnets utilized in television sets. The most expensive magnets.

12

The chief artist of a large advertising agency in your state. How he or she possesses the talent to put selling punch into drawings. The artist's favorite kinds of assignments. Use of children and animals in illustrations. Is the artist also a photographer? Has any of the work been exhibited?

Do tall women have more fun than short ones? Confessions of local members of the younger generation—from blondes to brunettes to redheads. Making the most of tallness and shortness. Spinoff: Tall and short athletes.

How the post office handles the Christmas rush. The processes the mail follows after it is deposited. Sorting for local and rural routes; parcel post packages and their delivery. Longest routes in the city; extra carriers. Record amounts of mail during past Christmas seasons. Various kinds of special or rush delivery; extra measures the post office takes to see that last-minute Christmas packages are delivered in time. How much attention do patrons pay to the numerous signs, notices, and warnings about mailing early and wrapping securely?

The records bureau chief at the local police station. Principal duties of the head and his assistants; busiest days, as on the weekend. The most common violations, as parking and speeding tickets and plain drunkenness.

13

Repairing of railroad cars in your state. The foremost repairs; the most difficult "doctoring" required; life span of a car. Dean of workers at the shop. Slant: Constant checking of railway cars and engines to prevent train wrecks. Cost of new railroad cars.

How to turn fears into confident living. The formula recommended by a psychologist of your section who speaks from his experiences with patients. The steps in converting negative emotions to positive ones. Dr. Norman Vincent Peale's famous philosophy of positive thinking; Dr. George W. Crane's Compliment Club in which a person bestows three compliments a day.

Favorite recipes of blind cooks in your city. Braille devices on the stove; how the persons get around and cope with the conceivable dangers. Typical meals prepared by the sightless cooks. Does smell play a part in the cooking? Speaking of smells, what are the sweetest smells to blind citizens locally?

Christmas on Main Street. A company that specializes in providing or selling yuletide decorations for cities. Kinds of decorations that lead in popularity; designing the biggest and the tallest decorations. The largest cities serviced by the firm; the fees. Spinoff: A company that makes animal figures and cartoon characters for use in Thanksgiving and Christmas parades.

14

The art of "dressing" store windows. Tricks of the trade from local window designers. Best ways to attract attention; special gimmicks, as mechanical devices. Use of colorful signs or banners. Are mannequins used as much as formerly? Planning seasonal displays, as for spring and fall. Rushing the season. Customers who insist upon getting merchandise from the window. How often are window displays changed?

The operator of a teachers' agency in your state. Slant: Keeping up with the educational picture in the United States and also overseas. School and college placements in teaching and administration; filling positions in virtually all sections of the nation. States with the highest salaries; the lowest. Foreign teaching opportunities. The agency's file; average number of applications each month.

Credit cards as the buyers'—and Santa's—best friend. Local stores who issue their own credit cards to customers in good standing in addition to accepting nationally-circulated cards. Abuse of credit cards. Unusual uses for credit cards. Cards with widest circulation.

What to give Wearers of the Cloth? What local members of the clergy—including the female clergy, such as nuns—have received from individuals and congregations in the past several years. The most cherished gifts. Presents for religious leaders from their wives. Homemade remembrances.

15

What can retired citizens do as volunteers? Make a survey in your city, covering the various community service agencies. Slant: How men and women in retirement can contribute to the welfare of the community while enriching their own lives. The continual need for hospital workers and clerical help, as well as unusual areas where retired people can help, such as businessmen who advise new businesses, "weekend grandparents."

The "Newspaper in the Classroom" program under newspaper sponsorship. How teachers are given instructions in how to use the newspaper—even the advertisements—as a teaching device. How different phases of the newspaper are used as educational tools. The director's evaluation of the program and also observations from an official of the state department of education.

The jukebox as a national institution. Its never-diminishing appeal in restaurants, amusement places, dance halls, and of course juke joints in your city. The number of records held by the largest jukebox; keeping the top tunes current. The longest-running hits during the past twelve months. The most common repairs by a jukebox serviceman.

Nature's gifts for December—mistletoe, holly, and of course the poinsettia, to name three favorites. How to make arrangements for the Christmas season, as told by a leading flower arranger. How Joel Roberts Poinsett of South Carolina introduced the poinsettia into the United States. Legends, customs, and superstitions related to Christmas greenery.

16

A public relations firm of your state. The smallest and the largest projects, as explained by a top consultant. The task of selling candidates in political campaigns; entertainment figures who are clients. Cities who employ the firm to supplement the work of the Chamber of Commerce in attracting tourists and industries.

The life of a bathtub salesman. How does one go about selling a bathtub? Features to stress, such as safety and unusual design. Average length of a tub; longest and largest ones. High-priced and luxury tubs. The evolution of tubs, as described by the salesman. Spinoff: Advantages—and cost—of a home whirlpool.

A well-known name analyst of your state. Slant: His or her contention that names affect people's personalities and can spell failure or success for an individual. The analyst's nominations for the best names to give—and the worst. Does he or she approve of nicknames? What about double names? How couples consult him or her about suitable names for their babies.

A long-time sparring partner in your state. The most prominent prizefighters who have engaged him for training; hardest punches he has taken in his career. His own victories in the ring; his selection of all-time greats in the various weight divisions. The fighter's plans for the future, including his ambitions for his children.

17

Leading subjects for calendar art. Have a look at the calendars in your city. The percentage featuring feminine beauty, children rank among the favorite subjects. Animals that win your heart via calendars. Calendar illustrations and photographs to suit a wide range of tastes; the timeless as well as new and different calendar subjects. Illustrators and photographers who devote their skills to calendars.

Are men or women better musicians? Match the dean of men musicians with the dean of women musicians in your city. Ask music teachers which sex learns music fastest. Instruments that men play more than women, and vice versa.

Wright Brothers Day. A "flying farmer" of your section can thank Orville and Wilbur Wright for aviation's impact on his life. How he pilots his own plane and has his crops dusted and sprayed from the air to control weeds and insects. Spinoff: The air-cargo industry in your city: The volume of shipping and the increase during recent months.

The task of directing local shoppers. Slant: A traffic officer needs the attributes of a Solomon and a Samson to carry out his duties on the busiest days. Street corners and intersections with the most activity, during the Christmas season and otherwise. The officers' most persistent problems downtown and at the huge and congested shopping centers. Finding packages—and money.

18

Mottoes of clubs and organizations in your city. The president of each group as your contact. The motto of Civitan International is "Builders of Good Citizenship," Kiwanis International has the motto "We Build," and the International Association of Lions Club says it in five words: "L-iberty, I-ntelligence, O-ur N-ation's Safety.'' Examples of how the local groups live up to their mottoes.

The truth about the teeth of animals, straight from the keeper of the largest zoo in your state. Which animal has the largest molars? The smallest? Kinds of teeth needed by herbivorous and carnivorous species. Bites suffered by the zookeeper—and patrons. You can glorify an animal dentist and dwell on tooth troubles in the animal world.

The oldest circuit court judge in your state in point of service. His education and positions before his judicial appointment. Length of service on the circuit bench and his observations about his career; number of trials at which he has presided. Suggestions for revision of criminal statutes.

The trend in mill villages. How industrial workers of your area have broken away from residence near the mill, which was a convenience once upon a time. Gradual sale of mill houses by the plants; renting of the dwellings. Spinoff: Model towns and villages in your state, elaborately planned to be "ideal."

19

Those precious baby locks! Experiences of long-time barbers of your city in giving first haircuts to children. Saving locks of hair as mementoes. Mothers who break into tears when the locks are shed. Have any cameras gone into action? Calming tots' fears about the clippers.

The first Christmas message from space—in the radio voice of President Dwight D. Eisenhower. The greeting consisted of fifty-eight words, including "America's wish for peace on earth and good will toward men everywhere," and were broadcast by a recording from a United States satellite, *Atlas,* on December 19, 1958.

Do you believe in love at first sight? Take a poll of the seniors at a local or nearby college. Do more women than men answer in the affirmative? Experiences of the students. The opinion of the college's teachers of the education-for-marriage course.

The popularity of state parks in the winter! Slant: How your state's operation of the parks both summer and winter reflects the growing trend of year-round vacations. Fixing the parks' cabins for the roughest winter; preparing piles of logs for the open fireplaces; favorite winter recreation at the parks, as hiking, cross country skiing, and sledding. The special adventure of "roughing it" in the winter.

20

A lawyer of your state who has written a number of legal textbooks. Drawing upon his years of experience in the profession of law as material for his volumes. Has he taught in a law school? How he has contributed articles to legal periodicals? Does he believe in capital punishment as a deterrent to crime? His opinions about the systems of justice in other countries.

A different kind of fish story for a change. This will be from a fisheries biologist with the wildlife and marine resources department of your state. Various experiments he has conducted; leading accomplishments so far. Has he had a hand in developing a strain of fish? His research concentration at present. The hatchery and rearing facilities of the department.

Special interest motion pictures. How movies on specialized subjects are shown by groups and businesses in your city; national companies and organizations supply the films gratis. Local clubs and schools that make extensive use of the films; how to obtain them.

The doorman of a large apartment house or a hotel in your city. How he escorts persons from the curb of the street to the entrance of the building. Making it a point to be as helpful and courteous as possible. Largest tips he has received. Does he wear special attire? His opportunity to observe human nature in all its aspects.

21

Beginning of winter. The oldest coal dealer in your city from standpoint of service. The years that witnessed the height of coal as fuel for home heating. Latter-day interest in coal as fuel. How much coal does the dealer keep on hand at all times? Various types of customers locally; the flood of orders when a severe cold wave strikes. Spinoff: An electric power company of your area as a leading user of coal. The operations at the coal-fired plant, and the amount of coal consumed monthly.

Forefather's Day. Anniversary angle: The Pilgrims landed at Plymouth, Massachusetts, on this day in 1620 and as they disembarked from the *Mayflower* supposedly stepped on Plymouth Rock. Captain John Smith applied the name of Plymouth in honor of Plymouth in England. Plymouth as a tourist center today, and relics in Pilgrim's Hall, like the charter of Plymouth Colony and the sword of Miles Standish.

Winter sports that beckon outdoor devotees of your state. Facts and figures from the management of resorts that go all out with such sports, as skiing, ice skating, sled riding, and artificial slides. How such resorts engage in winter-watching and hope for cold and snow for business. Instructors at the resorts, and rental of equipment. Sports celebrities.

The bloodhounds of a rescue squad in your county. How the dogs have found small children and others who have become lost. The most lengthy searches with the bloodhounds as the heroes. The keeper and trainer of the dogs.

22

Classical music in your city. Is the popularity increasing, judging by the sale of classical records? The reports of record store operators. Classical best-sellers and the stars. Owners of the largest libraries of classical albums. Spinoff: A pianist of your city who is noted for his or her interpretation of classical music. His or her concert career.

The smallest and the largest Santa Clauses in stores in your city. The problem of finding the right size in costumes. Mastering the knack of ho-ho-ing. Preventing some children from becoming over-enthusiastic. Qualities a Santa-hirer looks for in applicants. The pay rate for impersonating this beloved character. What the local Santas would like for Christmas.

The fate of old school buildings. Conversion to their new roles as community centers, dwellings, or stores. Slant: The widespread evidence of the sentimental attachment for the schools. Disposal of the desks, tables, and other equipment. Principals of the institutions down the years.

A local collector of miniature paintings. The oldest paintings in the collection and their worth. Unusual stories behind some of the art work. Paintings on watches and also ivory, as well as in lockets; the painters. Spinoff: Other kinds of miniatures, as figurine sets, porcelain plates, milk glass bowls and vases, dollhouse furniture, peddler's wagons, and old-time parlor sets of furniture.

23

A dress factory in your state. The machinery and the evolution of a dress from a pattern and the cloth. Slant: The precise and unromantic work involved in producing beautiful clothes. Planning styles for the coming year; worst problems of fashion designers.

A day with the local commander of the Salvation Army. Slant: How seven days a week he ministers to the food, shelter, and clothing needs of persons in addition to their religious needs. The attention given children and young people; boys' clubs and homes for girls. Devotional services and street-corner singing; gaining converts. Fund collecting at Christmas. The commander's wife and her devotion to the cause.

The barrel-making industry in your state today. Out of what materials are most barrels made today? Machines used in the manufacture of barrels; daily protection of metal barrels, or drums, and their uses. Demand for wooden barrels; coopers with the longest records of service.

A school of midwifery in your state. Does the state department of health supervise the practice of midwives? The number of midwives in the state; number of births they attended last year. An aged midwife of your section who has delivered an unusually high number of babies.

24

Christmas Eve at a local bakery. Best-sellers of the yuletide season. Is fruitcake the leader? Kinds of cakes available; cookies with holiday design. Baking all night in order to fill orders. Making cakes for birthdays on Christmas Day.

How the city and county officials will spend their Christmas holidays. Trips to visit relatives. Main yuletide attractions for the officials. Fond memories of Christmases of long ago: "Groaning" tables of food, fireworks, and hunting.

Real life reindeer. The importation of reindeer to Alaska. Eskimos and Indians killed so many caribou by 1892 that the United States Office of Education imported 1,280 reindeer to Alaska. How the Alaskans value the descendants of those reindeer because of their numerous uses as food, draught animals, and sources of hide for clothing. Reindeer's association with Santa Claus, including the song "Rudolph, the Red-Nosed Reindeer." Spinoff: A zookeeper of your section who will share his fund of reindeer knowledge.

The couple of your section who have adopted the most children from foreign countries. The procedure; requirements for adoption. Are any of the children war orphans? How the kids have adapted themselves to life in the States, and their excitement on Christmas Eve. Spinoff: How families of your city contribute to the support of needy children overseas in an adoption program. How prospective adopters are contacted.

25

Christmas at the largest trailer village in your county. The most unique yule decorations; unusual aspects of the Christmas celebration in this closely knit community.

Observance of Christmas in different countries. An armchair tour via interviews with local residents who emigrated to the United States or foreign students in colleges in your section. How Americans have borrowed yuletide customs from various countries—the Christmas tree from Germany, evergreens and mistletoe from northern Europe, the burning of yule log from the Balkans and elsewhere, and the distribution of gifts, from a practice dating back to the ancient Romans. How colonists continued the Christmas customs of their native lands. Spinoff: Christmas activities in the Holy Land.

The most elaborate Christmas decorations of churches. Are some of the decorations homemade, maybe by youngsters? The manger scene as a traditional highlight. Children who go caroling, especially for shut-ins. Features of the Christmas services.

Favorite Christmas poems of the poet laureate of your state.

Yuletide verses he or she includes in public readings. Christmas poetry he or she has written; the inspiration. Were most Christmas poems "born" during that season? Most memorable Christmases of the poet laureate.

26

The state director of vocational rehabilitation. Has he or she overcome a handicap? Members of the staff, and their combined years of experience. Number of handicapped persons who have been prepared for employment and placed in jobs during the past twelve months. Types of work that have the largest number of handicapped men and women. Rehabilitating releases from the state hospital and also prisons.

The knitting needle at a retirement home. The agility of the knitters' fingers and the average output per month. Knitting ribbon dresses and other attire. Knitted presents for friends and relatives. Learning to knit in advanced age.

Bringing the theater to the people. The operator of touring professional theater company appearing in your state. The productions and the number of players. Average number of shows for colleges and other audiences per week; meeting deadlines in travel. Transporting scenery and keeping the performers' voices in trim.

An instructor for a sewing machine company in your city. Slant: The satisfaction of the expert in passing her or his skill on to countless others. Average time it takes to teach a person to sew; main faults of beginners. Mothers and daughters who receive instructions at the same time.

27

The great American custom—stores' super sales, as those after Christmas. Christmas-related items, as decorations and cards, going, going, gone at bargain prices. What local store managers have found to be the sales with the greatest pulling power. January sales, Washington's Birthday sales, Fourth of July sales, and Thanksgiving sales as banner ones. Marking down goods near the end of the season; going out of business or liquidation sales.

The operator of a bus service for rural areas in your county. Number of trips per day; meeting places. Connecting small and outlying towns, especially with the county seat. The height of patronage; workers who commute. Safety records of the drivers. Main problems in rural bus service.

The perennial appeal of fireplaces. The latest in fireplaces, in design and energy-saving, according to the operator of a fireplace business in your city. The Franklin-style fireplace; wall-hung fireplaces with electric heater logs; free-standing units.

Vice President John C. Calhoun and President Andrew Jackson as bitter enemies. How "The Great Nullifier" from South Carolina clashed with Old Hickory over the protective tariff of 1828 and became the first vice president to resign, which he did on this day in 1832. His service in the United States Senate afterwards and his battle against the chief executive's policies.

28

A veteran maker of turtle stew in your county. Slant: His acclaim as the champion turtle hunter and stew cook. How the demand for his services keeps him on the go; his recipe for turtle stew. The best turtle "hunting grounds" in the county. The latter-day scarcity of turtle as the softshell and green are overhunted.

A frozen-food locker plant in your city. Slant: How farmers, city residents, and sportsmen benefit from the availability of storage space. Sale of bulk meat to the public. Capacity of the plant.

Skilled trades taught in your state's school for delinquent girls. Courses that are creating the most interest among the inmates; the teachers and their methods of instruction. How learning aids girls in the rehabilitation program.

The Woodrow Wilson Memorial Museum in Columbia, South Carolina. Tribute to the twenty-eighth president of this anniversary of his birth in 1956. How the twenty-eighth president who received the Nobel Peace Prize in 1919, spent part of his youth in the house built by his parents. That dwelling as a popular shrine.

29

A woman who occupies a forest watchout tower in your section. Keeping constant watch for any signs of fire; the radius covered by the "eagle eye" of the observer. What happens when she spreads an alarm. The fire-fighting equipment. The height of the tower; coping with loneliness.

Here comes the efficiency engineer. Industrial plants in your area employ this specialist to study and modify methods of operation to achieve more efficiency from the equipment and workers. Positioning machines to aid worker's production; Taking advantage of automation. Elimination of waste.

The critics' choice. How many movies, plays, books, and records do the critics of your city pass judgment on in a single month? Factors in making evaluations for the benefit of the public. The critics' recommendations of the best of motion pictures, drama, literature, and music at this time.

The decline of the revolving door. Do any remain locally or in neighboring cities? Early ones in your city, as recalled by an elderly citizen. The door's invention in the United States around 1880 and the advantages. Spinoff: The most ornate and striking doors of mansions, churches, and other places in your city.

30

Programs for young people emphasized by the Catholic Daughters in the Americas, in existence since 1903. Leaders of the programs in your state, and the number of members. Community service by CDA, among the largest Catholic women's groups in the world.

The driver of the local airport bus that transports passengers from the airport. Average number of persons carried daily; meeting celebrities; the matter of luggage. How the bus driver enlightens the new arrivals about your city and the attractions; recommending lodging places and restaurants. How his courtesy and friendliness have given him close ties with travelers. Going the so-called extra mile for patrons.

Question of qualifications for coroners in your state. Do citizens believe a coroner should have medical training? The role of a coroner at an inquest. The practice of electing handicapped persons as coroners over the years. Is this changing now?

The milkman—not from house to house but from store to store. How he is not a dairy operator himself but delivers the milk for a large dairy of your city and puts them on the stores' shelves. Number of establishments served in a day; sanitary regulations and freshness dating.

31

The ten top stories of the year locally in the judgment of city officials. Political events as newsmakers. Forecasts about the local political scene in the coming year. Subjects that aroused the most controversy.

A veteran orchestra leader who regularly plays at New Year's Eve parties. Songs that are a must at such gatherings. How elderly couples, as well as younger ones, join in the festivities. What the orchestra leader considers the greatest songs of the year. Spinoff: "Auld Lang Syne," the traditional song of New Year's Eve, as probably the best-known lyric by Robert Burns. How Burns declared that he took the words "from an old man's singing."

A truck weighing station maintained by the highway department, in your locality. Weight limits. The point of danger. Do most trucks meet requirements? Out of the ordinary cargoes; discovering mechanical deficiencies. Number of weighing stations over the state. Determining how much weight an ordinary bridge will stand.

The plastic world of tomorrow. Crystal-ball gazing by a plastics chemist who serves a plastic manufacturing company of your state. How his profession has spawned miracles in industry; from toys and household necessities to textiles and aircraft. Envisioning the future as a result of plastic innovations. Does the chemist predict plastic or semi-plastic homes and light-weight plastic cars?

Index

Acrobats, 59

Adoption: of foreign children, 246; overseas support programs, 246

Advertising: agency, artist in, 237; on billboards, Billboard Spoilers, 98; false, 237; pulling power of classified, 175; on walls, 121; What's in a brand name?, 94

Africa: David Livingston and Morton Stanley, 123; emergence, 123

Agriculture: firsts, 57; harvesting machine improvements, 132; machinery, 101; major grain elevators, 132; new crop of farming graduates, 78; research, 57; soil testing, 70

Air: cargo industry, 241; heroes of WW II, 132; show star, 20

Aircraft: crop dusting, 150, 241; balloons, 188; flying at the turn of the century, 127; helicopter use in spraying insecticide, 189; homebuilt, 26; illness on, 91; National Aviation Day, 158; pilots, female, 67; pilots, farmers, 241; for rent, 55; traffic officer in sky, 57; use on ranches, 140; Wright brothers, 158; Wright Brothers Day, 241; zeppelin, 127

Airline, manager of, 34

Airport: air traffic controllers, 162; baggagemen, 26; boom in private, 140; bus driver goes the extra mile, 249; groundskeeper at, 120; as jetport, 158; ramp servicemen, 199; secretary to manager of, 87

Alcoholism: Allied Youth, Inc., 135; hospital for, 53

Ambulance: of local fire department, 75; of rescue squad, 12

American Chemical Society, 141

American Red Cross, anniversary, 98

Amish: craft and food-selling enterprises, 162; farming, as part of religious beliefs, 162

Amundsen, Roald, flying explorer, 93

Amusement, business side of arcades, 149

Amusement parks, since Disney, 233

Amusement Rides, safety of, 101

Anesthetist, champ, 90

Animals. See also specific species: with best memory, 214; breeding of dwarf, 30; busy beavers, 129; cost of, in zoo, 71; deer preservation, 90; and exterminators, 135; first aid to, 198; fur, 143; game preserves, 90; going to market, 117; as grass mowers, 160; most stubborn, 83; mule dealer in space age, 136; photographic portraits of, 107; raising ducks, 74; raising peacocks, 109; raising rabbits, 59; sale of, 157; snails, the world of, 191; SPCA, 13; speed of, 52; ten leading myths, 160; trapper of, 213; truth about teeth of, 242

Antique: automobiles, 10; clock restoration, 188; early American, 136; hearses, 194; household items, 194; the older the higher priced?, 136; pianos, 99; pocket watches, 188; snuffbox, popularity and use of, 173; spinning wheel, 180; thefts, 86; weather vane, 131

April Fool's Day, 66

Aquarium, maintaining public, 162
Arbor Day, 79
Archery: showman, 178; women archers and marksmen, 100
Architecture: barrier free, 184; of city, Washington D.C., 196; decline of revolving door in, 249; homes of the future, 162; landscape, 175; latest city hall, 170; the perfect house, 133; Spanish dwellings in St. Augustine, Florida, 164; striking city doors, 249; unusual local staircases, 215
Arson, in your community, 88
Art: for calendar, 241; exhibit judge, 16; of giving titles, 155; largest private collection in state, 162; miniature painting collection, 245; natural materials used in, 221; outdoor murals, 123; portraits of state founder, 140; restoration of paintings, 126; sculpture of heads, 46; stimulated by state commissioner, 96; on wheels, 49
Artificial eyes, art and production of, 120
Artificial insemination: births by, 99; extent among state's population, 99
Artificial kidney, use of, 127
Artisans and craftsmen: caner, 102; gift shop for, 102; indian pottery of, 115; jewelry designer and maker, 210; local, 90; organ builder, 171; violin maker, 91
Artist: in advertising agency, 237; animal illustrator, 235; battlefield scenes by, 134; bird painter, 58; chalkboard, 103; collage, 27; largest colony in state of, 25; opinions on sunset and sunrise by, 150; papier-mache, 89; silhouette, 88
Astronomy: amateur, 20; research at local planetarium, 164
Athletes. *See also* Sports; and specific sport; baseball stars, 19; biorhythm of, 191; on church teams, 118; college, pranks of, 66; Fellowship of Christian, 180; highest paid pro in state, 199; junior golf champ, 24; in prison, 11; raise money for worthy causes, 143; summer jobs of, 110; tall

vs. short, 238
Atomic Bomb Day, 135
Atomic Energy Commission, 150
Attorney: dean of city attorneys, 7; dean of city solicitors, 164; female, 4; patent, 15, 159; as textbook author, 243
Auction: school for, 63; Sheriff Sales, in county, 128
Stephen F. Austin, Father of Texas, 212
Automobile: with adaptations for handicapped, 222; antique, 10, 118; bumper stickers, 185; daredevil drivers, 40; first salesman of, 118; hearses and limousines, 194; license plate manufacturing, 219; license plate messages, 185; makes that bit the dust, 227; Motor Vehicle Bureau, 93; opening locked cars, 50; state motor club, 135; trouble at drive-ins, 28; wash of your choice, 189; wild and wooly driving tests, 93
Automobile dealers: auction, 13; recollections of, 227
Automobile racing: driver builds own car, 3; midget car racing, 16; stock car track operator, 83
Automobile repair: high school course in, 25; highway patrol car mechanics, 8

Baby: abandoned, 152; adoption of, 92, 246; leap year, 41; locks of, 242; new year, 2
Babysitting: finding in neighborhood, 147; hotel service, 147
Badminton, college, 9
Baggagemen, 26
Bakery: Christmas Eve at local, 245; Pretzel, 120
Balloons: friendship via, 59; hot air, 188; manufacture and peddling of, 92
Band director: at girls' college, 12; as good or bad matrimonial merchandise, 180
Bands: in Christmas parades, 232; of fraternal or service organization, 108
Banks: armored car service, 49; bad checks, 192; blood, 190; Christmas Club at, 233; demand for safety

deposit boxes at, 176; mattresses and jars as, 8

Barber: bald, 217; college operator, 129; female, 79; first haircut, 242

Barbershop quartet, 217

Barnaard, Christian, M.D., heart transplants, 232

Barns: converted to homes, 87; unusual, 87

Barrelmaking, 245

Barry Day, 176

Baseball: batter up, college, 44; fan not missed Series in 20 years, 164; Hall of Fame, 123; minor league farm teams, 61; president of league, winter, 18; stars, 19

Basketball, girls, 13

Beauty: beauty parlor comes to hospital, 28; cosmeticians advice on, 237; do tall women have more fun, 238; drugstore cosmetics, 237; everyone loves a mirror, 198; first haircut, 242; hair for a price, 202

Beer and ale making, at home, 90

Bees: husking, 152; as villains, 57

Beginning the day's work, 146

Better Business Bureau, activities of, 237

Bible: children's favorite biblical characters, 29; Clement Clarke Moore, as scholar of, 134; as family record, 225; minister's collection of, 16; discussed by religious leaders, 205

Bicycling, families, 121

Billiard, champion, 28

Bills: collection, excuses, excuses, excuses, 222; preparing monthly statements, 151

Bird: attempt to make turkey official U.S., 222; feeder, 217; for sale, 148; painter of, 58; speed of, 52; trainer, 15; welcoming spring, 47

Black Poetry Day, 199

Black Press Day, 54

Blind: champion reader, 4; color-, 212; cooking by, 238; new sights, 2; talking book program for, 4; weddings of, 231; White Cane Safety Day, 198

Blood: commercial bank, 190; donor clubs, 190; firemen and police as donors, 101; transfusions for dogs, 172

Boats. See also Ships; factory, 52; houseboats, large and luxurious, 180; racing, full speed ahead, 198; sailboats. (see sailboat)

Books: dictionary as best seller, 198; dream, 184; famous first novels, 190; Gone with the Wind, 215; Horatio Alger, 224; rare book dealers, 7; state residents as characters in, 221; textbook depository, 163; textbook, legal, 243; textbook market, changing styles in, 183; used book stores, 27; Uncle Remus: His Songs and His Sayings, 236

Bosses, 232

Bottles, bottles, bottles: recycling, 158; in soft drink plant, 158

Bowling: instructor, 232; youth, 141

Bricklaying, 96

Bridge: champion players, 172; favorite menus, 173

Bridges: Brooklyn Bridge, 100; covered, 35; drawbridge, 205; evolution of bridge construction, 100; safety and strength in, 100; tollbridge, 205

Buffalo: meat, 220; ranches, 220

Buildings: tallest building in state, 51; want to buy a church, 79; what's new for old school, 244

Burbank, Luther, Day, 48

Bureau of Vital Statistics, 101

Bus: airport drivers, 249; baggagemen, 26; busman's holiday, 127; illness on, 91; information at bus terminal, 130; mechanics at company, 60; old, 36; rural service, 247; school, articles forgotten on, 90; traffic manager of company, 76

Business: boxmaking is his business, 137; community cannery, 140; complaints of complaint department, 61; decoration specialty shop, for cities, 239; diaper service, 94; downtown malls, 214; give-away candies as business booster, 98; franchises, 200; if at first you don't succeed, 97; ladder factory, 217; laminating, 203;

livewire, electrical contractor, 112; parade animal and cartoon character producer, 239; parties with a sales pitch, 130; playground equipment, 6; storage company, 153; success secrets on cassettes, 77; suggestion box, 92; United States-Japanese, 234; welcoming newcomers, 140
Business cards: bilingual, 108; take a card, 108

Calculators, of all descriptions, 189
Calendar: reform, 60
Camera, repairman, 148
Camping: and campers, 98; popularity of campsites, 98; and religious services, 103
Carilloneur, 18
Catt, Carrie Chapman, suffragette, 7
Canals: building today, 213; Erie, formal opening of, 212
Candy: cotton candy and candy apples, 190; given to children by business, 98; a look at what people like, 69
Card: personalized holiday greetings, 231; shop, 198
Cartoons: cartooning to fame and fortune, 149; religion on the drawing board, 79
Cash registers: ornate classics to electronic scanners, 98; repairman, 98
Cassettes, success secrets on, 77
Cats, 190
Celebration, See also Festival; centennial, 156; 89ers, 220; ethnic, 202; Touch of Scotland, 202
Cemetery: epitaphs in oldest, 80; gravedigger, 131; upkeep of lots, 14, 159
Chain letter craze, 151
Chainstores: magnate, 94; what's the best location, 152
Champagne: french process vs. domestic, 174; popping the cork, 174
Chaplains. See also clergy; at hotels and motels, 56; of legislature, 27; at state penitentiary, 138
Charity: activities of organizations, 236; drives, 143; for fire department, 155;

haven for homeless and vagrant, 179; organizations at Christmas, 236; religious telethons, 173; sharing crops with needy, 175
Chef: barbecue master, 161; broadcasting culinary expert, 67; at country club, 201; favorite salads of, 182; turtle stew cook, 248
Chemist: with national reputation, 141; paint, 231; vs. criminal, 19
Cherokee Strip Day, 177
Chewing gum, 175
Children. See also Babies; Youth; affect of fairytales on, 123; boys choir, 138; edibles given to, 98; of former beauty queens, 80; education of mountain, 192; handicapped, 113; high fashion boutique for, 180; Junior Red Cross activities, 98; juvenile air bureau and delinquency, 114; museum, 177; in orphanages, 100, 119; pediatric unit playroom, 95; of professional wrestlers, 12; runaways, 33; section of library, 36; storyteller for, 128; student safety, 170
Chimney sweeps, ups and downs of, 11
Christmas: charitable organizations at, 236; Clement Clarke Moore, 134; credit cards at, 239; decorations in church, 246; eve at local bakery, 245; favorite poems of poet laureate, 246; first message from space, 242; holly decorations, for, 233; how government officials spend, 245; largest and smallest Santa Clauses, 244; on Main Street, 239; memories of past, 246; observance in foreign countries, 246; parade float, 235; parades, 232; post office handles rush at, 238; reindeer, 246; services in church, 246; at trailer village, 246; unique decorations, 246; unusual celebrations on, 246
Churches. See also Religion; athletic teams, 118; bells and chimes, 196; Christmas decorations, 246; Christmas services, 246; fate of old, 79; largest nurseries, 81; libraries, 12; literature, 78; perfect attendance, 89; oldest building, 99; oldest sun-

day school class, 51; photography in,
3; provisions for handicapped, 112;
scheduling weddings in, 191; steeples, 62; supply salesman, 111;
theatre group, 36
Churchill, Winston, as phrasemaker, 46
Circus: a day with the circus ringmaster,
169; mini, 197
Citizenship Day, 178
City: annexation to, 161; auditorium
manager, 140; codes vs. state codes,
200; downtown mall, 214; fast-grow-
ing, 201; first lady of, travels and activities, 78; founders and their descendants, 62; history of city hall, 14;
honorary citizens of, 201; with Indian name, 53; key to, 201; key troubles in, 172; latest city hall architecture, 170; names, 194; newcomers
reaction to, 140; newcomers welcome
to, 140; parks, 109, 158; printing,
139; producing the city directory,
114; reference library, 71; river, 224;
school carpenter shop, 204; seal, 39;
served as state capital, 213; wedding
customs in, 117; what's average in,
71; zoning board, 232
Civil War: Fort Sumter, 73; organizations, 69; as used by Margaret
Mitchell, 215; War is Hell, 236
Clergy: campsite and resort services by,
103; collects Bibles, 16; female, 115;
gifts to, 239; mail to, 8; with most
baptisms, 142; opinions on proper
age to marry, 70; with part-time occupations, 175; raises and rides
horses, 218; at school for deaf, 33;
serving in retirement homes, 194;
wedding in home, 53; wife of evangelist, 74
Climatologist, as walking weather
bureau, 9
Clothing. See also Costumes; Fashion;
belts or suspenders, 227; donations
of, 74; children, fashion boutiques,
180; furs, 143; hat lady, 110; inside
dress factory, 245; manufacturing
center of state, 122; professional
home economist plans family
clothing, 234; rental uniforms, 82;

sportswear and swimsuit manufacturing, 176; spring fashions, 56;
trials and tribulations of men's suit
salesman, 163; unique aprons, 219;
upswing in down popularity, 212;
what are hats made of, 40; zippers
and other fastenings, 204
Clowns: and animals, 38; dunking, 181;
silence and the chase are golden, 223
Clubs: fan, 231; flying, 226; garden, 120;
gun, 117; hiking, 83; Home Demonstration Council, 132; largest state
writers, 16; liars, 88; mottoes of, 241;
neighborhood, 219; Parents without
Partners, 11; qualifications to join
local, 70; saddle, 39; sailboat, 106;
square dance, 236; state motor club,
135; Toastmasters International,
153; woe's of program chairperson
of, 174; women's political, 172;
Women's Press Club, 19; YMCA,
1000-mile swimming club, 113
Coach: coach's wife, mom to team, 55; of
girls basketball team, 13; memories
of, my first job as, 32
Coal: dealer, 243; electric company
powered by, 243
Coin dealer: leading in state, 112; in
nickels, 95
Collections: bark, 112; Bibles by ministers, 16; of coins, 52; of debt, 222;
early phonograph records, 153; first-
day covers of stamps, 173; of Indian
pottery, 115; largest private art, in
state, 162; of medical journals, 19;
miniature   paintings,   245;
miniatures, 245; nature, 112; pocket
knife, 202; shell, 55; of war weapons,
143; of whips, 38
College: athletic programs, 97; average
student, 224; badminton, 9; band
director, 12; baseball, 44; conservatory, 54; debating team, 94;
females at technical, 204; football, as
big business, 172; founder of state
university, 18; graduates of
agricultural, 78; illness strikes students, 177; largest state choir, 91; as
newsmakers, 50; photographers, 68;
pranks of athletes, 66; professor of

meterology at, 25; registrar of, 224; scholarships, private, 116; six worst problems of campus police, 40; term paper, 197; theses for sale, 197; water polo, 49; wrestlers in, 218; writer-in-residence at, 168

College placement bureau, 171

Columbus Day, 195

Comedian, serious side of, 19

Comic Strips, battle of the sexes in, 45

Common cold, battleground of science and superstition, 47

Community: cannery, 140; Christmas at trailer village, 246; Indian villages, 102; mill village trends, 242; model towns and villages, 242; planned, 196; private villages, 91; straddling two states, 75

Confucius: claim to fame, 185; Teacher's Day (Taiwan), 185

Constitution: analysis of handwriting of signers of U.S., 178; state, 75

Construction, tightrope walkers, 231

Consumers and consumerism: consumer-owned rural electric system, 111; consumer watchdog, 123; generic or no-name brands at lower prices, 157; precautions for consumers, in gasoline use, 235

Contests: cat shows, what makes a champ, 190; foods, eating like a hog pays off, 93; horse shows, 142; what are past Miss America candidates doing today, 173

Conventions: bringing them in, 95; singing, 223

Cooperatives: appliance and household goods, 104; crafts, co-ops and communes, 90; more food for your money, 104

Costumes: for centennial, 156; country music costume maker, 99; rental agency, 207; for square dance, 236

County: named for war heroes, 214; with the smallest seat, 234

County agent: bulletins from, 24; as photographer, 51

County deed registrar, 58

County fair: carnival time, cotton candy and candy apples, 190; highlight of fall for farmer and family, 168

County farm, 177

Coupon clippers, 25

Court: clerk, Supreme Court, 127; librarian, 127; reporter, 127; stenographer, 17

Courthouse: custodian of county, 13; oldest in state, 31

Crafts, co-ops and communes, 90

Crime: antique thefts, 86; bad checks, 192; chain letter game, 151; old rackets, 55; pyramiding and other swindles, 151; shoplifters will be prosecuted, 211; reenactment of slayings, 132

Crime lab: combatting criminals with portable equipment, 37; the chemist vs. the criminal, 19; the ink detectors, 218; soil that spells doom for criminals, 218

Criminal, ballads about infamous, 170

Crop: demand abroad, 168; dusting, 150, 189; predictions, 110; sharing with needy, 175

Custer, General George A., the man vs. the movies, 120

Dairy Association: contrast between old and new, 102; milk and ice cream consumption promotion, 102; predictions, 102

Dams: busy beavers, 129; highest in state, 164; prevention of disasters, 49

Dance: acrobatic, 59; ballet teacher, 29; belly-dancing teacher, 110; clogging team, 47; fifty years ago, 69; local dancer makes name on stage, 10; longest career of teacher, 19; square dance, 236; as therapy, 123

Dare, Virginia, what happened to, 157

DAR, historian of, 62

D-Day recollections, 109

Deaf: church provisions for, 112; clergyman at school for, 33

Debating team, what makes a winner, 94

Debt collection, excuses, excuses, excuses, 222

Dentistry: advances in technology, 17; headaches of local dentists, 174; making tooth care fun, 160; plate mishaps, 138; truth about animal teeth, 242; winning ways of local pedodontist, 160

Desserts: birthday cakes, 237; record-holding cake baker, 236; top five, 76

Devil, what does he look like, 28

Dial-a-prayer, 35

Dialects, research, 88

Diapers, keeping diapers off the line, 94

Diaries: as a dying art, 139; prized by the state historical society, 139

Diary of Anne Frank, 113

Dirt: eaters, 11; is not dirt cheap, 102

Diseases: arthritis and rheumatism, 196; Arthritis Foundation, 197; cancer, 237; common cold, 47; gout, no longer for kings, 197; heart, 200; occupational, 51; venereal, rates in county, 204

Disposal: of chemical wastes, 74; of county garbage, 164; of sewage, 132

Diving: commercial, mission dangerous, 171; for sport, 171

Dogs: blood transfusions for, 172; bloodhounds of the rescue squad, 244; bravest breed, 116; kennels known for hunting dogs, 194; military, 227; police and customs dog detectives, 227; that saved lives, 116

Dolls, rag, 74

Dream study, 13

Drug Abuse, youth group combatting, 135

Dry cleaners: button-sewing expertise at, 116; items left behind at, 116

Duels, earliest on record in state, 122

Earhart, Amelia, as writer, 98

Earthquake: present-day engineering for protection against, 77; the San Francisco holocaust, and other famous, 77; in state, 227

Easter: egg trees, 59; rabbit raising, 59

Education: with closed-circuit television, 136; library films for, 95; for marriage, 242; for midwives, 245; of mountain children, 192; movie making in school, 63; newspaper in classroom, 240; nursing schools, local, 134; parent-teacher association, 234; radio, 117; reform in, 88; school for auctioneers, 63; school days for law enforcement personnel, 60; schools for mentally retarded, 143; science projects in, 211; sex in school, 38; substitute teachers, 211; theological school, 233

Employment. See also Occupations; and specific listings; for hire, typist, editors, etc., 155; jobs for shut-ins, 102; longest strike in state history, 218; original way to apply for job, 139; self-employment, 220; state employment statistics, 155; state labor commissioner's duties, 179; vocational rehabilitation, 247

Energy: coal, 243; consumer-owned rural electric system, 111; windmill, as energy source, 97

Entertainers: comedian, the serious side of a comedian, 19; of the 4-H club, 76; high wire walker, 137; impersonator, state amateur or professional, 136; local dancer makes name, 10; pantomimist, 150; portraying famous personalities on stage, 174; understudies in theater, 78

Entertainment. See also Dance; Theater; Circus; capital of state, 6; city auditorium managers, as bookers for, 140; critics choice, 249; how about a pass, 153; library films as, 95; parties with a salespitch, 130; pioneer amusements, 220; puppetry, 57; public relations in, 240; what price, 214

Environment: anti-litter officer, 174; beautification of, 73; conservationist and humane society attack trapping, 213; energy conservation progress, 235; and insecticide use, 189; insulation talk, 235; recycling bottles, 158; war on noise pollution, 185; World Environment Day, 109

Ethnic celebrations, 202

Excavations: Indian mounds and relics, 102; what construction works uncovered in your town, 136

Explosives: bomb squad, 46; down on the farm, 48; fireworks, 131

Exterminators, SOS calls about insects and animals, 135

Fairytales: implications of, by child psy-

chologist, 123; universal appeal of, 123
Faith healer, 63
Family tree: of state historian, 28; tracing, by local geneologist, 173
Farm: county farm for prisoners, 177; crop dusting on, 150; crop predictions, 110; demand for state crops abroad, 168; egg market economics, 97; explosives down on, 48; firewood for urban fire places from, 223; irrigation, 170; latest improvement in harvesting machine, 132; model, 147; news department in radio-television, 181; new inventions for, 199; as part of Amish religious beliefs, 162; pigeon, 232; research on, 57; scarecrow of seventies on, 142; seed growing for nation, 126, 156; windmills, as energy, 97; woodpiles on, 223
Farm Bureau, origin, 56
Farm women's organization, 91
Father: life with father by centenarian, 116; what my father wanted me to be, 156
Fathers Day, 116
Females: in agricultural and industrial sales, 101; as archers, 100; as barber, 79; as cattle rancher, 62; as clergy, 115; as detectives, 114; as embalmer, 157; farm organization of, 91; fastest runner, 80; first physician in county, 154; as forest ranger, 248; largest professional sorority of, 82; as lawyers, 4; as mail order business owner, 143; as marksmen, 100; as mayor, 5; as motorcycle salesperson, 196; as pageant director, 3; as philanthropist, 102; as pilots, 67; as police, 10; as probate judge, 10; prisoners, as escape artists, 79; as pro wrestlers, 159; suffragette, 7; at technical college, 204; trades taught to delinquent, 248; trapshooter champ, 100
Fence: builder, 31; stone, 225
Fertilizer: factory, 37; manure boom, 192
Field, Cyrus W., linking Europe with America by telegraph, 142

Filibusters, 52
Fire Department: ambulances of, 75; arson in your community, 88; blood donors in, 101; cuisine, 183; Fire Prevention Week, 193; fund raising projects, 155; hoaxes perpetrated on, 67; musicians in, 18; and Salvation Army, 216; secretary to, 87; volunteer, 52, 193
Fire hydrants, 134
Fireplaces: perennial appeal of, 248; wood for, 223; wood stoves as, 159
Fire Prevention Week, 193
Firsts: babies of new years, past, 2; born in America, 157; famous first, 221; and favorite movies of town luminaries, 140; medical school in state, 88; men in county to die in wars, 70; newspaper in state, 156; presidential election, 6; presidential inauguration, 84; settlement, St. Augustine, 164; state, World War II heroes, 132; steam locomotive, 11
Fishing, 56; pay pond, 153; tagged, 71
Fish stories of a biologist, 243
Flag, daily raising of, 231
Flag Day in Samoa, 76
Flag Day in U.S., 114
Florist: deliveryman, 197; greenhouse of, 212; interview with wholesale, 26
Flowers: bulbs, 82; conservatory of local college, 54; at funerals, 235; garden club president names favorites, 120; male wild flower collector, 130; manufacture of artificial, 19; mixing business and flowers, 157; patenting of, 189; and plants at hospital, 44; of state, 179; in state parks, 62; vendor, curb market, 138; where do all the flowers go, 197
Folklore: animal roles in, 107; casting spells against warts, 186; herb doctor, 225; Indian legends never die, 184; and medical cures, 142; and musical composers, 134
Foods. See also Chefs; Food preparation; Restaurants; broker, 34; Buffalo meat, 220; candy, 69; dairy promotion of, 102; and drink for longevity, 181; fast foods, 195; five most nutritious fruits produced in

state, 137; gourds, champion, 159; government inspection of meat, 40; government testing of, 176; grapes, king, 118; ham, expert in, 142; increased use of commercial foods, 213; meals-on-Wheels, 68; mobile catering, food where and when you want it, 45; for New Years, 2; planned by prison dietician, 25; pretzels, 120; rattlesnake meat and other wild, 206; salads, 182; sanitation inspection of, 222; state dish, 17; strawberries, 106; sunflower seeds, 156; top five desserts, 76; transportation of perishables, 9; turtle stew, 248; when eating like a hog pays off, 93

Food packaging: that art of, 157; no-name brands trend, 157

Football: chain gang in, 194; as big business for colleges, 172; television debut, 186

Forest: insecticide use in, 189; in state, 77; timber, 193; of tomorrow, 5

Forest Service: authority describes tree contribution to naval stores, 185; smoke jumper, 108; wildlife's best friend, 200; woman forest ranger, 248

Fort Sumter Day, 73

Founders: city founders and their descendants, 62; portraits of state founders, 140; of state universities, 18

Founders Day, Harvard, 205

Four Freedoms Day, 5

4-H Club, entertainers, 76

Fourth of July: fifty years ago, 128; patriotic commemorations on, 128; Spirit of 1776, 128

Freeloading, 18

Frozen food locker plant, 248

Fruit: developed by Luther Burbank, 48; five most nutritious fruits produced in state, 137; highest fruit-producing county in state, 137

Fruit company operation, 56

Fruit store operator, 161

Fund raising: anything to help a drive, 143; for fire department, 155; telethons, 173

Furniture: bed styles, 194; caning, 102; of the future, 162; woodworking, 116

Furs: controversy over fur use, 143; designing and caring for furs, 143

Future Farmers of America, 147

Gamblers Anonymous, 121

Gambling: laws, 224; odds on beating the habit, 121

Games: checkers and chess masters, 225; champion bridge players, 172; playing by mail, 225; street games, 83; video, 223; wide range of, 223

Gandhi, Mahatma, 189

Gardener: of city, 152; of state capital, 12; top bulb grower, 82

Gardening: best-selling garden sculpture, 67; conservatory of local college, 54; gazebo in, 190; grass seed or sod, 175; rock gardens, 226; topiary, 190

Gavels, historic gavels in use by judges, 51

Gems and Mineral Society president, 77

Ghosts. See also Spiritualism; scientists' opinions of, 24

Giants, tall problems, 138

Girl Scouts, with foreign pen pals, 68

John Glenn Day, 36

Gold Rush: the magic cry of gold, 16; voyage of California, 40

Golden Spike Day, 92

Golf: lost and found golf balls, 39; municipal golf course, 189; youth champ, 24

Goodies, for small children, 98

Government: five ways to improve it, 123; food testing by, 176; longest and shortest session of state legislature, 129

Government officials. See also State; and specific title; attorney general, duties and laws, 139; city electrical inspector, 215; county deed registrar, 58; experiences of Motor Vehicle Bureau official, 93; food sanitation inspector, 222; how spend Christmas, 245; legal aid by governor, 129; meat inspectors, 40; sisters of, 39; state commissioner stimulates culture, 96; state labor commissioner, 179; tax

collector, talking with, 160
Graphologist: analyses U.S. Constitution signatures, 178; deducing traits from handwriting, 178; testimony in court of, 195
Ground Hog Day, 25
Growers. See also Farmers; of gourds, 159; as grape king, 118; of mushrooms, 39; of nuts, 143; as seed growers for nation, 126, 156; of sunflowers, 156; of watermelon, 149
Guinness Book of Records, 69
Guns: collectors of war weapons, 143; gunsmith, 57; largest gun club, 117
Gypsies, lifestyle of, 126

Hall of Fame: baseball stars in, 19; craze, 123; state members of, 47
Halloween, 207
Handicapped: absenteeism among workers, 169; children, swimmers, 113; helping retarded adults, 35; marriage of, 150; modification of cars for driving, 222; phys-ed for, 31; progress in barrier-free architecture, 184; provisions in church for, 112; recreational therapy for psychologically handicapped, 78; school for mentally retarded, 143; stuttering cure, 206; vocational rehabilitation for, 247
Handicrafts: bed spread making, 173; coops and communes, 90; embroidery and needlework, 205; expert hand lace maker, 69; gift shop for, 102; local artisans and craftsmen, 90; male needleworker, 39; spool craftsman, 50; thread market, 205; young people in, 90
Hats: number one hat lady in town, 110; what are hats made of, 40
Hawaii: cost of haven, 112; Kamehameha Day, 112
Hayrides, 179
Health Department: maternal and child care by, 119; prenatal care by, 137; visiting nurse, 76
Hemingway, Ernest, 138
Hermits, 139
Herpetologist, amateur, 78
Highway department: construction bar-

riers, 234; a day with paving crew, 196; information desk, 51; secretary-treasurer of, 81
Highway: beautification of, 73; line painting on, 94; tales of street sweepers, 132; zoos, by side of, 129
Hiking, 83
Hitchhiking, laments, 203
Hitler, Adolph, interest in, 78
Hoaxes, perpetrated on vital services, 67
Hoboes, 84, 179
Home: architecture of the future, 162; to celebrities, 111; converted from barns, 87; Home Demonstration Council, 132; mobile, 94; modular, 95; new uses for glass in, 203; perfect house, architect builds own, 133; poison-proofing your home, 121; whirlpool in, 240
Honeymoon trips, 32
Horse: interview with winning jockey, 184; Kentucky Derby, 96; minister raises and rides, 218; popularity of, 111; racing, 184; saddle club, 39; shows, 142; trainer, 50
Horseshoe pitching, 128
Hospital: admittance office of, 72; switchboard operator at, 38
Hotel: ambitions of bellboys, 165; babysitting service at, 147; chaplains at, 56; doorman, 243; housekeeping at largest hotel, 141; local interior decorator, specializing in, 148; problem with sticky-fingered tourists, 141; reservations, 87; residential, 192
Hot lines, 8
Houseboats, large luxurious, 180
Housemother for college women, 27
House painters, records of, 217
Human Rights Day, 237
Humor, first grade, 176
Hudson, Henry, explorer, 163
Hunting: dogs, 194; for buried treasure, 108; fox hunt customs and etiquette, 202; for historical secrets, 17; most versatile hunter in county, 114; on safari, 61; preserves, as sportsmen's paradise, 153; turtle, 248
Hypnotism, 14

Ice: dry, 178; sculptor, 147
Ice Age, past and future, 121
Ice cream man, 111
Ice skating: juggling while, 17; rink maintenance, 163
Indian: authority on relics of, 74; chiefs and peace treaties, 225; cities with Indian names, 53; craft, 193; legends never die, 184; pottery, 115; romance and marriage of Pochahontas, 69; villages, mounds and relics, 102; welcome to the reservation, 131
Industry: courting, 159; industrial education, with closed-circuit television, 136; industrial machinery saleswoman, 101; industrial psychologist, 81; has mining lost its romance, 203; magnets in, 237; new uses for glass in, 203; power plant lingo, 95; public relations in, 240; rehabilitation office, 169; research in, 92; state association of nurses in, 96; use of radioactive substances in, 237
Insects: bugging the entomologists, 220; and insecticides, 189
Insurance: confidential investigations by, 150; experiences of adjuster, 215; in the sports world, 235; unusual policies, 192
Interpreter, local, 20
Inventions: of Robert Fulton, 157; indifference to, 173; new, in farming, 199; patent laws about, 159; phonograph and record, 153
Inventors: Thomas A. Edison, 153; explain patent laws, 159; Robert Fulton and his inventions, 157; lucky discoveries by, 144; National Inventor's Day, 30; state's most prolific, 215
Investment: counselor, 63; foreign, in state, 169; once a stockbroker always a stockbroker, 164
Irrigation, practiced by leading orchard owner, 170

Jackson, Andrew, 7; vs. Calhoun, 248; dispute over birthplace, 53
Jackson, Stonewall, 14
Jamaica: discovery of, 89; as resort, 89

James, Jesse, 68
Jefferson, Thomas, bookworm, 20
Jewelry designer, 210
Jokes: on apprentices, 20; favorite practical, 66; Irish, 54; pranks of college athletes, 66
Jukebox, as national institution, 240
Juries, duties and authority of Grand Jury, 131
Juvenile aid bureau, and juvenile delinquency, 114

Keller, Helen, as writer, 122
Kentucky Derby, family witnesses race, rain or shine, 96
Key, Francis Scott, 147
Kites, 45

Lacemaker, 69
Landrush, Oklahoma, 177
Landslides, 165
Language: bilingual business cards, 108; body, 206; foreign newspapers, 211; interpreter, 20; power plant lingo, 95; singing in foreign, 233; pros and cons of universal, 208; Yiddish, 136
Largest: church nurseries, 81; college choir in state, 91; gun club, 117; gymnastic team in state, 73; private art collection in state, 162; shoe size, 133; state's Toastmaster International, 153; state writers' club, 16; women's professional sorority, 82
Law: citizen's arrest on the increase, 182; common law marriage, 227; duties of a grand jury, 131; filing bankruptcy, 204; gambling, 224; grounds for annulment, 192; international patent laws, 159; introduction of income tax, 38; legal aid allowed by governor, 129; Legal Aid Society, 220; public defender, 220; quarantine, 46; shoplifters will be prosecuted, 211; state code vs. city code, 200
Leap year, 41
Lectures, on law enforcement, 61
Lee, Robert E., 71
Left-handed blues, 20
Lewis, Sinclair, 8

Liars Club, 88
Liberty Day, 58
Librarian: as etiquette authority, 84; for court, 127
Library: children's section of, 36; children's storyteller in, 128; church, 12; with films for entertainment and education, 95; maps in, 55; municipal reference, 71
Lifesaving: CPR, 34; lifeguard, 141
Lightning, and death and damage, 122
Lincoln, Abraham: Birthday, 30; women in life, 30
Little People of America, Inc., 109
Locks, opening locked cars, 50
Love: are love letters eternal, 138; computerized courtship, 217; at first sight, poll, 242; object: matrimony, 217; and William Shakespeare, 86
Lumber: and science, 83; state trees best for, 16

McCormick, Cyrus, gold mine in reapers, 118
Magna Carta Day, 114
Mailing list: companies that sell, 161; might get you, 161
Mail order: catalog ordering, 28; female owner of business, 143
Mann, Horace, educational reform, 88
Manufacturing: activities of lobbies, 160; of sportswear and swimsuit, 176; state association for, 160
Maps: demand for city and county, 130; in the library, 55
Marble shooting, herald of spring, 48
Maritime Day, 99
Marksmen, feats of trick marksmen, 27
Marquis de Lafayette, hero's name lives on, 171
Marriage: are bandleaders good or bad material for, 180; agencies, 217; bridal consultant, 41; common law, 227; foreign war brides, today, 90, 168; and grounds for annulment, 192; laws, 41; longest in town, 219; of mayor, 32; most popular gifts for, 13; of Pocahontas, 69; proper age for, 70; tapes and films of, 100; wheelchair, 150; in White House, 107
May Day, festivities at school, 86

Mayor: as club joiner, 54; courtship and marriage of, 32; hobbies of, 224; salaries of, 37; woman as, 5
Meals-On-Wheels, 68
Meat inspectors, 40
Mechanics, at bus company, 60
Memorial Day, observances and customs, 104
Memory, improvement methods, 135
Microfilm, taking over record keeping, 92
Military: dogs, 227; recruitment, 181
Millionaires: county of state most inhabited by, 108; what drives them crazy, 3
Milkman, from store-to-store, 249
Missing persons: search via newspapers, 139; search via radio-television, 139; tracing lost relatives, 10
Mississippi River, exploration of, 115
Mitchell, Margaret, using the Civil War, 215
Mobile homes, transportation of, 94
Modeling: agent, 40; male, 180
Modular home, 95
Money: bankruptcy, 204; credit cards, 239; how to give away a fortune, 102; lifespan of a dollar bill, 133; lucky breaks for country's well-to-do, 226; nickels, 95; swindles, 151; that goes up in smoke, 133; worn-out cash, 133
Monkeys, 165
Monuments: battle to save Mt. Vernon, 37; mountain memorials, 59; Washington Monument, 36
Moon Day, 137
Morse, Samuel, partners in developing telegraph, 70
Mother: do's and don'ts for expectant mothers, 82; with largest number of adopted children, 92
Mothers Day, 92
Mountain climbing, 99
Mummies, 126
Murders, reenactment of, 132
Music: classical, in city, 244; costumes for country, 99; drama behind symphony orchestra, 151; five headaches of opera house manager, 28; George Gershwin, 183; and jukeboxes, 240; orchestra leader

chooses favorites, 96; sheet music sale, 67

Musical instruments: church bells and chimes, 196; organ, builder, 171; pianos, antique and player, 99; sale of, at pawnshop, 184; violin making, 91

Musician: are men or women better, 241; barbershop quartets, 217; Boy Scout bugler, 198; boys choir, local, 138; carillonneur, 18; classical pianist, 244; country fiddler, 38; cymbal player, 30; day of organ teacher, 171; evangelistic, 177; largest college choir in state, 91; orchestra leader chooses favorite music, 96; other jobs of, 215; piccolo players and other unusual instrumentalists, 100; in police and fire departments, 18

Mysteries: exploring local mystery creature legends, 160; local speculation about Bigfoot, Abominable Snowman, the Loch Ness, etc., 160

Names: analysis and affect on personality of, 240; bridge, 35; changes in, and reaction to, 176; city, shortest and longest, 194; hero's name lives on, 171; odd cafe diner or nightspot, 172; political nicknames, 97; pro baseball club nicknames, 148; pro baseball players nicknames, 148; of rivers, 100; *royalty* names, in phone book, 110; state nicknames, 177; what's in a brand name, 94

Napoleon's Day, 155

National Guard, activities, 115

Naturalist, 91

National Aviation Day, 158

National Hospital Day, 93

National Inventor's Day, 30

National Magic Day, 207

National Rose Month, 107

Needles: knitting, 247; use of, 185

New Years: first babies, 2; foods, 2; new sights, 2; predictions, 3

New Years Eve, 250

Newspaper: breaking into journalism, 14; in the classroom, 240; clipping service, 50; country correspondent for, 207; days of O Henry, 174; first in state, 156; grandads and grandmas as carriers, 116; Hemingway as newspaper reporter, 138; image of newspaper people in movie vs. real life, 29; as missing person bureaus, 139; morgue, 9; newsgirls, 116; old newspapers are news, 183; pulling power of classified, 175; retired publisher of, 135; technological advances in, 56; work, good or bad for novelists, 138

Newspaper press, installer and repairman of, 86

Nickels, history of, 95

Ninety-Nines, Inc., 67

Nuclear power: advances in industry, 162; armaments today, 135; Atomic Bomb Day, 135; crusades against, 162; Manhattan Project, 135

Numbers: assigning house numbers, 133; what's in a, 156

Nurses: nursing schools, local, 134; queen of shot givers at county health department, 36; state association of nurses in industry, 96, 134; surgical sisters, 122; visiting, 76

Occupational diseases, 51

Occupations. *See* individual occupation

Oceans, 201

Oil, 163

Old West: ballads about infamous outlaws, 170; characters who died with their boots on, 147; legend vs. reality, 147

Olympics, winter, 26

Orchestra leader. *See also* Band director; chooses favorites, 96; conducting rehearsal, 226; synonymous with New Years Eve, 250; youngest, 191

Pacific Ocean Day, 183

Panama Canal, 156

Parents Without Partners, 11

Parking: how profitable are private lots, 99; municipal parking tax to encourage alternate transportation, 99

Parking meter, 131-132

Parole board, state, 162

Parties with a sales pitch, 130

Pascua Florida Day, 67
Pawnshops, pawning wedding and engagement rings, 112
Pattern Department, 34
Peace Officers Memorial Day, 95
Pearl Harbor Day, 234
Peary, Robert E. and Josephine, 89
Penn, William, 119
Pen pals: as tape pals, 89; Girl Scouts with foreign, 68
Perfumes, lure of, 120
Phonographs, early record collection, 153
Photocopying machine, 112
Photographer: college, 68; county agent as, 51; opinions on sunrise and sunset, 150; reminiscences of traveling, 133; school for, 46; secrets of glamour, 236; for senator, 8; television sports, 72; wildflower, 130
Photography: aerial, 45; animal portraits, 107; in churches, 3; George Eastman, camera pioneer, 133; pleasing the customers, 183; postcard, 119; restoration of photographs, 126; specialist, 186; stock photos, 93; tips for better photographs, 30; tips for travelers, 134; what everyone wants to know about, 216; wildlife, 89
Phrenology, reading the human body, 206
Physician: allergies and allergists, 181; clubfoot specialist, 31; the doctors are married, 223; first female in county to be, 154; heart surgeon, 200; local always on call, 169; plastic surgeon, 214; surgical instruction by closed-circuit television, 136
Picnicking, 82
Pigeon: farming, 232; racing, 9
Pioneers: amusements of, 220; dye making, 52; Forefathers Day, 244; Frontier Days, 182; Pilgrims at Plymouth, 244
Pipe smokers, 82
Plastic world, 250
Play, source of plots, 193
Pocahontas, romance and marriage of, 69
Poetry: Black Poetry Day, 199;

Christmas, 246; magazine publisher of, 80
Poe, Edgar Allen, child wife, 13
Poets: city vs. farm, 148; favorite Christmas poems of poet laureate, 246; who are prisoners, 4
Poisoned, 120
Police: attitudes of, 95; auxiliaries, 8; as blood donors, 101; bomb squad, 46; care of equipment, 52; dogs, 227; equipment, 52; hoaxes perpetrated on, 67; ink detectives, 218; lectures, 61; moonlighting of off-duty cops, 146; musicians, 18; Peace Officers Memorial Day, 95; policewoman, 10; portable crime lab of, 37; protection for, 201; records bureau chief, 238; reenactment of murders by, 132; school days for, 60; secretary of department of, 87; six worst problems of campus, 40; traffic, 241; traffic officer in sky, 57
Population, statistics, 214
Postage meter, 33
Postage stamp, 126, 173, 227
Posters, for safety promotion, 54
Postman: good deeds, 77; oldest rural mail carrier, 104; postal inspector, detecting mail fraud, 96
Post office: the box story, 94; county with most, 161; General Delivery, 126; handling Christmas rush, 238; questions, complaints and bouquets for, 117; regional director of, 74; vehicle manager of service at, 3
Poultry: bantam raiser, 199; broilers, 127; developments in hen house, 127; oriental, 199; research, 31
Preservation: deer, 90; game preserves, 90; of old buildings, 4; wildlife refuges, 153
Presidency: Dwight D. Eisenhower in, 197; first election for, 6; first inauguration, 84; Andrew Jackson in, 248; political opponents of, 159, 248; role of first ladies, 107; security measure for, 172; White House marriages, 107, 212; Woodrow Wilson in, 248
Press room: humor in, 151; superintendent of, 151

Pretzels, 120

Printing: city, from tax forms to parking tickets, 139; house production manager of, 211; high school yearbook, 57

Prison: dietician, 25; factory, 222; operating on business basis, 222

Prisoners: as athletes, 11; conjugal rights for, 148; county farm for, 177; as escape artists, 79; as guinea pigs for drug testing, 198; medical treatment of, 197; parole of, 162; as poets, 4

Private detective: female, 114; want a private eye, 74

Prize fighting, sparring partner in, 241

Probation officer, 73

Proofreaders, 81

Prospector, old-time mineral, 168

Psychiatry: and emotional problems after mastectomy, 165; how to turn fears into confidence, 238; kleptomania, 211; village facilities, 158; visiting state mental institute, 201

Psychologist: child, on fairytales, 123; industrial, 81

Publisher: of city magazine, 11; of poetry magazine, 80; retired, newspaper, 135

Public relations: in entertainment, 240; in industry, 240; in selling candidates, 240; in tourism, 240

Puppetry, pulling strings, 57

Puzzles, from crosswords to jigsaw, 204

Quarries, products and recreational facilities of, 87

Racing: boat, 198; car driver, 3; foot up Pike's Peak, 219; horse, 184; marathon, 213; midget car, 16; pigeon, 9; raft, 76; sailboat, 106

Radio: broadcasters association, 176; control engineer at station, 54; culinary expert on, 67; educational 117; farm news department of station, 181; interview with scriptwriter for, 149; manager of christian station, 173; missing person bureau ,of the air, 139; program research department of station, 222; queries to local stations, 87; and selling religion, 173

Raft racing, 76

Rag dolls, 74

Rag laundry operator, 29

Railroad: baggagemen, 26; business office of, 48; car repair, 238; experience of Railway Express agent, 129; flagman on, 109; Golden Spike Day, 92; highest trestle, 218; illness on, 91; model, fad with girls, 117; obsolete, 58; old box cars, 81; snow plows, 12; timetable of, 215

Rainbows, 91

Rainmakers, 146

Rancher: aircraft use by, 140; of buffalo, 220; and cattle branding, 188; day on a cattle ranch with, 117; female, 62; sale day at cattle barn, 157

Rape Prevention Program, 225

Real estate: largest deal in county, 225; prices from pioneer times to present, 89

Recreation, 87

Reindeer, 246

Religion. *See also* Churches; Clergy; Amish craft and food selling enterprises, 162; Amish farming, 162; Bar Mitzvah, Bat Mitzvah, 110; campsite and resort services, 103; Catholic Daughters in the Americas, 249; changing attitudes in, 89; Dial-a-Prayer, 35; faith healer, 63; Fellowship of Christian Athletes, 180; and home for retired, 39; Mennonites, 228; Mormon membership in state, 140; printing house of, 211; revivals, 177; selling, on airwaves, 173; surgical nursing sisters, 122; telethons to raise funds for, 173; theological school, 233

Religious cartoonists, 79

Rentals: of airplanes, 55; of costumes, 207; of uniforms, 82; what you can rent in your city, 189

Research: agricultural, 57; arthritis and rheumatism, 196; astronomical, 164; by commercial seed company, 126; industrial, 92; local, any subject, 141; by radio-television program department, 222; for term paper, 197; using prisoners for, 198

Rescue: ambulance squad, 12; blood hounds to the, 244; bomb squad, 46; life guard, 141; park rangers to the, 171

Resort areas, day with owner promoter, 118

Restaurant: fast food star rises, 195; increased commercial food use, 213; preparation, 113; salad bar, 182; supply house, 213; welcome truck drivers, 35

Restoration, of portraits and photographs, 126

Rhode Island, heritage of, 103

Rivers: and cities, 224; exploration of Mississippi, 115; favorites with travelers, 100; how named in your state, 100

Role of first ladies: city, 78; national, 107

Roller skating, 26

Roofing: easy as falling off, 139; repairs and perils of, 179; trends in, 139

Roses, 107

Runaways, 33

Runners: fastest girl, 80; marathon, 213

Safari, 61

Safes: company built on distrust, 113; demand for bank deposit boxes, 176

Sailboat, building and racing own, 106

St. Augustine, Florida, 164

St. Patrick's Day, 54

Sales: best-selling merchandise door-to-door, 165; business or liquidation, 247; garage and rummage, 225; Great American super, 247; sales day at a cattle barn, 157; of sheet music, 67; sheriff sale, 128; what will people buy, 200

Salespeople: agricultural and industrial machinery, 101; of church supplies, 111; computer, 150; day with organ, 171; first automobile, 118; life of bathtub, 240; tent, in camping boom, 117; motorcycle, 196; samples of, 123; tombstone, 72; trials and tribulation of men's suit, 163

Salvation Army: and firemen, 216; Founder's Day, 72; local commander of, 245

Sandblaster, the life of, 61

Sandman business, 97

San Francisco earthquake, 77

Sauna, 193

Saving money: bargain basement goodies, 154; generic "no-name" brands, 157

Scales, size, type, uses, 103

Scarecrows of the seventies, 142

Scholarships to college, 116

Scissors, cut to fit, 221

Scott, General Winfield, 113

Sculptor: of heads, 46; in scrap metal, 98

Sculpture: of animals, 235; community reaction to modern, 163; garden, 67

Secretary, 87, 133

Senior citizens: bedspread making among, 173; centenarian describes life with father, 116; county with most centenarians, 45; day centers for, 154; on the go, 15; knitting needles at retirement home, 247; medicare and government programs for, 103; privileges for, 103; religious home for, 39; as volunteers, 239

Seward's Day, 62

Shaw, George Bernard, 141

Sheet music, sale of, 67

Shakespeare, William: festival, 112; love and, 80

Shell collector, 55

Ship. See also Boat; battleships named after state, 60; freighters and cruises, 206

Shoes: built-ups, 11; largest size, 133; repair shop, 60

Shoplifters will be prosecuted, 211

Signmakers, 34

Skateboard, daredevils on, 215

Skiing: snow, 30; water, 170

Skydiving, champ, 75

Slingshot wizard, 227

Snuff box: antiques, 173; today, 173

Soapbox cars, homemade, 81

Soil: dirt is not dirt cheap, 102; testing, 70

Songs: Auld Lang Syne, 250; ballads about infamous outlaws, 170; favorites of other nationalities, 82; foreign, 233; official state songs, 141;

replacement for *Star Spangled Banner,* 147; singing telegrams, 226
Souvenir, business, 152
Spanish-American War, *Maine* Memorial Day, 32
SPCA, 13
Speaker: before women's groups, 77; booking, 174; filibuster by, 52; Mr. Toastmaster, 230; what makes a winning debating team, 94; Winston Churchill as, 46
Speech, restoration of, 83
Spelling, hardest words to, 15
Spies, in enemy hands, 181
Spiritualism: faith healer with reputation for cures, 63; fortune tellers, 182; ghosts, 24; psychics, fake or real, 207
Sports. *See also* individual listings; accidents to sports officials, 7; camps, 110; college athletic program funding, 97; Fellowship of Christian Athletes, 180; high school letters, 31; insurance in, 235; nicknames in, 148; television cameraman for, 72; training rules, too rigid or too loose, 130; winter, 244
Staircases, unusual, 215
Stars: early recordings of, 35; hollywood comes to your state, 121; hometown to, 111; idol worship of, 160; interview with president of largest fan club, 231; interviewing, 113; in person, 144
State: battleship named for, 60; code vs. city code, 200; constitution, 75; contributions to Navy, 136; dish, 17; flower, 179; history of, 33, 55; landmarks of and elevations in, 122; nickname for, 177; parole board, 162; real estate board, 144; society in Washington DC, 117; song, 141; tallest building in, 51; tourist bureau, 154; twin states, 158; vacation capital in, 158
State capital: cities served as, 213; damage to buildings in, 4; gardener for, 12; statues and busts at, 163
Statehood Day, 106
State Employment Security Commission, 155

State House, cleaning of, 87
State legislature, 6; chaplains of, 27; longest and shortest session of, 129; pages in, 6; sergeant-at-arms of senate, 15
State Parks: care of flowers and shrubs in, 62; director talks about other state systems, 118; popularity of campsites in, 98
Statues, 163
Steam locomotive, first, 11
Steeplejacks worst scares, 72
Steeples, erection and manufacture, 62
Stockbroker, 164
Stock car track operator, 83
Stores: alteration tailor in, 25; book, 27; breakage of fragile items in, 7; chain store magnate, 94; confidential investigation by, 150; country, 220; department store buyers, 200; engraver, jewelry store, 151; experiences in layaway, 137; fashion buyer in, 16; great American super sale, 247; milkman for, 247; outlet, 154; personal shopper in, 169; seconds at, 228; shoplifters will be prosecuted, 211; toy department in, 73; window dressing at, 239
Strawberry, 106
Street games, 83
Street sweeper, tales of, 132
Student Memorial Day, 88
Summer, 118, 119
Sundial, 216
Superstitions, 44; animal roles in, 207; chain letter game, 151; at Christmas, 240; of farmers, 3; medical, 142; owl in ghost stories, 207
Surfing, 128
Swindles, pyramiding and others, 151
Symphony, drama behind orchestra, 151

Tape: exchange of tapes through mail, 89; voices from the past, 203
Tattoos, unfading interest in, 71
Tax: collector, 160; municipal parking to encourage alternate transportation, 99
Taxidermy, school of, 59
Taxi: drivers experience with animals, 6; passengers as humorist, 231

Teacher's pet, 219

Telegraph: communication sattelites making cables obsolete, 142; Cyrus, W. Field and the Atlantic Cable, 142; Morse' partners, 70; singing telegrams, 226

Telepathy, as hobby, 70

Telephone: action line, 38; first in city, 48; hot line, 8; how cheap—or dear—is talk, 110; male operators, 92; *royalty* in directory, 110; traveling, and other mobile communications, 205

Television: broadcasters association, 176; closed-circuit for industrial and professional instruction, 136; crusades of editorialist, 103; culinary expert on, 67; ETV magazine editor, 117; farm news department of, 181; football debut on, 186; forecast equipment of, 211; interview with scriptwriter, 149; investigative reporters on, 104; as missing person bureau of air, 139; muckrakers, 104; program research department of, 222; queries to local stations, 87; recollections of first set owners, 186; sports cameraman, 72

Tennis, Davis Cup, 129

Testing: drug testing on prisoners, 198; experiences of Motor Vehicle official, 93; eyesight at drivers license bureau, 25; government, food, 176; by home economist, 176; passing judgment on new products, 186; products, 228; soil, 70; by test driver, 185; and wild and wooly driving, 93

Thanksgiving Day, 223

Theater: bringing theater to the people, 247; church group, 36; dinner, guiding to success, 91; Little Theater, 78; marquees of, 45; portraying famous personalities on stage, 174; stage manager of, 114; troubles of ushers in, 221; understudies in, 78

Thefts, antiques, 86

Therapy: for cancer with radioactive substances, 237; cure for stuttering, 206; dance as, 123; learning to use prostheses in, 188; recreational, for psychologically handicapped, 78; for

vocational rehabilitation, 247

Thermometers, types of, 169

Timber, 193

Time capsule, dedication and opening of, 107

Titles, art of giving, 155

Tobacco, 113

Tombstone salesman, 72

Tourism: as business stimulant, 154; cruises, 206; foreign, 115; guided tours of city, 35; host (local) to foreign visitors, 115; Jamaica and, 89; Plymouth Rock as center of, 244; public relations in, 240; souvenirs, 152; tour director as Marco Polo, 149; tourist bureau, 107; tourist (local) rate natural wonders, 134; travel by freighter, 206; vacation capital of state, 158; welcome to the Indian reservation, 131

Toys: Christmas spirit comes early for wholesalers, 205; in local stores, 73

Trade journals, 61

Traffic: and air traffic controllers, 162; latest state surveys on, 160; limiting truck traffic, 160

Traffic cop in congested shopping area, 241

Traffic manager of bus company, 76

Traffic officer in sky, 57

Transportation: of mobile homes, 94; of perishables, 9

Trapshooter, 100

Travel. *See also* Tourism; Around the world in 80 days, 218

Treasure: buried, hunting by metal detector, 127; when trash is, 143

Trees: best for lumber, 16; cherry, 68; contribute to naval store, 185; dogwood, 73; doctor for, 134; holly, demand for, 233; traimming of, by utility company, 76; young bark collector, 112

Triplets, amusing experiences, 60

Trucks: drivers and truck stops, 35; limiting truck traffic, 160; weigh stations, the rules are, 250

Tunnel, 218

Turkey: attempts to make U.S. bird, 222; National Wild Turkey Federation, 221

Twins: Do twins work alike, 2; fraternal twins in city, 101; states that are twins with yours, 158; twin mothers of large families, 130
Typewriter, repairmen, 27

Understudies, in Little Theater, 78
Uniforms: athletic, 100; rental, 82
United Nations: Eleanor Roosevelt and, 195; Human Rights Commission, 195; Human Rights Day, 237
United Nations Day, 203
U.S. Air Force Academy, 132
United States Congress, youngest member from state, 165
United States Marine Corps, 216
United States Navy: Barry Day, 176; Stephen Decatur as naval hero, 5; naval stores, 185; Navy Day, 205; state's foremost contribution to, 136
Utility company: meter checking, 169; tree trimming, 76

Valentines Day, 32
Amerigo Vespucci Day, 50
Veterans Day, 216
Veterinarian: blood transfusions for dogs by, 172; boarding pets with, 101; government, 153
VE (Victory in Europe) Day, 90
VJ (Victory in Japan) Day, 155
Vietnam Day, 18
Violin making, step-by-step, 91
Voting: machines, 32; registration, 179; woman's suffrage and Carrie Chapman Catt, 7

War: air heroes of WW II, 132; American Gold Star Mothers, 179; American Revolution, 195; battlefield scenes in art, 134; battlefield visits, 51; brides, 90, 168; cannons and other relics, 211; Civil, as used by Mitchell, 215; counties named for war heroes, 214; D-Day recollections, 109; first county men to die in, 70; Fort Sumter Day, 73; Gold Star Wives of America, Inc., 179; introduction of military tanks, 177; is hell, 236; on noise pollution, 185; Pearl Harbor Day, 234; VE Day, 90;

VJ Day, 155; weapons, 143; women in, 216; Yorktown Day, 200
Washington, George, 37
Wastebasket, what's in a, 175
Water: flood control, 39; highest waterfall, 81; polo, 49; skiing, 170; surfing, riding the waves, 128
Waterloo Day, 116
Water polo, college, 49
Water tower, unique, 55
Waterwheel, survival of, 36
Wax museum, 83
Weather: bureau, 29, 169; coldest spot in state, 231; lightning, death and damage, 122; rainmakers, 146; stormwarnings, 185; television forecasting equipment, 211; thermometers, 169; vane, 131
Wedding: of blind, 231; catering of, 106; customs of city, 117; decorator, 58; gift delivery for, 111; invitations, 79; of Lincoln, 212; in minister's home, 53; in retirement home, 194; scheduling church, 191; singer at, 32; tapes and films of, 100; ten most popular gifts for, 13; veteran caterers of, 106; in White House, 107
Weekend fever, local "R&R", 26
Weightlifting, 106
White House: cornerstone laid, 196; burned, 161; marriages in, 107
Wildlife: photography, 89; refuges, 153
Windmills, as energy, 97
Window washing, cleanest career in city, 154
Winemaking, at home, 90
Winter: begins, 243; of long ago, 15; popularity of roughing it in, 242; sports, 244
Winter Olympics, 26
Witches, most frightening stories about, 75
Wood: on the farm, 223; stoves, 159; for urban fireplaces, 223
World Environment Day, 109
Wrestlers: female pro, 159; high school, 218
Wright Brothers Day, 241
Writers: of articles in church weekly, 53; autobiographies by, 69; conference, 119; Amelia Earhart as, 98; famous

first novels by, 190; gag, depending on wit for income, 142; Ernest Hemingway, 138; in-residence at college, 168; Helen Keller as, 122; largest state club of, 16; of legal texts, 243; Sinclair Lewis, 8; Margaret Mitchell, 215; newspaper work, good or bad for novelists, 138; paperback, 182; scriptwriters, 149; George Bernard Shaw, 141; Mark Twain, 228

Youth: bark collector, 112; as bird trainer, 15; bowlers, 141; breaking into journalism, 14; combatting drug abuse, 135; in crafts, 90; gold champ, 24; martial arts, 33; as pantomimist, 150; runaways, 33; teenage coin collectors, 52

Zenger, John Peter, freedom of the press, 148
Zoo: blessed events at, 178; cost of animals in, 71; reindeers at, 246; roadside, 129

Books of Interest From Writer's Digest

The Beginning Writer's Answer Book, edited by Kirk Polking, Jean Chimsky, and Rose Adkins. "What is a query letter?" "If I use a pen name, how can I cash the check?" These are among 567 questions most frequently asked by beginning writers — and expertly answered in this down-to-earth handbook. Cross-indexed. 270 pp. $8.95.

Bylines & Babies, by Elaine Fantle Shimberg. The art of being a successful housewife/writer. 256 pp. $10.95.

The Cartoonist's and Gag Writer's Handbook, by Jack Markow. Longtime cartoonist with thousands of sales, reveals the secrets of successful cartooning — step by step. Richly illustrated. 157 pp. $9.95.

A Complete Guide to Marketing Magazine Articles, by Duane Newcomb. "Anyone who can write a clear sentence can learn to write and sell articles on a consistent basis," says Newcomb (who has published well over 3,000 articles). Here's how. 248 pp. $7.95.

The Confession Writer's Handbook, by Florence K. Palmer. A stylish and informative guide to getting started and getting ahead in the confessions. How to start a confession and carry it through. How to take an insignificant event and make it significant. 171 pp. $7.95.

The Craft of Interviewing, by John Brady. Everything you always wanted to know about asking questions, but were afriad to ask — from an experienced interviewer and editor of *Writer's Digest.* The most comprehensive guide to interviewing on the market. 244 pp. $9.95.

The Creative Writer, edited by Aron Mathieu. This book opens the door to the real world of publishing. Inspiration, techniques, and ideas, plus inside tips from Maugham, Caldwell, Purdy, others. 416 pp. $8.95.

The Greeting Card Writer's Handbook, by H. Joseph Chadwick. A former greeting card editor tells you what editors look for in inspirational verse . . . how to write humor . . . what to write about for conventional, studio and juvenile cards. Extra: a renewable list of greeting card markets. Will be greeted by any freelancer. 268 pp. $8.95.

A Guide to Writing History, by Doris Ricker Marston. How to track down Big Foot — or your family Civil War letters, or your hometown's last century — for publication and profit. A timely handbook for history buffs and writers. 258 pp. $8.50.

Handbook of Short Story Writing, edited by Frank A. Dickson and Sandra Smythe. You provide the pencil, paper, and sweat — and this book will provide the expert guidance. Features include James Hilton on creating a lovable character; R. V. Cassill on plotting a short story. 238 pp. $8.95.

Law and the Writer, edited by Kirk Polking and Leonard S. Meranus. Don't let legal hassles slow down your progress as a writer. Now you can find good counsel on libel, invasion of privacy, fair use, plagiarism, taxes, contracts, social security, and more — all in one volume. 249 pp. $9.95.

Magazine Writing: The Inside Angle, by Art Spikol. Successful editor and writer reveals inside secrets of getting your mss. published. 288 pp. $10.95.

Magazine Writing Today, by Jerome E. Kelley. If you sometimes feel like a mouse in a maze of magazines, with a fat manuscript check at the end of the line, don't fret. Kelley tells you how to get a piece of the action. Covers ideas, research, interviewing, organization, the writing process, and ways to get photos. Plus advice on getting started. 220 pp. $9.95.

Mystery Writer's Handbook, by the Mystery Writers of America. A howtheydunit to the whodunit, newly written and revised by members of the Mystery Writers of America. Includes the four elements essential to the classic mystery. A comprehensive handbook that takes the mystery out of mystery writing. 273 pp. $8.95.

1001 Article Ideas, by Frank A. Dickson. A compendium of ideas plus formulas to generate more of your own! 256 pp. $10.95.

Writing for Regional Publications, by Brian Vachon. How to write for this growing market. 256 pp. $10.95.

One Way to Write Your Novel, by Dick Perry. For Perry, a novel is 200 pages. Or, two pages a day for 100 days. You can start and finish your novel, with the help of this step-by-step guide taking you from blank sheet to polished page. 138 pp. $8.95.

Photographer's Market, edited by Melissa Milar. Contains what you need to know to be a successful freelance photographer. Names, addresses, photo requirements, and payment rates for 3,000 markets. 672 pp. $12.95.

The Poet and the Poem, by Judson Jerome. A rare journey into the night of the poem — the mechanics, the mystery, the craft and sullen art. Written by the most widely read authority on poetry in America, and a major contemporary poet in his own right. 400 pp. $9.95.

Sell Copy, by Webster Kuswa. Tells the secrets of successful business writing. How to write it. How to sell it. How to buy it. 288 pp. $10.95.

Songwriter's Market, edited by William Brohaugh. Lists 1,500 places where you can sell your songs. Included are the people and companies who work daily with songwriters and musicians. Features names and addresses, pay rates and other valuable information you need to sell your work. 480 pp. $10.95.

Stalking the Feature Story, by William Ruehlmann. Besides a nose for news, the newspaper feature writer needs an ear for dialog and an eye for detail. He must also be adept at handling off-the-record remarks, organization, grammar, and the investigative story. Here's the "scoop" on newspaper feature writing. 314 pp. $9.95.

Successful Outdoor Writing, by Jack Samson. Longtime editor of *Field & Stream* covers this market in depth. Illustrated. 288 pp. $11.95.

A Treasury of Tips for Writers, edited by Marvin Weisbord. Everything from Vance Packard's system of organizing notes to tips on how to get research done free, by 86 magazine writers. 174 pp. $7.95.

Writer's Digest. The world's leading magazine for writers. Monthly issues include timely interviews, columns, tips to keep writers informed on where and how to sell their work. One year subscription, $15.

The Writer's Digest Diary. Plan your year in it, note appointments, log manuscript sales, be prepared for the IRS. With advice such as the reminder on March 21 to "plan your Christmas story today." It will become a permanent annual record of writing activity. Durable cloth cover. 144 pp. $8.95.

Writer's Market, edited by William Brohaugh. The freelancer's bible, containing 4,500 places to sell what you write. Includes the name, address and phone number of the buyer, a description of material wanted and rates of payment. 960 pp. $14.95.

The Writer's Resource Guide, edited by William Brohaugh. Over 2,000 research sources for information on anything you write about. 488 pp. $11.95.

Writer's Yearbook, edited by John Brady. This large annual magazine contains how-to articles, interviews and special features, along with analyses of 500 major markets for writers. 128 pp. $2.50.

Writing and Selling Non-Fiction, by Hayes B. Jacobs. Explores with style and know-how the book market, organization and research, finding new markets, interviewing, humor, agents, writer's fatigue and more. 317 pp. $9.95.

Writing and Selling Science Fiction, compiled by the Science Fiction Writers of America. A comprehensive handbook to an exciting but oft-misunderstood genre. Eleven articles by top-flight sf writers on markets, characters, dialog, "crazy" ideas, world-building, alien-building, money and more. 197 pp. $8.95.

Writing for Children and Teen-agers, by Lee Wyndham. Author of over 50 children's books shares her secrets for selling to this large, lucrative market. Features: the 12-point recipe for plotting, and the Ten Commandments for Writers. 253 pp. $9.95.

Writing Popular Fiction, by Dean R. Koontz. How to write mysteries, suspense, thrillers, science fiction, Gothic romances, adult fantasy, Westerns and erotica. Here's an inside guide to lively fiction, by a lively novelist. 232 pp. $8.95.

Writing the Novel: From Plot to Print, by Lawrence Block. Practical advice on how to write any kind of novel. 256 pp. $10.95.

(1-2 books, add $1.00 postage and handling; 3 or more, additional 25¢ each.
Allow 30 days for delivery. Prices subject to change without notice.)

Writer's Digest Books, Dept. B, 9933 Alliance Road, Cincinnati, Ohio 45242